How To...

SIGHT SING

BY CHAD JOHNSON

To access audio visit:
www.halleonard.com/mylibrary

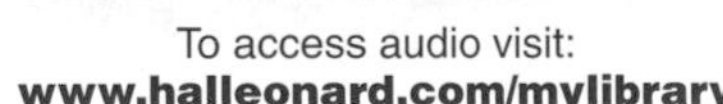

3591-8557-3595-1386

7777 W. Bluemound Rd. P.O. Box 13819 Milwaukee, WI 53213

ISBN 978-1-4950-5778-6

Copyright © 2017 by HAL LEONARD LLC
International Copyright Secured All Rights Reserved

No part of this publication may be reproduced in any form or by any means without the prior written permission of the Publisher.

In Australia Contact:
Hal Leonard Australia Pty. Ltd.
4 Lentara Court
Cheltenham, Victoria, 3192 Australia
Email: ausadmin@halleonard.com.au

Visit Hal Leonard Online at
www.halleonard.com

CONTENTS

INTRODUCTION

How to Sight Sing aims to help you master the art of singing a melody correctly upon first glance. Though this may seem a daunting task initially, like any other skill, it simply takes practice to master. Much the same as learning a new language, there are fundamentals to learn and drills and exercises to cement the concepts, but there are other helpful tools to make the process enjoyable and productive.

We'll begin with a primer in reading music. If you already know how, skim through this section to be sure you haven't missed anything along the way and that you understand all the terminology used in this method. Then we'll look at some basic music theory that will help prepare your ear and mind for the task at hand. Even if you're familiar with this subject, read through it once, because it's a critical part of the method.

Armed with this knowledge, we'll then tackle the rest of the book, covering along the way the most common keys and scales used in Western music. We'll introduce new musical concepts to provide you with a well-rounded understanding of written music. This knowledge will be applicable to any other instrument you choose to play.

Some sight-singing methods treat the subject almost as a parlor trick, encouraging shortcuts and "cheats" in the spirit of shortening the time needed to master the art. While this type of thing can be helpful on occasion, the entire method should not be built upon such flimsy ground. With this book, we seek to endow you with an understanding of why and how you're doing what you do. To use our language analogy once more, you're not just going to be learning a new language by parroting a native speaker; you'll also be learning a good bit of grammar as well. Aside from the obvious benefits this deeper comprehension affords, it will aid you in other areas of the complete musical experience, including communication with other musicians and the composition of your own music.

Have fun with this process. Singing is a joyous activity on its own. There's no reason learning to sight sing has to be any different. There's a great sense of achievement in it—not to mention much confidence in your overall musicianship, which is transferrable to any instrument. Let's learn to sight sing!

HOW TO USE THIS BOOK

This book is designed to be used with the guidance of an instructor—either privately or in a classroom setting—but it can serve as a self-teaching method if no formal instruction is available. As there is strength in numbers, going it alone is not ideal, but if you're dedicated to the course of action, there's no reason you can't do it. Nevertheless, references to an instructor will be made at times throughout the book for those in the preferred setting. It is not designed as a reference book and should be studied sequentially. This is important, as each subsequent chapter builds upon concepts learned in previous ones.

After the introductory material on reading and music theory, the book begins with basic exercises and progresses in difficulty throughout. As it's divided into chapters that concentrate on various keys, the exercises in the key of C major (Chapter 3) will be easier than those in the key of B major (Chapter 12). However, one of the skills we'll learn over the course of the book is *transposition*—the act of writing and/or performing a piece of music in a different key. By the end of the book, you'll be armed with the knowledge to transpose any of the exercises—in any chapter—to any other key. (Your instructor will be able to help in this area, if necessary.)

Each chapter follows an established format that includes the following topics:

- Major and minor scales
- Rhythm study
- Interval study
- Sight-singing exercises
- Melodic dictation
- Echo drills

Along the way, we'll introduce new musical concepts as they become relative to the learning process.

For the melodic dictation and echo drills, the instructor will play the exercises. Alternatively, and/or if you're working through the book without an instructor, audio demonstrations are included for these exercises and drills. (Use the 16-digit code on the title page to access the online audio files.) **Note to instructors:** The notation for the echo drills and dictation exercises is found at the back of the book (pages 151-166).

After the major/minor chapters, we'll look at a few more scales and modes common in Western music, including pentatonic and blues scales, the Mixolydian mode, the Dorian mode, and two other types of minor scales: the harmonic minor and the melodic minor. These chapters span various keys—a concept with which you will be familiar at that point in the book. We'll also look at the topic of reading charts—so you'll know how to find and keep your place in a piece of real music—a skill applicable to any instrument.

The Appendix contains numerous helpful aids, including information on vocal ranges, solfège syllables, and the Circle of Fifths.

Although mentioned in the Appendix, the solfège system is not used in this book. If the instructor prefers to use the system, it can easily be implemented by substituting the proper syllable for each note. See the Appendix if you're working through the book alone for an explanation of the system and how it's applied. Otherwise, you can simply sing "la," "da," "dee," or any other one-syllable word while working through the exercises. Another possibility is the number system, in which you sing the number of the scale degree. In other words, a C major arpeggio (C–E–G) in the key of C could be sung as any one of the following:

- 1–3–5 (number system)
- Do–mi–sol (solfège system)
- La–la–la (or Da–da–da, etc.)

CHAPTER 1
READING MUSIC

You may already know how to read music, but if you don't, it's time to bring you up to speed. It's a shame some people shy away from learning to read music, because there's nothing to it!

THE STAFF

Music is written on a *staff*, which consists of five horizontal lines. The notes are written along the *lines* and *spaces* of the staff and are read from left to right. The pitch of a note is dictated by its vertical placement on the staff: higher notes are high, lower notes are low.

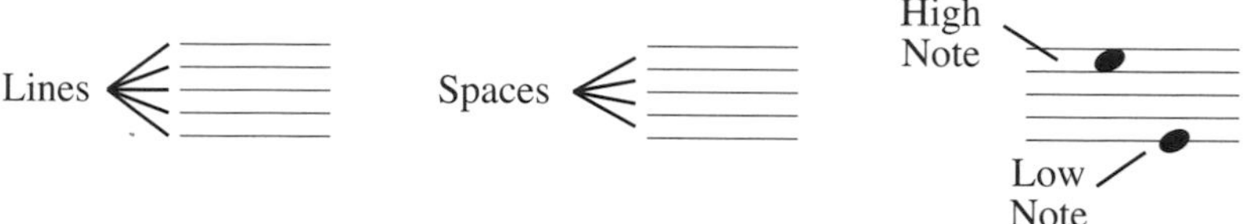

A symbol at the beginning called the *clef* tells us what notes are assigned to these lines and spaces. The two most common types of clefs are the *treble clef* (used for higher-pitched instruments) and the *bass clef* (used for lower-pitched instruments).

Mnemonic devices are often used to remember the notes on the lines and spaces of each clef. For the treble clef, the lines can be remembered, low to high, as "**E**very **G**ood **B**oy **D**oes **F**ine." The spaces spell the word "**FACE**."

For the bass clef, the lines can be remembered as "**G**ood **B**oys **D**o **F**ine **A**lways," whereas the spaces can be remembered with "**A**ll **C**ows **E**at **G**rass."

When we need to move above or below the notes of the staff, we use temporary staff extenders called *ledger lines*.

The C note on the ledger line just below the treble clef and just above the bass clef is the same pitch. It's known as *middle C* because it can be found in the middle of a piano keyboard. So, the notes of the treble clef and bass clef can overlap when using ledger lines.

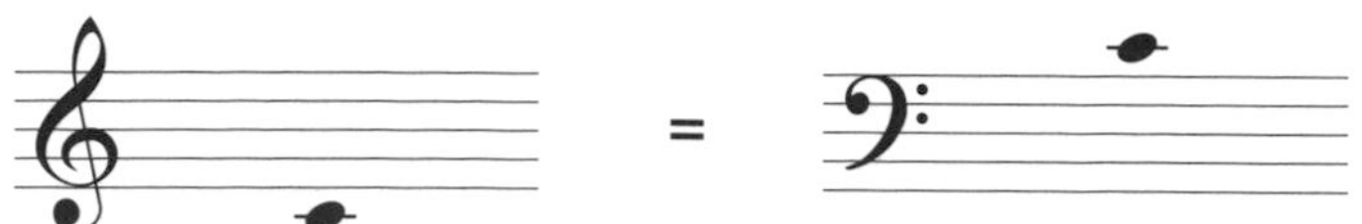

Bar lines divide the music into measures, which makes it easier to keep your place—just like punctuation does in written text. A double bar line is used to signify the end of an exercise or sometimes the end of a section in the music. A *terminal bar* line signifies the end of a piece of music.

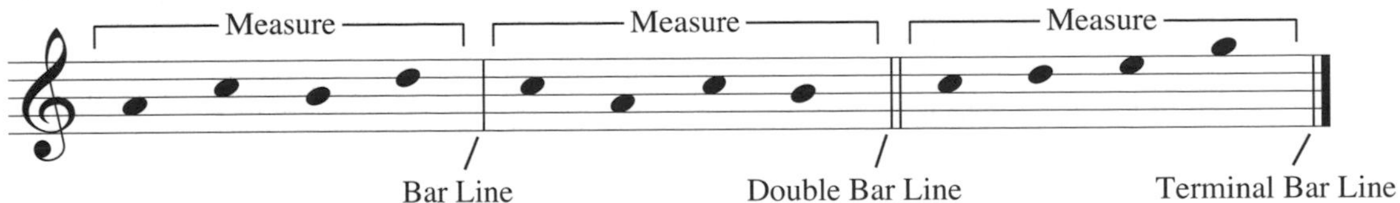

RHYTHM

Aside from the pitch of a note, represented by its vertical placement on the staff, a note also has a rhythmic quality. The *rhythm* tells us when and for how long to play notes and/or to play nothing (rest). Rhythm is displayed with the use of different types of *stems* and *note heads*.

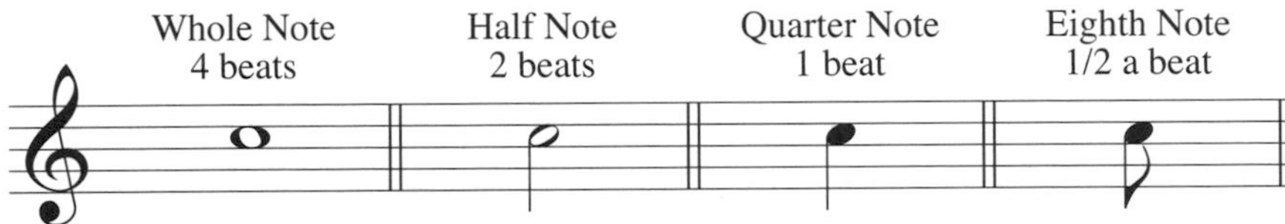

Similarly, different *rest* symbols tell us to be quiet—i.e., play nothing.

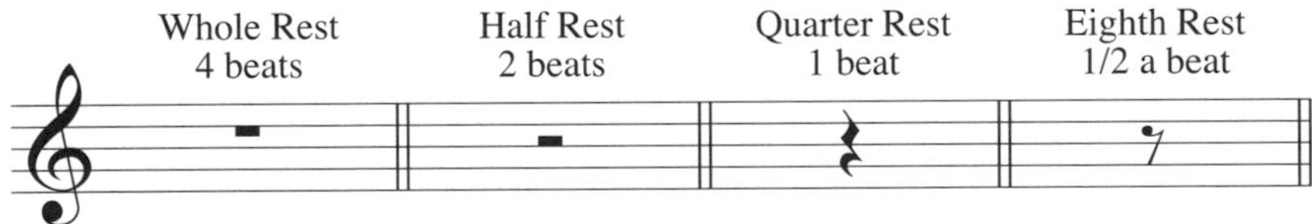

The *beat* is what propels the music along. At the beginning of a piece of music, a *time signature* appears after the clef, telling us how the beat will be counted—also known as the *meter* of the piece. It's comprised of two vertically stacked numbers and looks like a mathematical fraction. The top number tells us how many beats will be in each measure, while the bottom number tells us which kind of note will be counted as one beat. The most common time signature of all is 4/4. It's so common, in fact, that it's also known as "common time" and will sometimes be represented as "C" instead of 4/4. They mean the same thing.

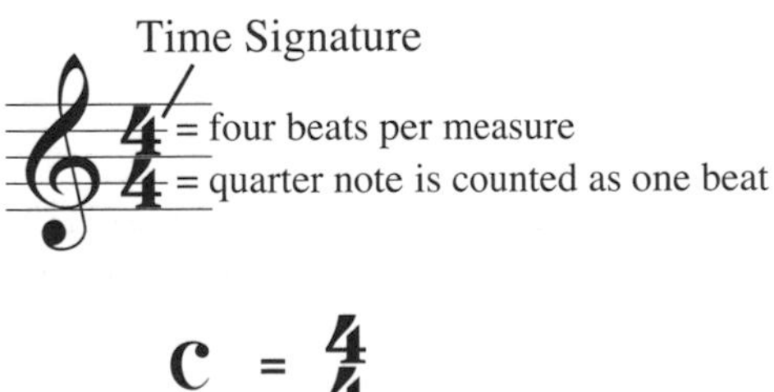

$$\mathbf{C} = \frac{4}{4}$$

So in 4/4 meter, the top 4 tells us that there are four beats in every measure. The bottom number tells us that the quarter note (think 1/4) is counted as the beat. (As we progress through the book, we'll look at other time signatures as well.) Here, then, are a few typical measures of music in 4/4 time, using different notes and rhythms. Note that, when several eighth notes are played in a row, they're connected by *beams* to make them easier to read. Also observe that the stems change direction depending upon the pitch of the note. Don't worry at all about trying to recreate this right now; just be aware of how it looks.

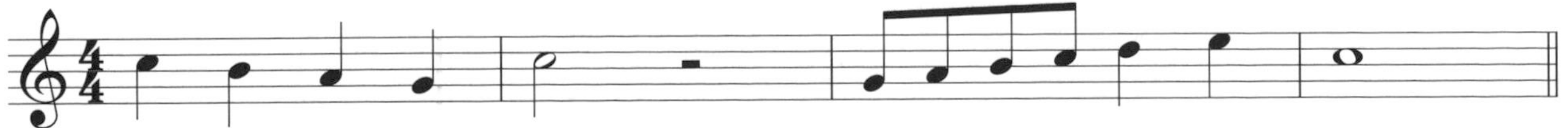

COUNTING

By *counting*, we mean keeping our rhythmic place in the music. Counting is something helpful to do, especially in the early stage of learning rhythms. Eventually, this will become second nature, and you won't have to rely upon counting except in cases of extremely complicated rhythms.

In 4/4 music, we count the quarter notes by default. There are four of them in a measure, so we say "1, 2, 3, 4" as we read them.

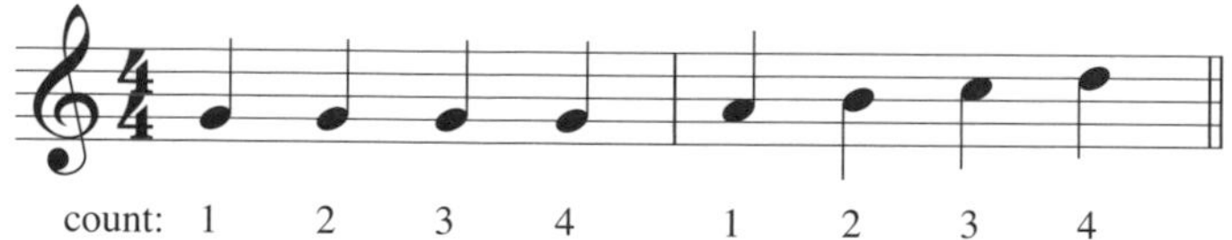

When singing, we obviously can't count while articulating other words, but it's always a good exercise to count the rhythms aloud with beat numbers before trying to sing a melody. That way, you'll be sure you have a grip on the rhythm. When counting whole or half notes, you'll sustain a note through one or more of the counts. In this case, you can count the sounded beats aloud and the sustained ones silently, like this:

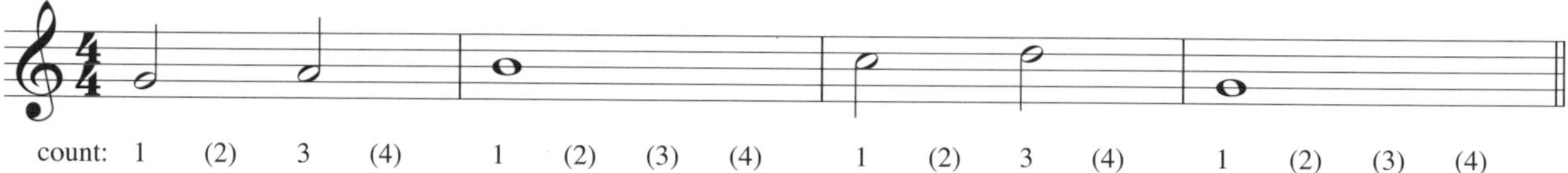

You can count rests the same way (silently).

To count eighth notes, we add the word "and" between the beats.

Any time you're counting rhythms, it's a good idea to either tap your foot or pat your hand on your leg. This will help you when counting through rests or whole and half notes in the beginning.

Others Are Counting on You!

Being able to keep a steady beat is a critical skill on any instrument. If you're in a band, for example, it's your job—not just the rhythm section's—to set the tempo. It doesn't matter who's rushing the beat; if someone's not on the beat, the whole ensemble will suffer. Therefore, be sure to pay close attention to this aspect of music from the beginning. If you're singing along to a click of some kind, listen closely and make sure you're not singing ahead of or behind the beat. Playing with musicians who have good rhythmic skills is a real joy. The same can't be said for the opposite!

CHAPTER 2

INTERVALS, THE MAJOR SCALE AND THE MINOR SCALE

Practically all Western music is comprised of various intervals and scales. To sight sing, you need to understand a few basic concepts in this regard. We'll want to put on our thinking caps a bit here before we start singing, but fret not; it's really not that bad.

INTERVALS

An *interval* is the musical distance between notes. There are different kinds of intervals with different names, but right now we're going to focus on two: the half step and the whole step.

A *half step* is the distance from a note to its closest possible neighbor. It's the smallest interval in Western music. On a piano keyboard, it's the distance of one key to the one right next to it—white or black keys included.

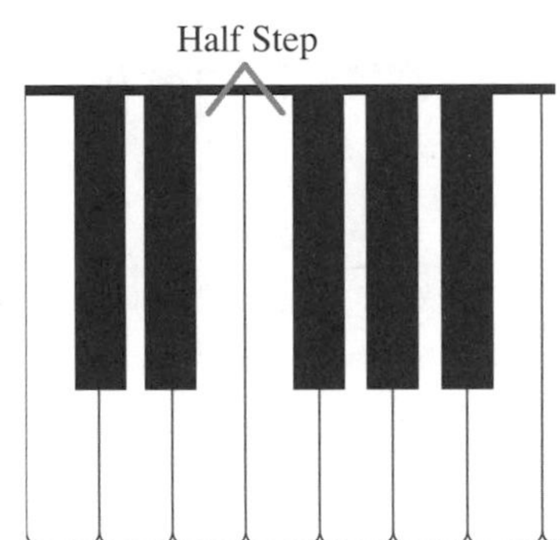

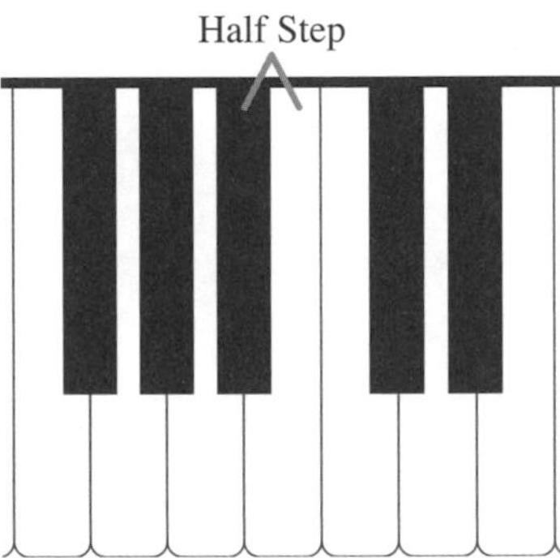

A *whole step* is twice that of a half step; it's the distance of two notes on the piano—white or black.

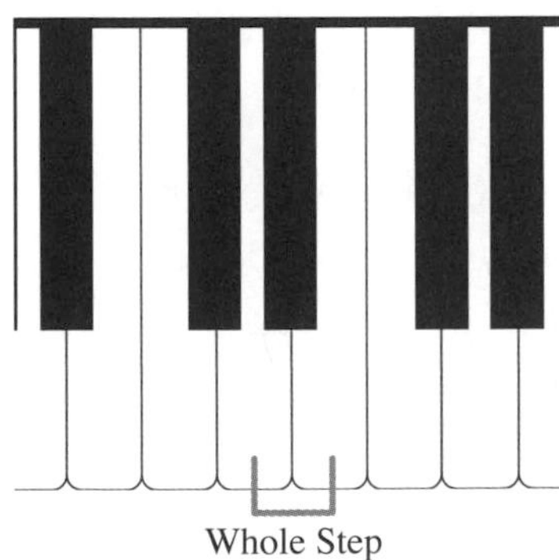

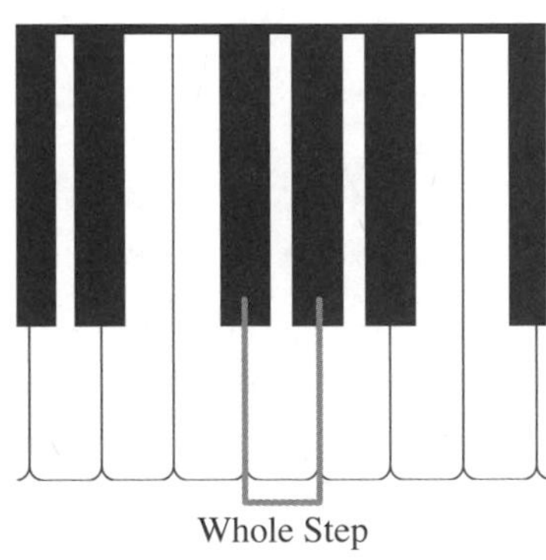

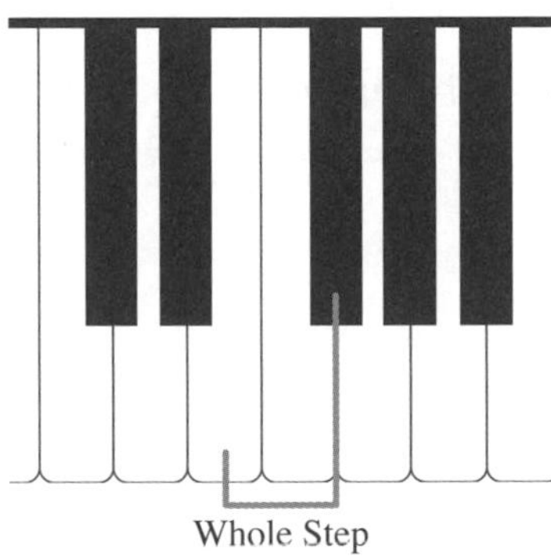

On the piano keyboard, we call the white keys *natural notes* and the black ones *accidentals*. The white notes simply run up through the musical alphabet, starting over afterward, throughout the length of the keyboard. One other interval we'll mention here is the *octave*: the distance from one note to a note of the same name, but at a higher or lower pitch.

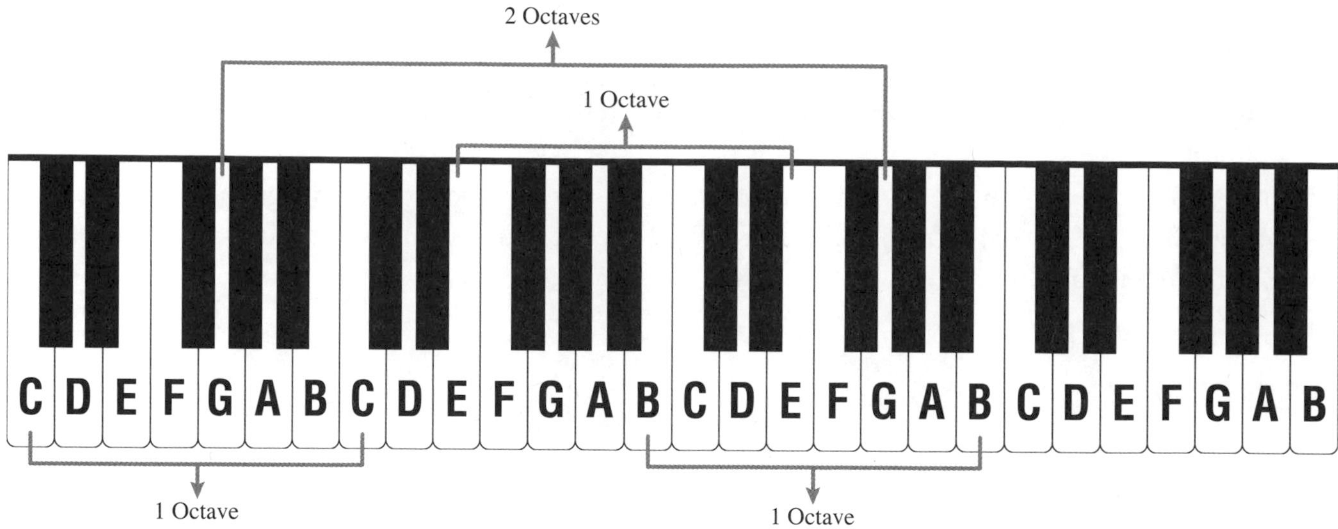

Accidental notes can have two different names, depending on their context: They're either a sharp note or a flat note. A *sharp* (♯) note is one half step higher than a natural note, whereas a *flat* (♭) is one half step lower.

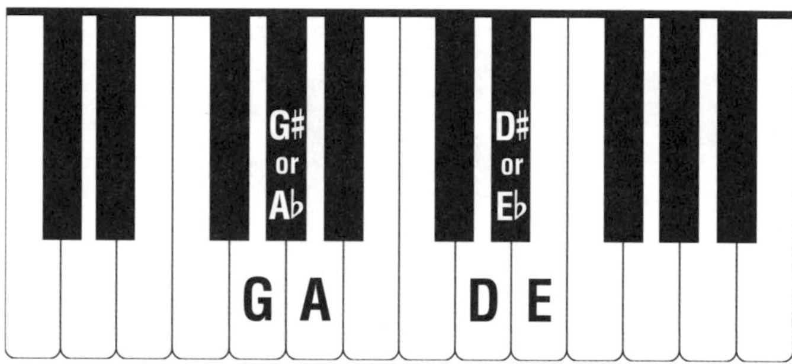

So the black key between G and A can be called G♯ because it's a half step higher than G. But it can also be called A♭ because it's a half step lower than A. Musical context dictates which it is. There's a little more to it than that, but you needn't concern yourself with anything further at the moment. This concept is called *enharmonic*, which is a fancy way of saying that a note can have two different names. For example, G♯ and A♭ are enharmonic to each other.

The piano keyboard graphics shown above are important because they tell us several things:

- On the keyboard, a note will always look the same, regardless of the octave it's in. In other words, a C note will always have the set of two black keys on its right side and a white key to its immediate left. An F note will always have the set of three black keys on its right side and a white key to its immediate left. A D note will always be the one sandwiched between the set of two black keys, and so on.
- There are two "natural half steps" on the piano keyboard, in which a white key lies a half step away from another white key: from B to C and from E to F. This has great importance when we look at different keys.
- Half steps and whole steps have nothing to do with black or white keys. In other words, either interval can involve either type of key (black or white). A half step can involve a black and white key or only white keys. A whole step can involve two white keys, two black keys, or a black and white key. The only combination that's not possible is a half step from a black key to a black key. There are no two black keys on a piano that are a half step apart.

THE MAJOR SCALE

A *scale* is a collection of notes used to create chords and melodies. The *major scale*, which contains seven different notes, is the most popular scale in all of Western music. It's used in pop, rock, jazz, classical, country, folk—you name it.

Every major scale follows the same intervallic formula of whole steps and half steps. Attention! You need to turn on your thinking cap here and memorize this pattern:

whole-whole-half-whole-whole-whole-half

Every major scale on the planet is built from this interval pattern. As an example, we'll look at the key of C—but first read the information in the gray box.

What's a Key?

In a piece of music, the *key* is named after the note that feels like home. If something is said to be "in the key of C," then the note C will feel ultimately resolved when you come to it. It's often the last note in a song, though not always. Think of "The Star-Spangled Banner," for example. The last line, "and the home of the brave," ends with "brave" on the tonic. The word *tonic* is another name for the note after which the key is named—i.e., home base. So if you sing "The Star-Spangled Banner" in the key of C, that last note is a C.

Think of the song again. Imagine how unresolved it would sound if you stopped after singing, "and the home of the." That's the power of *diatonic* music—music built upon a certain key. It can create a powerful effect on the listener, and certain phrases (such as "and the home of the") want to resolve to home base. Just as there are 12 different keys on the piano (seven white ones and five black ones) before starting over in another octave, there are 12 different keys. We'll look more at this subject as we advance through the book.

To build a C major scale, we start with the tonic note—C, in this case—and progress through the intervallic formula of whole and half steps given above. We end up with this:

C D E F G A B C

We can confirm these are the right notes by checking the intervals on the piano keyboard, remembering that half steps are one key apart and whole steps are two keys apart:

- From C to D is a *whole* step
- From D to E is a *whole* step
- From E to F is a *half* step
- From F to G is a *whole* step
- From G to A is a *whole* step
- From A to B is a *whole* step
- From B to C is a *half* step

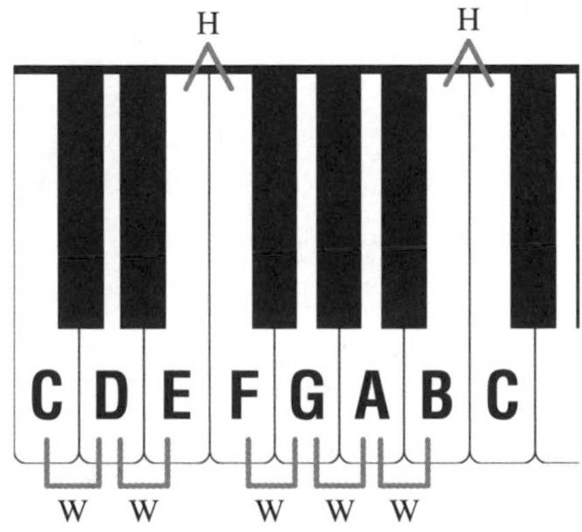

And here's what that looks like on the staff, starting from middle C.

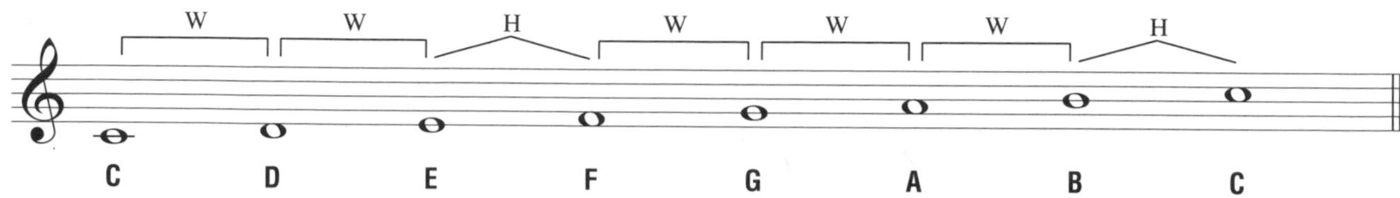

So we don't need accidentals to play a C major scale. Coincidentally, C major is the only key like this. Any other major scale will involve the use of one or more sharps or flats.

THE MINOR SCALE

The *minor scale* is another popular scale. Whereas the major scale sounds upbeat and cheerful, the minor scale sounds sad and dramatic. It's used in all musical styles.

The minor scale has a different intervallic formula than the major scale:

whole–half–whole–whole–half–whole–whole

Like the major scale, there are seven intervals comprised of five whole steps and two half steps—but the order has changed. Let's look at the key of A minor. (We'll discuss why we chose A minor in just a bit.) If we apply the above intervallic formula to an A tonic, we arrive at the following:

A B C D E F G A

We can again confirm this by checking the intervals on the piano keyboard.

- From A to B is a *whole* step
- From B to C is a *half* step
- From C to D is a *whole* step
- From D to E is a *whole* step
- From E to F is a *half* step
- From F to G is a *whole* step
- From G to A is a *whole* step

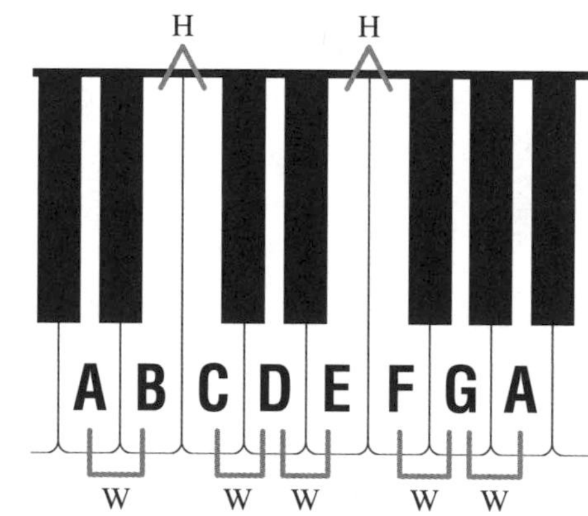

And here's what the A minor scale looks like on the staff.

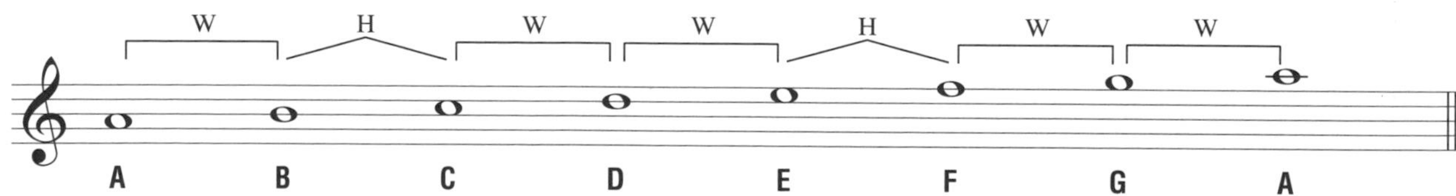

We didn't need sharps or flats to make the A minor scale. It's the only minor scale like that. Every other minor scale will involve one or more sharps or flats.

RELATIVE KEYS

We started with the A minor scale because it uses the exact same notes as a C major scale. The only difference is that we're treating A as the tonic instead of C. Because of this, these two keys—A minor and C major—are said to be relative to each other. In other words, A minor is the relative minor of C major, and C major is the relative major of A minor. Think of them as using the same "family" (therefore, they're relatives) of notes. Every major scale has a relative minor scale and vice versa. And again, C major and A minor are the only keys that contain no sharps or flats.

Now that we've exercised the noodle a bit, let's begin exercising the ear and the voice. The information in this chapter will help inform the skills you'll learn in the following chapters, and those skills in turn will help cement this information. Don't worry too much if you don't understand it all right now. If necessary, you can come back and reference this chapter later on. Now it's time to start putting some of this knowledge to work.

CHAPTER 3
EXERCISES IN C MAJOR AND A MINOR

We'll begin our journey in the key of C and its relative minor, A minor. Remember that neither of these scales requires any sharps or flats and can therefore be played using nothing but the white keys on the piano.

THE SCALES

To get the sound of these scales in your ear, listen to the instructor play them.

C Major Scale

Here's the C major scale. Listen to see if you can hear the difference between the whole step intervals and the half-step intervals.

TRACK 1

A Minor Scale

Now here's the A minor scale. It contains the same notes as the C major scale, but we're treating the note A as the tonic of the scale. Listen closely to see if you can hear how the arrangement of whole and half steps has changed.

TRACK 2

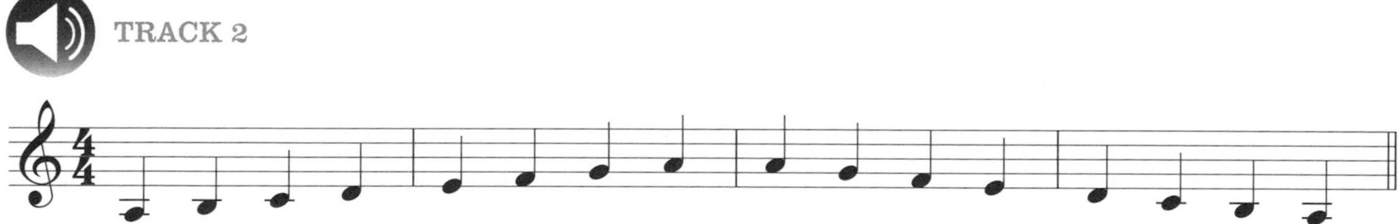

RHYTHM STUDY

The notes are only half of every melody; the other half is the rhythm, so it's critical that we're able to read rhythms correctly. We'll begin simply, with whole notes, half notes, and quarter notes.

Rhythmic Drills

Clap the following rhythms together as a class or in smaller groups. When counting through a rest or a sustained note (such as a whole or half note), count quietly to keep your place.

Rhythmic Dictation

Listen to the following rhythms and write them down. Although the rhythm is the sole concern here, these examples are played with sustained piano notes so that the duration (length) is clearly defined for each. Be sure to listen closely to the duration of each note and account for it in the music. The rests are just as important as the notes! Each example should be played twice. Example A is done for you.

INTERVAL STUDY

As mentioned in Chapter 2, there are many kinds of musical intervals, with all sorts of names. Learning to sing melodies at sight requires being familiar with the sound of these intervals. There are additional names for the two intervals we already know: the whole step and half step.

- Half step = *minor* 2nd.
- Whole step = *major* 2nd.

This relationship between minor and major intervals plays out time and again when dealing with other intervals. Remember this basic rule: A major interval is always one half step larger than its companion minor interval. So, a major 2nd is one half step larger than a minor 2nd.

Whole steps and half steps are common names we use when talking about scales, but most interval names are discussed in terms of two parts: a *quantity* and *quality*. The quantity is easy; it tells you how many note names are involved. For example, from C up to D is a 2nd, because two note names are involved: C (1) and D (2). From C up to E is a 3rd because three note names are involved: C (1), D (2), and E (3).

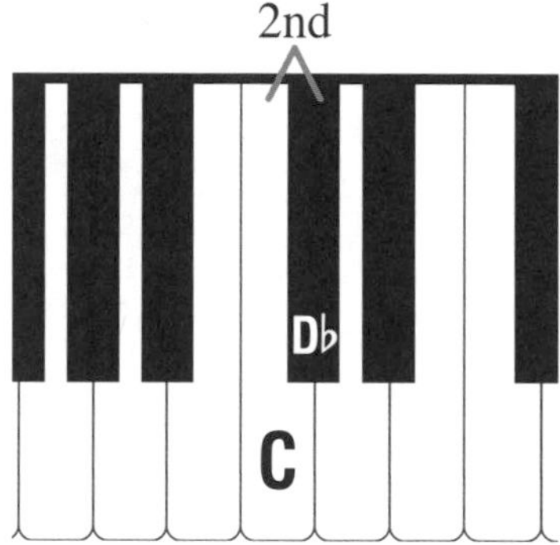

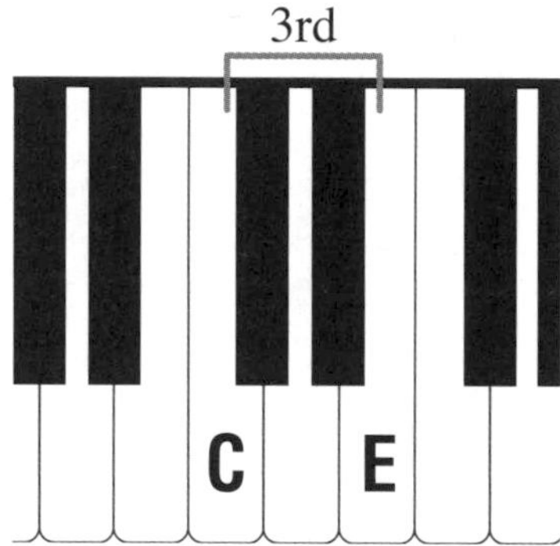

The quality refers to how many half steps comprise the interval. In the case of 2nds, for example, the minor 2nd contains one half step, and the major 2nd contains two half steps (or one whole step, if you prefer).

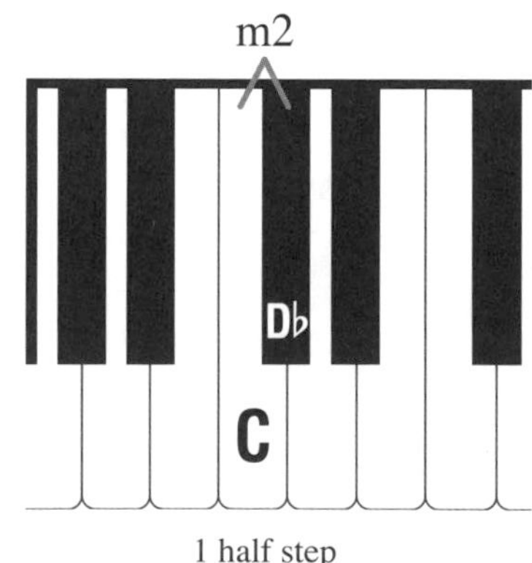

1 half step

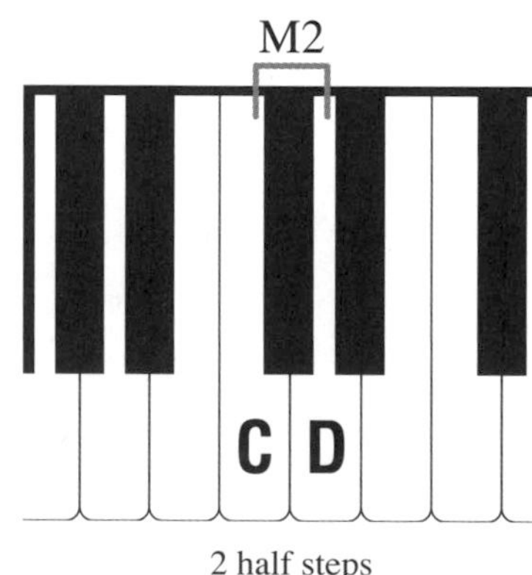

2 half steps

In the interval name "m2," the lowercase "m" stands for minor, and the "2" stands for 2nd. An uppercase "M" means "major."

Listen to the sound of a major 2nd, from C to D:

And now here's the sound of a minor 2nd, from C to D♭:

Interval Dictation

That's enough talk for now. What's really important is being able to hear these intervals. Listen to the following intervals and determine if they are minor 2nds (m2) or major 2nds (M2). Each interval will be played twice; the first one is done for you.

TRACK 13

A) M2

B) ___

C) ___

D) ___

E) ___

F) ___

G) ___

H) ___

SIGHT-SINGING EXERCISES

Let's combine our rhythmic and melodic reading skills and try our first sight-singing exercises. At first, sing these together as a class or in small groups. Then you can try singing them by yourself. If you're working through this book alone, check the notes against a piano keyboard while you sing them, to verify you're singing the right notes.

Key of C Major

We're going to start with the basics, using only 2nds as we work through the C major scale. You can sing "la" if you prefer, or you can sing the number of the scale degree, as shown in Example A that follows. The tonic is always the number 1, so in this case, C =1, D = 2, E = 3, etc.

A Note on Ranges

Although male tenors read treble clef, they actually sing an octave lower. In other words, if you were to play the G note on the second line of the treble clef at the piano, you would hear that it's quite a high note for a male to sing. You'll sometimes see an "8" dangling from the bottom of the treble clef, which means to sing an octave lower than written. However, it's become so commonplace these days that it's largely assumed. Therefore, for all these exercises, females will sing the notes as written, and males will sing an octave lower.

Likewise, when we introduce the bass clef into exercises, start on the octave that's comfortable for you. That goes for ladies and gents!

Remember to concentrate on the rhythm as well! Tap your foot or pat your leg as you sing along to help you keep the beat.

TRACK 21

B)

TRACK 22

C)

TRACK 23

D)

TRACK 24

E)

TRACK 25

F)

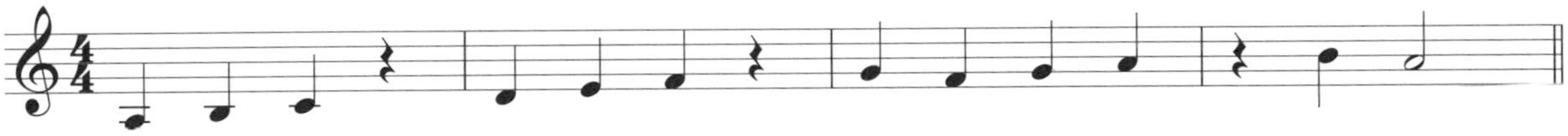

MELODIC DICTATION EXERCISES

This is where we concentrate on *ear training*—i.e., training your ear to recognize pitches and patterns in melodies. Sight singing and ear training go hand in hand; you can't really study one without studying the other. In these exercises, you'll hear the instructor play a melody twice, and you'll write it down by ear. (The online audio plays the melody only once.) For all the melodic exercises in this book, the first note will be provided for you as a reference pitch. Example A is done for you. (**Instructors:** See Appendix for notation of these exercises. Alternatively, these can be found on the accompanying audio.)

Key of C Major

TRACK 26

A)

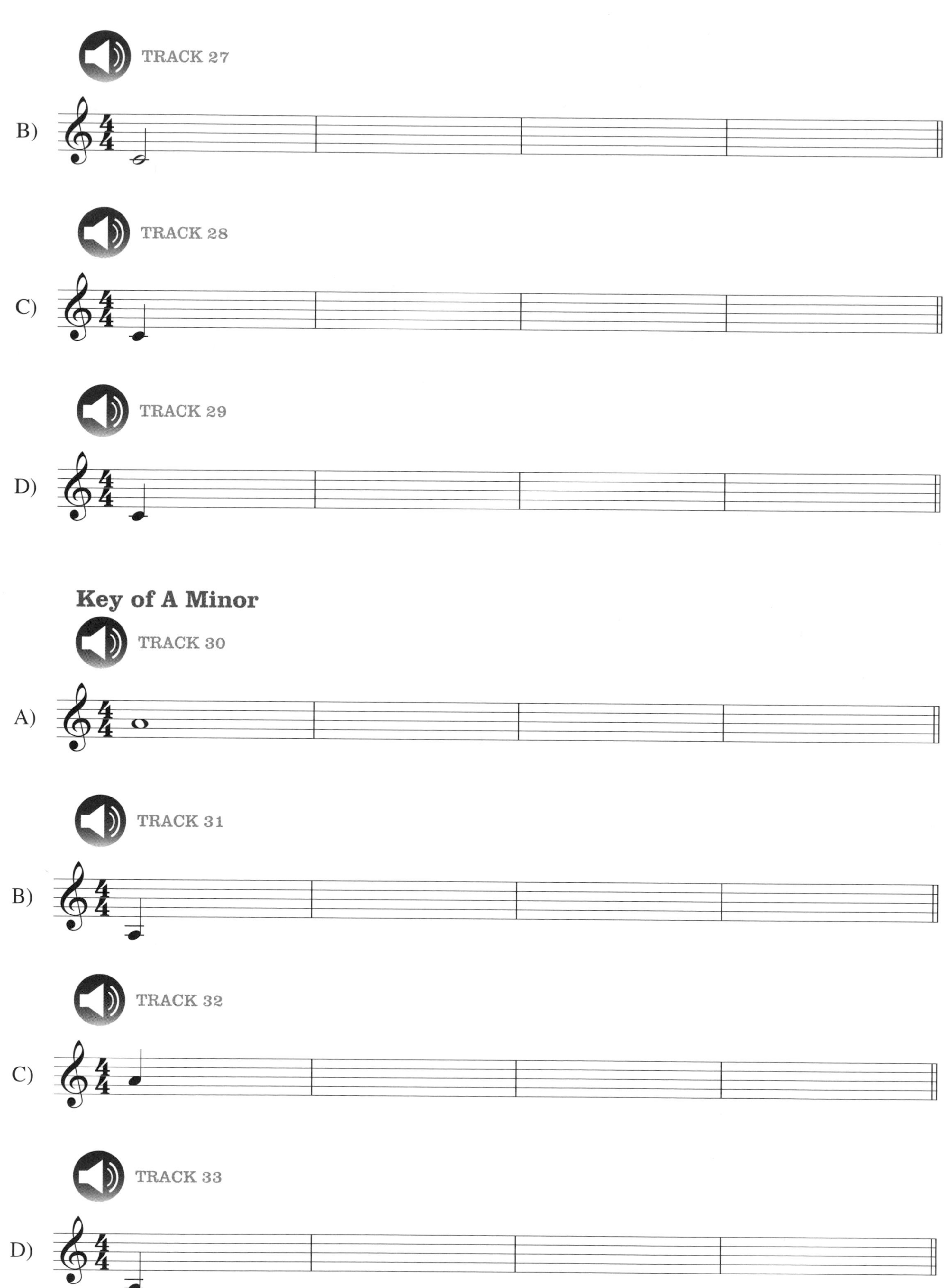
TRACK 27
B)
TRACK 28
C)
TRACK 29
D)
Key of A Minor
TRACK 30
A)
TRACK 31
B)
TRACK 32
C)
TRACK 33
D)

ECHO DRILLS

For these drills, you'll listen to a phrase and then echo it back. This helps with your ability to memorize musical information in chunks. When you start to sight read or sight sing more complicated music, this is an essential skill that allows you to keep up and also read ahead. The idea is to concentrate on listening and repeating without thinking about it too much. (**Instructors:** See Appendix for notation of these exercises. Alternatively, these can be found on the accompanying audio.)

Rhythm Echoes

In these four exercises, you'll hear a one-bar rhythm followed by one bar of silence. Clap the rhythm back during the break.

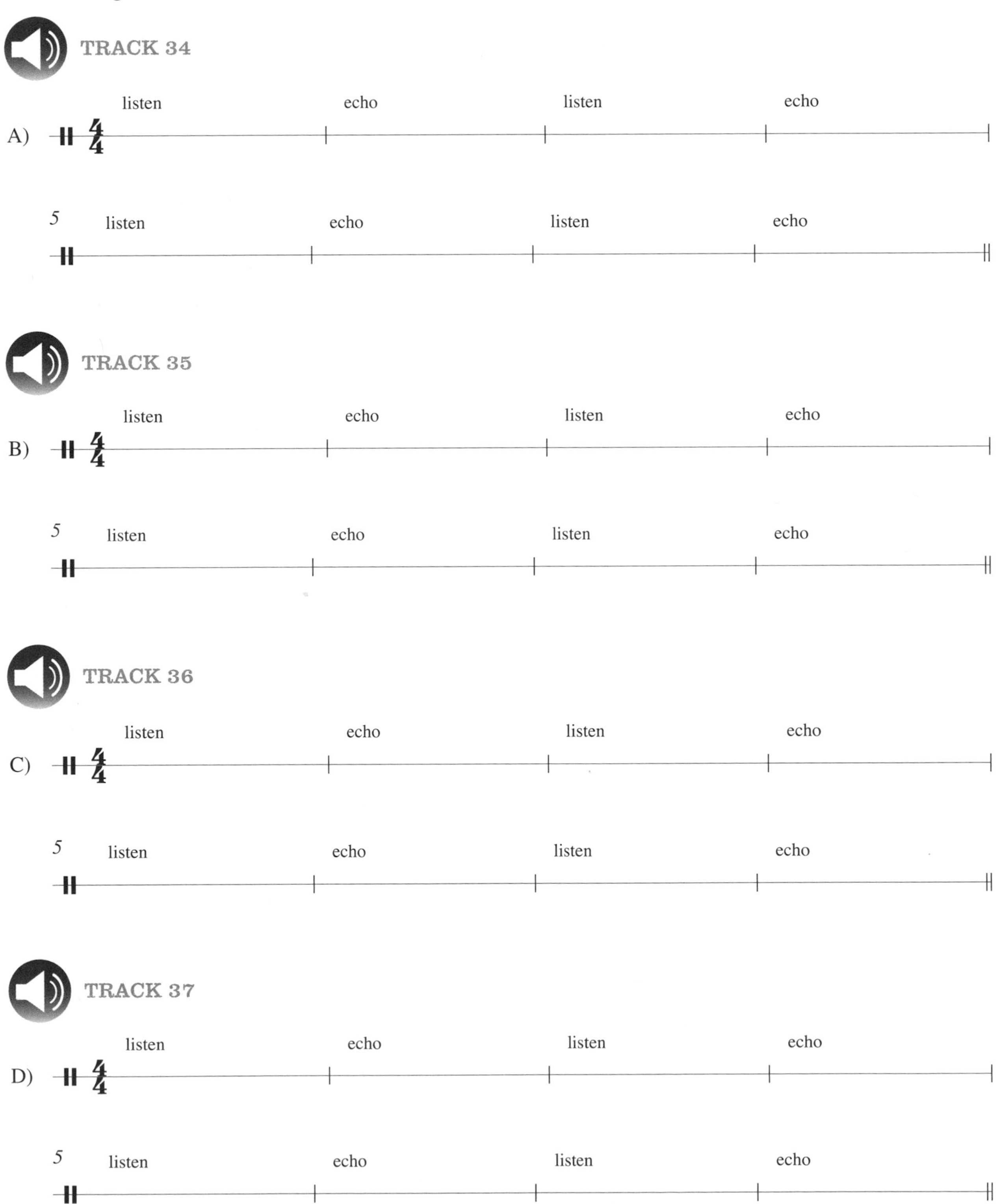

Melodic Echoes

In these six exercises, you'll hear a one-bar melody followed by one bar of silence. Sing the melody back during the break.

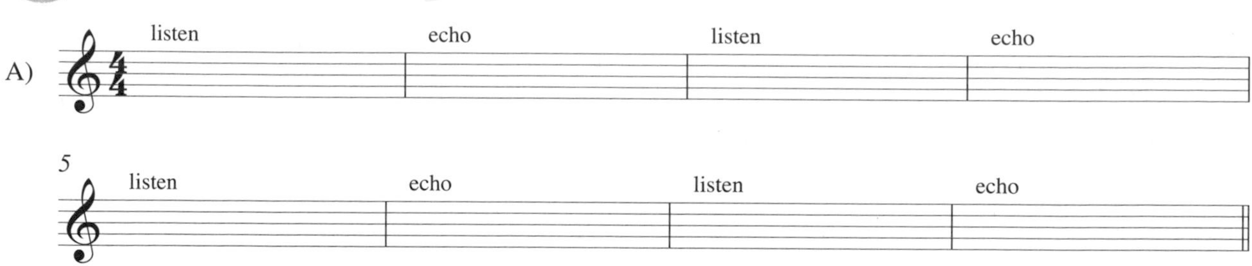

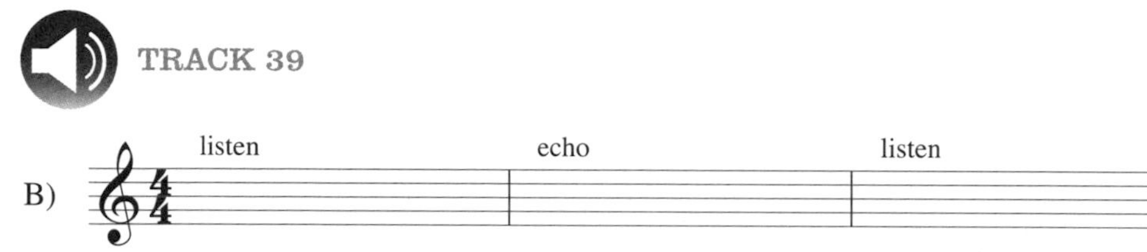

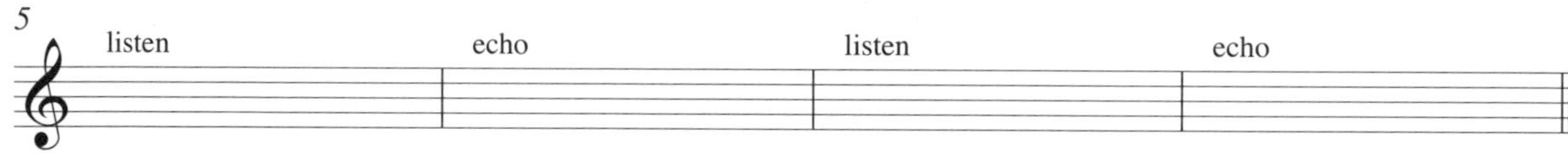

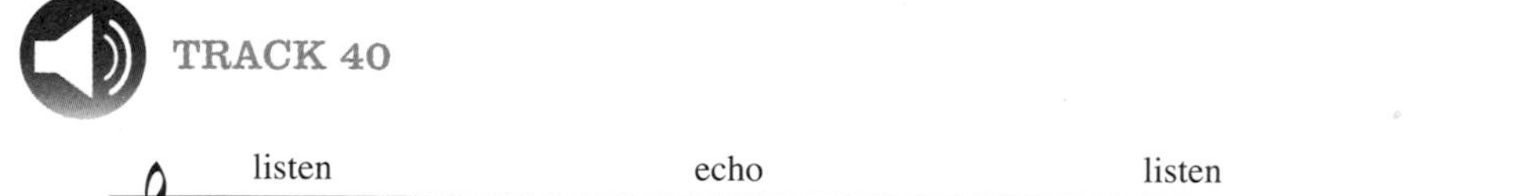

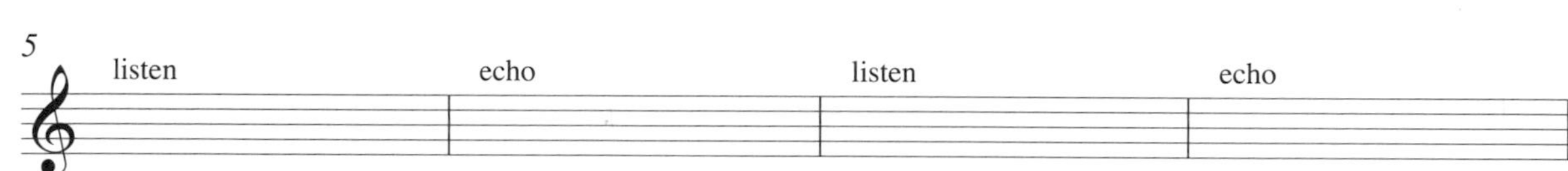

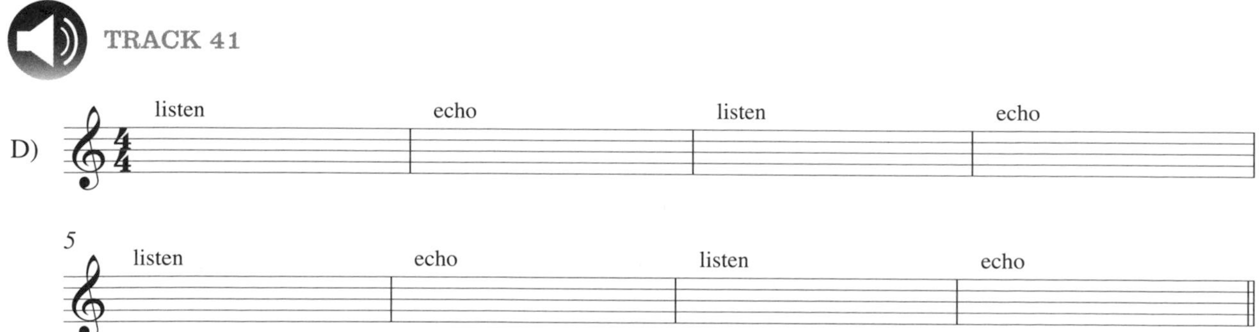

E)

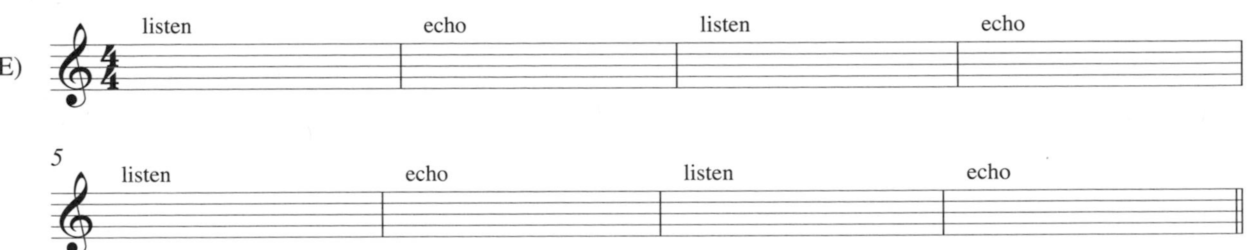

F)

listen echo listen echo

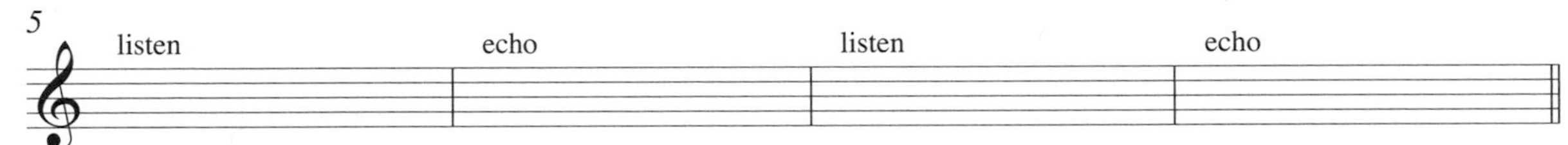

CHAPTER 4

EXERCISES IN G MAJOR AND E MINOR

In this chapter, we'll learn about the key of G major and its relative minor, E minor.

THE SCALES

As mentioned earlier, the only major scale that contains no sharps or flats is C major, and the only minor one is A minor. Going forward, then, sharps or flats will be added into the mix. In the case of G major and E minor, we'll add F♯.

G Major Scale

We know that every major scale follows the intervallic formula W-W-H-W-W-W-H. Let's see how that applies to the key of G major. To spell any new major scale, write only the note names from the tonic up to an octave higher. Don't worry about any details yet. G major looks like this:

G A B C D E F G

Be a Good Speller!

Any major scale *always* has each of the seven letters represented once and only once. (The tonic at the end of the scale is the beginning of another octave.) If you find yourself with both an A and A♯, for example, or both a G and G♭ when writing out a scale, you'll know something's wrong. Use the enharmonic equivalent for the accidental in this case, ensuring that each letter name is present in the scale.

When we look at these notes on a piano keyboard and compare them against the intervallic formula, we discover a problem:

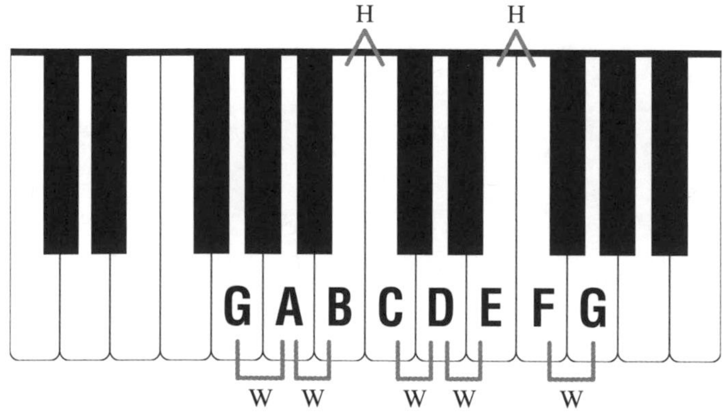

The formula begins correctly with W-W-H, but concludes with W-W-H-W instead of W-W-W-H. What's the solution? Raise the F note a half step up to F♯, and everything is perfect!

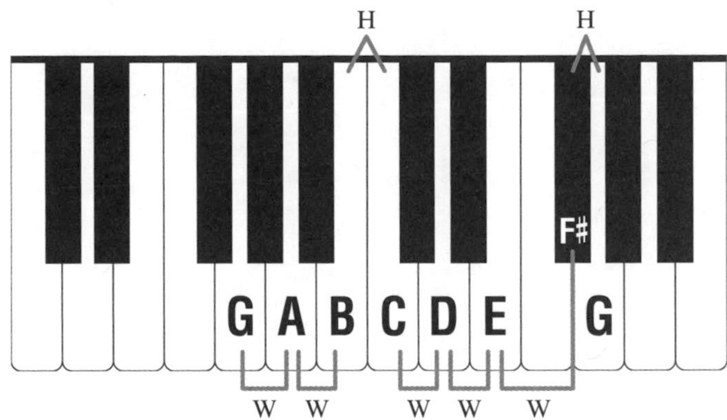

We now know that the G major scale is spelled G–A–B–C–D–E–F♯.

TRACK 44

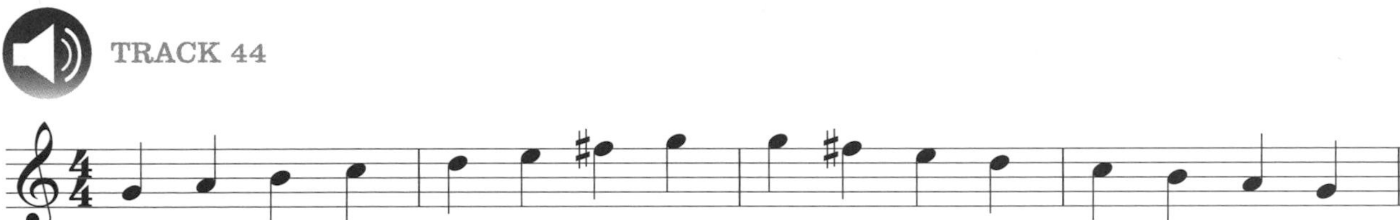

E Minor Scale

Just as with A minor and C major, E minor is the relative minor of G major; it contains the same notes. We progress through those notes, but start on E instead.

TRACK 45

RHYTHM STUDY

We're going to introduce the eighth note here and there in this chapter, while keeping the rhythms relatively simple. Remember that eighth notes can be counted by saying "and" in between the beats: "1 and 2 and 3 and," etc.

Rhythmic Drills

Clap the following rhythms together as a class or in smaller groups. When counting through a rest or a sustained note, count quietly to keep your place.

Rhythmic Dictation

Listen to the following rhythms and write them down. Each example will be played twice. Be sure to listen closely to the duration of each note.

INTERVAL STUDY

The next interval in line is the 3rd. A 3rd involves three note names, such as from C up to E: C (1)–D (2)–E (3). And just as with 2nds, we can have major and minor 3rds. Again, the major 3rd is one half step larger than the minor 3rd.

- Major 3rd = four half steps (or two whole steps)
- Minor 3rd = three half steps (or one and a half steps—"one step" is another name for a whole step)

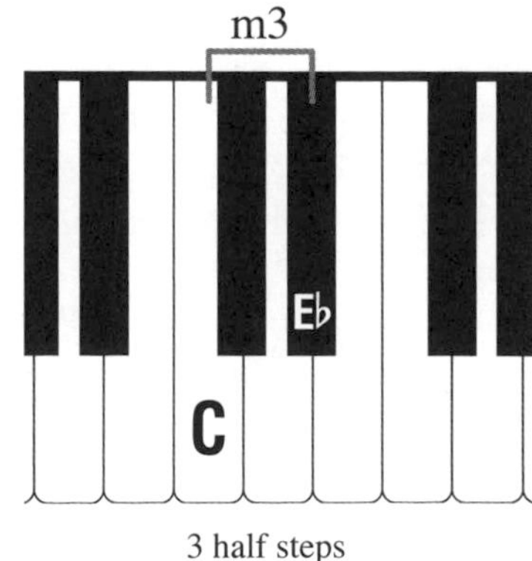

3 half steps

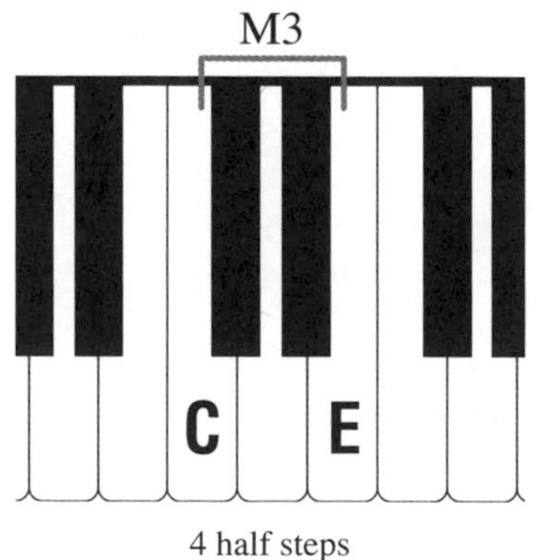

4 half steps

Enharmonic Reminder

Just as scales require all seven notes in their spelling, intervals technically work the same way. In other words, an interval requires three letter names to be called a 3rd. Though the note E♭ can be called D♯, we don't call it that because there are no longer three note names involved. Thus, a minor 3rd above C is the note E♭, not D♯. Granted, it sounds the same either way, but to transpose melodies, we need to know how to spell scales and intervals properly.

Our chordal system is built upon 3rds, so this interval is one of the most common in music. We'll talk more about this idea later on, but suffice it to say that 3rds sound good to our ears. When you hear two people singing in harmony, they're often singing a 3rd apart. You've probably heard something like this, which consists of 3rd harmony, many times:

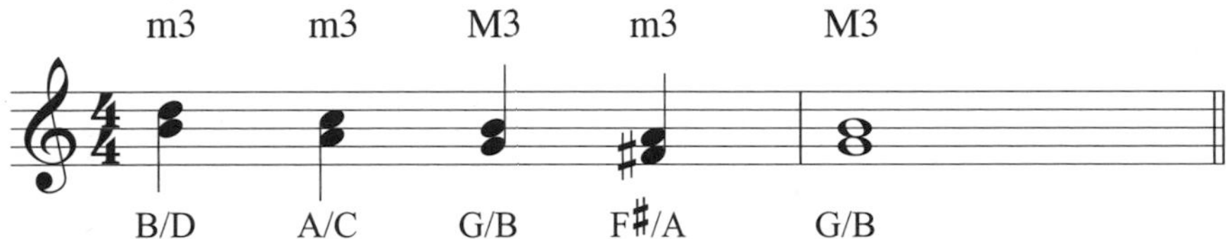

TRACK 50

Listen to the sound of a major 3rd, from C to E.

TRACK 51

And now here's the sound of a minor 3rd, from C to E♭.

Interval Dictation

It's important to recognize major 3rds and minor 3rds when you hear them. From now on, we'll play these intervals two different ways: 1) melodically (one note at a time); 2) harmonically (both notes played together). Using both methods makes for excellent ear-training practice.

Listen to the following intervals and determine if they are major 3rd or minor 3rd intervals.

TRACK 52

A) ___

B) ___

C) ___

D) ___

E) ___

F) ___

G) ___

H) ___

SIGHT-SINGING EXERCISES

Now let's look at some sight-singing examples in the keys of G major and E minor. We'll incorporate 2nds, 3rds, and eighth notes throughout these examples.

Key of G Major

As you sing through these exercises, be aware of what the tonic note sounds like. It should be in your mind as a reference pitch, and should be the easiest note for you to sight sing. Notice the sharp on the F line at the beginning of each staff. This is called a key signature, and it tells you to play/sing an F♯ instead of F every time. We'll look at key signatures a bit more closely in the next chapter.

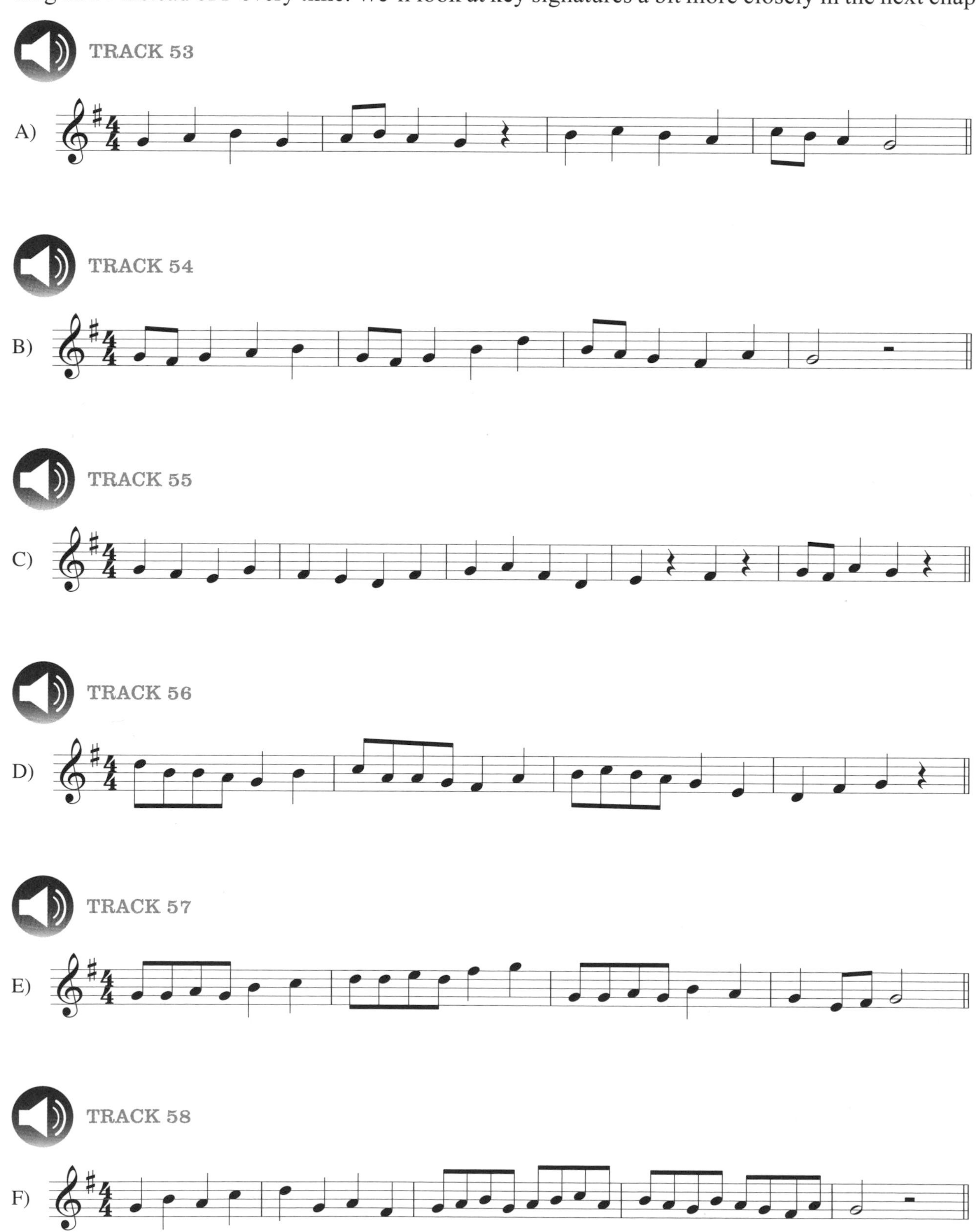

Key of E Minor

Remember to acknowledge the rests. Don't sustain the notes across them.

TRACK 59

A)

TRACK 60

B)

TRACK 61

C)

TRACK 62

D)

TRACK 63

E)

TRACK 64

F)

MELODIC DICTATION EXERCISES

In these exercises, you'll hear the instructor play a melody twice. Write it down by ear, remembering to account for the rests. (**Instructors:** See Appendix for notation of these exercises. Alternatively, these can be found on the accompanying audio.)

Key of G Major

A)

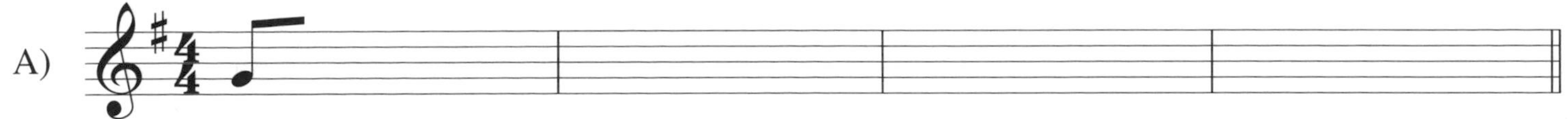

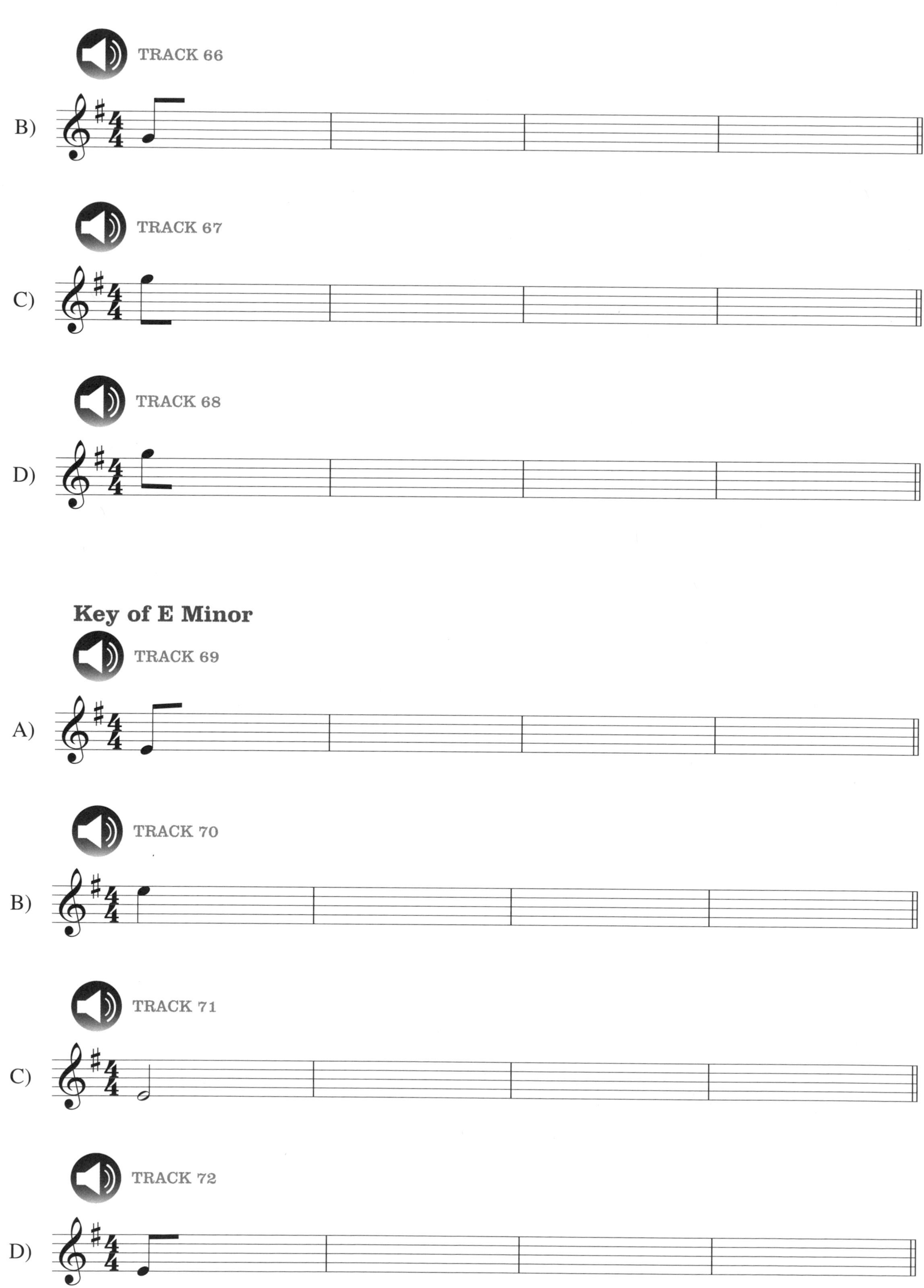
TRACK 66
B)
TRACK 67
C)
TRACK 68
D)
Key of E Minor
TRACK 69
A)
TRACK 70
B)
TRACK 71
C)
TRACK 72
D)

ECHO DRILLS

For these drills, listen to the phrase and then echo it back. (**Instructors:** See Appendix for notation of these exercises. Alternatively, these can be found on the accompanying audio.)

Rhythm Echoes

In these four exercises, you'll hear a one-bar rhythm followed by one bar of silence. Clap the rhythm back during the break.

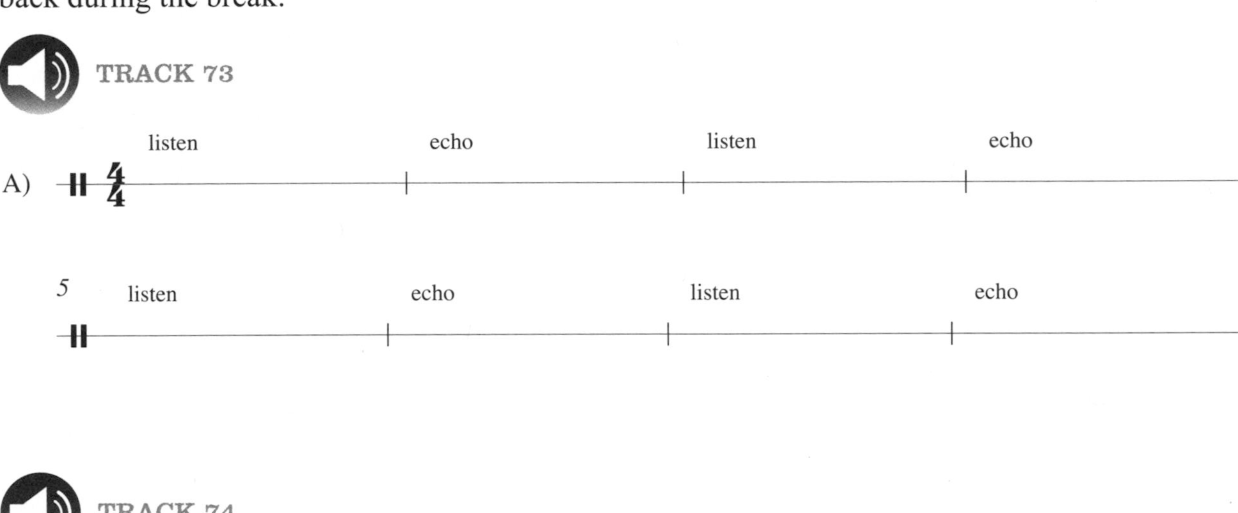

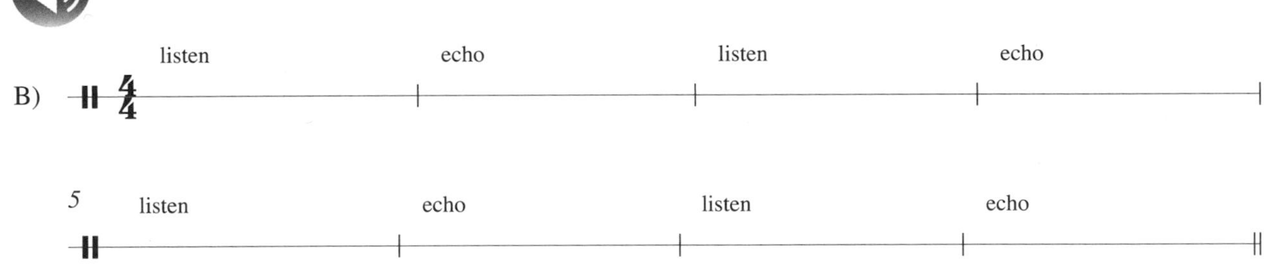

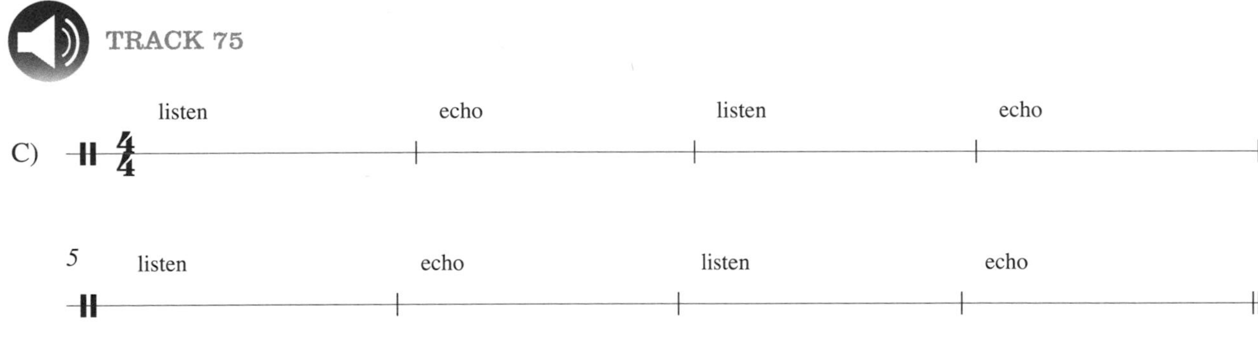

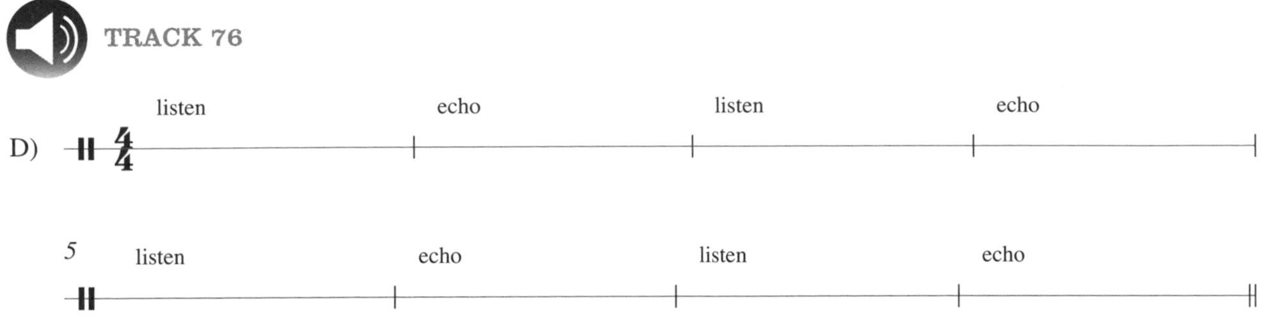

Melodic Echoes

In these four exercises, you'll hear a one-bar melody followed by one bar of silence. Sing the melody back during the break.

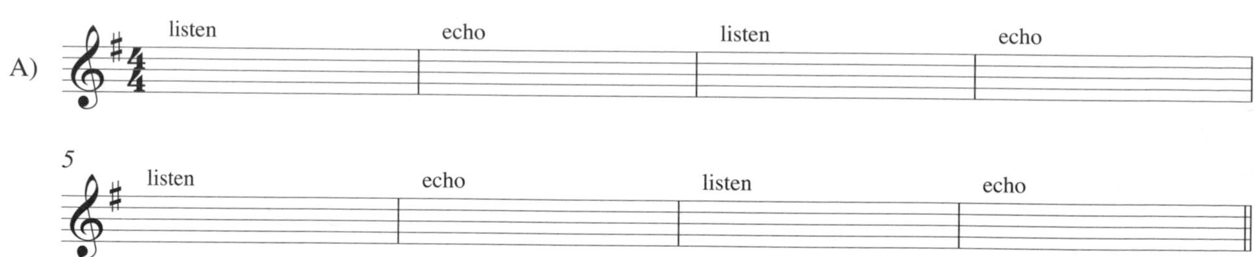

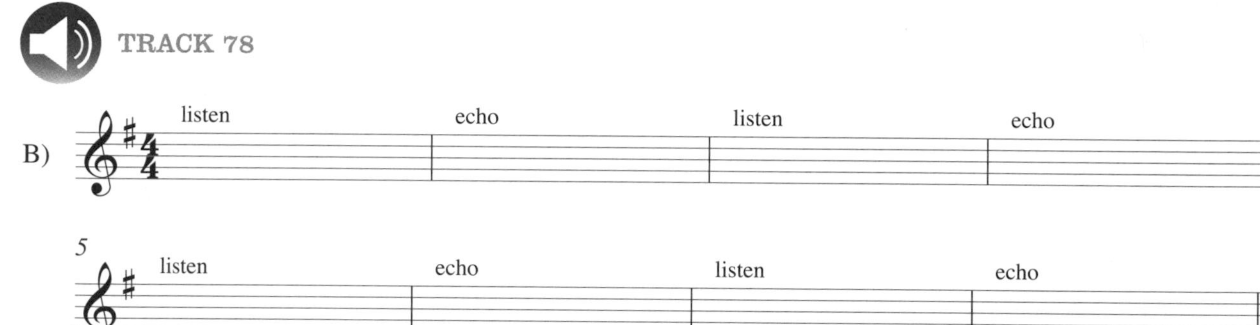

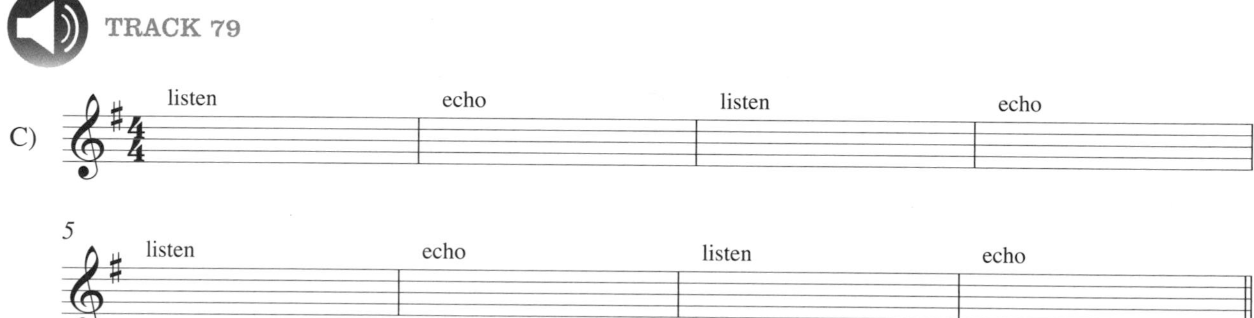

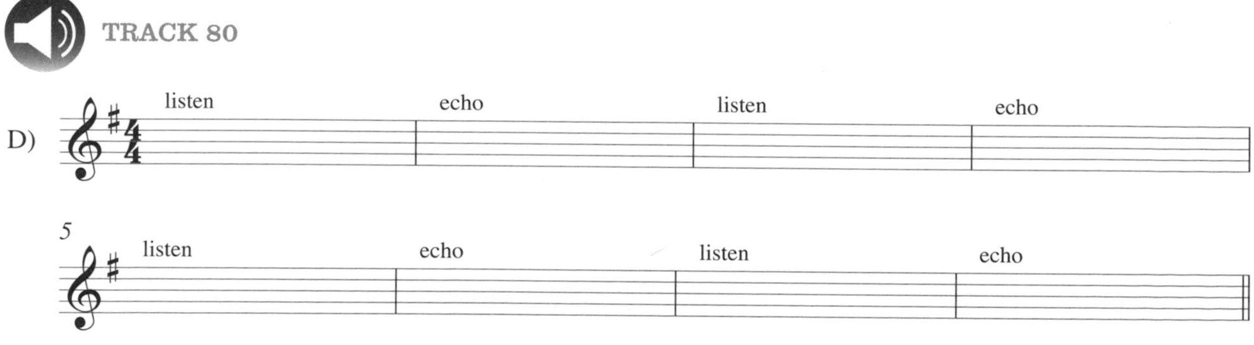

CHAPTER 5

EXERCISES IN F MAJOR AND D MINOR

In this chapter, we'll venture into our first flat key.

THE SCALES

F Major Scale

As we learned in Chapter 4, the first step in building a new scale is to write out the letter names starting and ending on the tonic. Since we want to build an F major scale, F is our tonic.

F G A B C D E F

When we look at these notes on a piano keyboard and compare them against the intervallic formula, we again discover a problem. It's different than when building a G major scale.

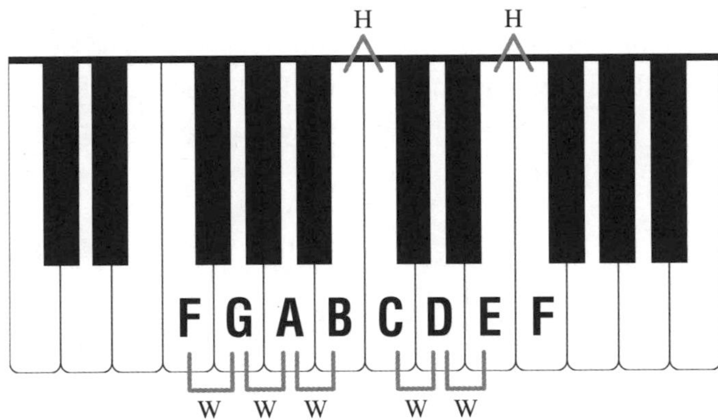

Instead of whole-whole-half in the beginning, there's whole-whole-whole, which doesn't match the formula. By lowering B to B♭, however, everything falls into place.

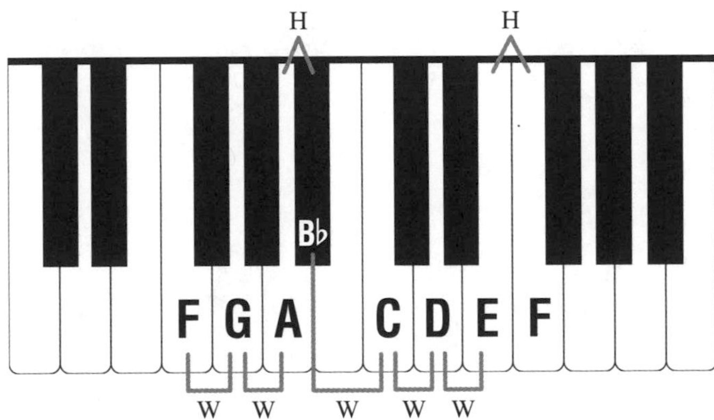

So, we now know that the F major scale is spelled F–G–A–B♭–C–D–E.

TRACK 81

The Wonderful World of Key Signatures

Think back to a time before smartphones—before computers, even. Okay, *imagine* a time before computers. Long before we could make copies of any and every little thing we wanted with just a mouse click, composers and music copyists had to write out by hand every bar of music on every page. They looked for ways to ease that burden, and they found plenty, several of which we'll look at in this book. One was a *key signature.*

A key signature is a collection of sharps or flats at the beginning of each staff that tells the performer the key of the piece. (It's placed before the time signature on the first staff.) By using a key signature, a performer knows that every time he sees a B note—in F major, for example—that he is to play B♭ instead. This way, the composer doesn't have to write a flat next to every B note in the piece. Of course, the other benefit is that it quickly lets the performer know the key of the music, which proves invaluable to the performance. A major key and its relative minor key share the same key signature, but the musical context will usually make clear which mode is being used.

What if there is no key signature, no flats or sharps at the beginning of a staff? What's up with that? In Chapter 3, we learned that there's a major key (and relative minor) that contains no sharps or flats: C major! So, a "blank" key signature tells you that you're in the key of C major or A minor. The other key we've looked at so far is G major/E minor, and its key signature contains an F♯.

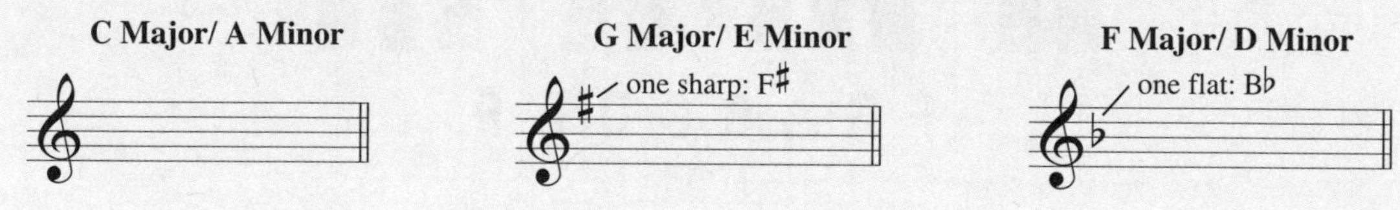

D Minor Scale

The relative minor of F major is D minor, so it's spelled D–E–F–G–A–B♭–C. Here's how it looks on the staff. Remember the key signature!

TRACK 82

Rhythm Study

In Chapter 4, we added the eighth note to our rhythm set. We'll continue to explore more complex eighth-note rhythms and look at two further rhythmic concepts: the dot and the tie.

Dots and Ties

A *dot* after a note lengthens its duration by half. A half note lasts for two beats, but a *dotted*-half note lasts for three beats. While a quarter note lasts for one beat, a dotted-quarter note lasts for a beat and a half.

A *tie* looks like a curved line connecting two notes, and there's good reason. It's used to combine the duration of two notes. For instance, if you see a half note tied to a quarter note, sing the half note and sustain it through the end of the tied quarter note, or three beats.

= 3 beats = 2 beats = 1 1/2 beats

We can notate the same rhythm by using ties and dots. For example, if you write a dotted-quarter note or a quarter note tied to an eighth note, they are the same rhythm. The general rule is this: use dotted rhythms (see A) unless crossing a bar line (see C) or the middle of the bar (from beat 2 to beat 3) in 4/4 time (see B). It's generally preferable to show beat 3. The one exception to the rule of showing beat 3 is when there is a half note on beat 2; this is permitted (see D).

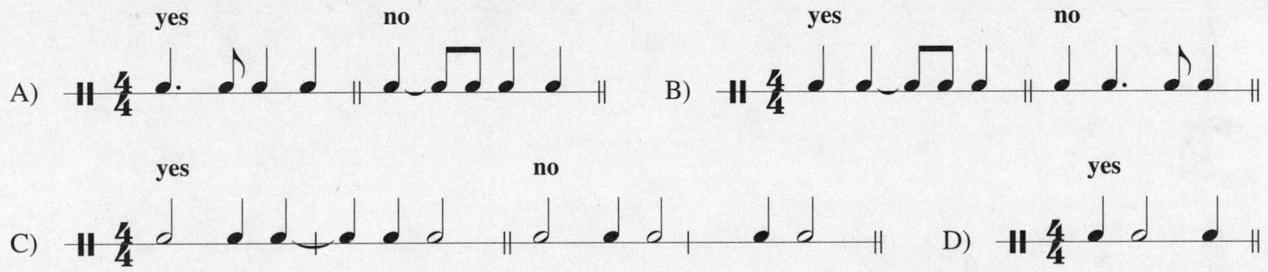

Don't worry too much about memorizing these rules right now. You'll learn to recognize the conventions by seeing them over and over throughout the book.

RHYTHMIC DRILLS

Clap the following rhythms together as a class or in smaller groups. Watch out for the dotted and tied notes. These won't be so evident with hand claps, because they don't sustain, but you'll need to recognize them in the dictations that follow. The counts have been included for these new elements.

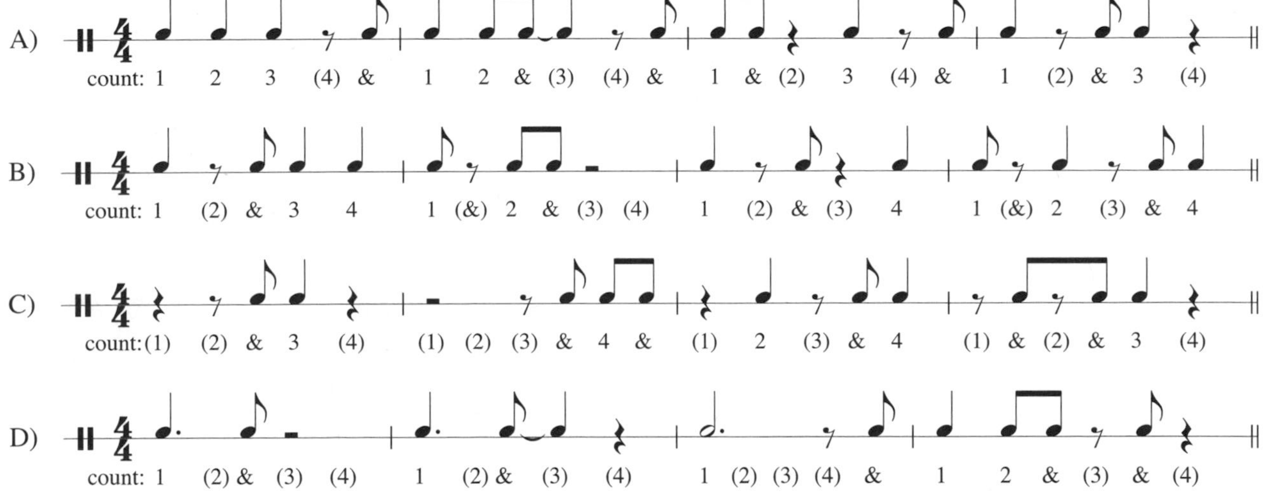

Rhythmic Dictation

Listen to the following rhythms and write them down. Each example will be played twice. Be sure to listen closely to the duration of each note. Note the ties and dots!

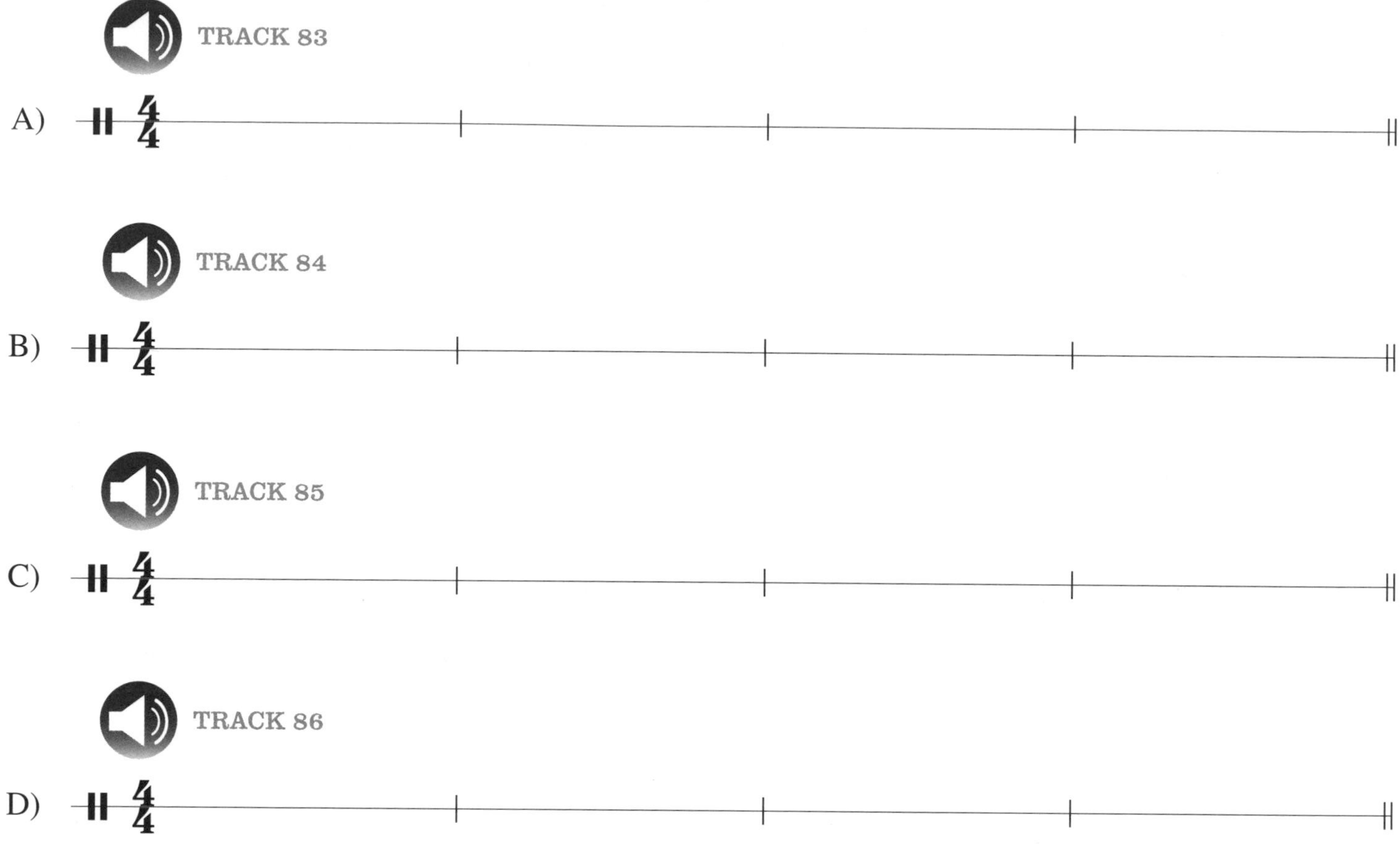

INTERVAL STUDY

Now that we have 2nds and 3rds securely in hand, let's expand our interval database to 4ths and 5ths. The same rule applies to the interval quantity here, so a 4th involves four letter names, and a 5th involves five. Therefore:

- from C up to F is a 4th
- from C up to G is a 5th

Unlike 2nds and 3rds, 4th and 5th intervals don't use major and minor descriptors for their quality: They use *perfect*, *diminished*, or *augmented*. (A 4th is usually only perfect or augmented, but a 5th can be any of the three.) In this chapter, we'll look at the perfect variety.

Perfect 4ths and Perfect 5ths

A perfect 4th (P4) is the distance of five half steps, or two-and-a-half steps. From C to F is a perfect 4th. Let's confirm this on the piano keyboard:

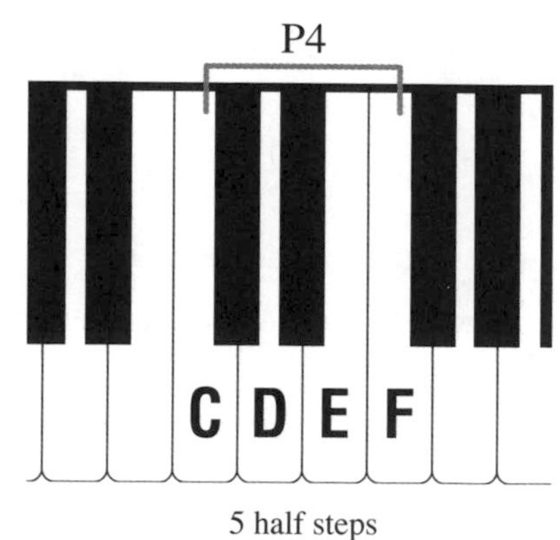

A perfect 5th (P5) is the distance of seven half steps, or three-and-a-half steps. From C to G is a perfect 5th. We can confirm this on the piano as well:

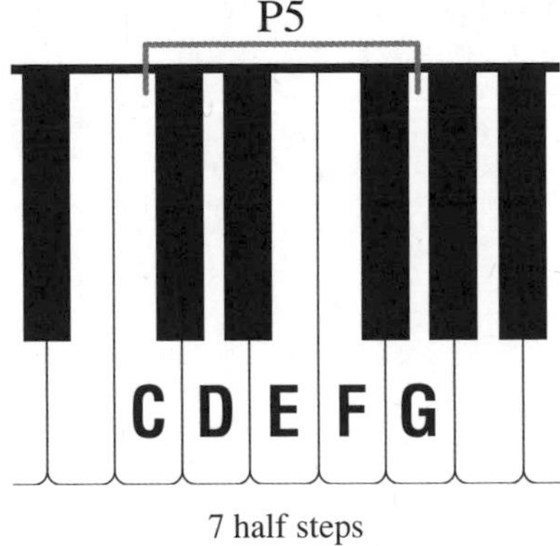

7 half steps

Listen to a perfect 4th, from C to F.

 TRACK 87

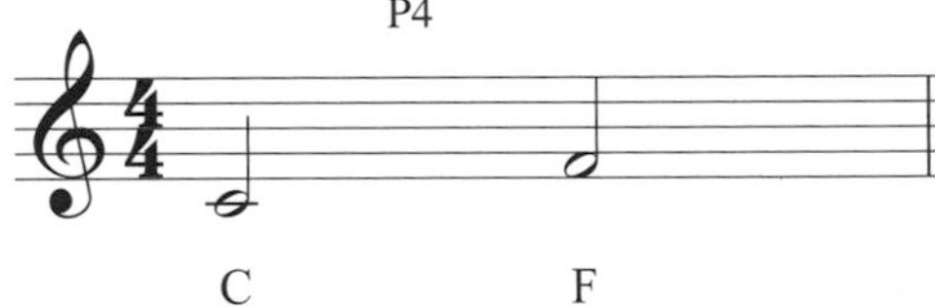

And here's a perfect 5th, from C to G.

 TRACK 88

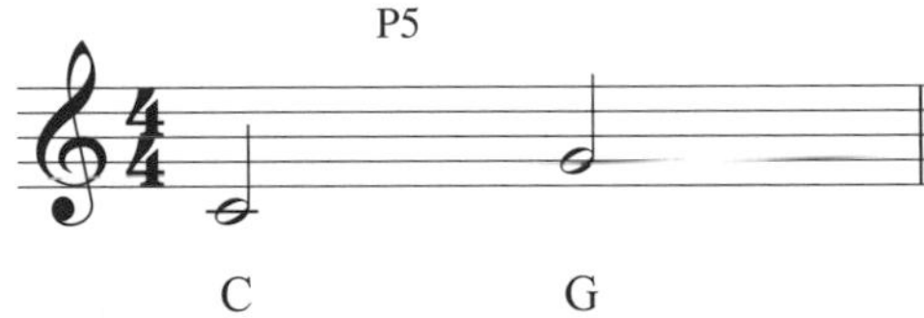

Interval Dictation

Listen to the following intervals and determine whether they are a P4 (perfect 4th) or a P5 (perfect 5th).

 TRACK 89

A) ___

B) ___

C) ___

D) ___

E) ___

F) ___

G) ___

H) ___

SIGHT-SINGING EXERCISES

These examples will feature all the intervals we've studied thus far: 2nds, 3rds, 4ths, and 5ths. Watch also for the dotted notes and tied notes.

Key of F Major

In F major, the key signature tells you that every B note is a B♭. As you sing through these examples, pay attention to the tendency of certain notes. What do you want or expect to hear after certain tones?

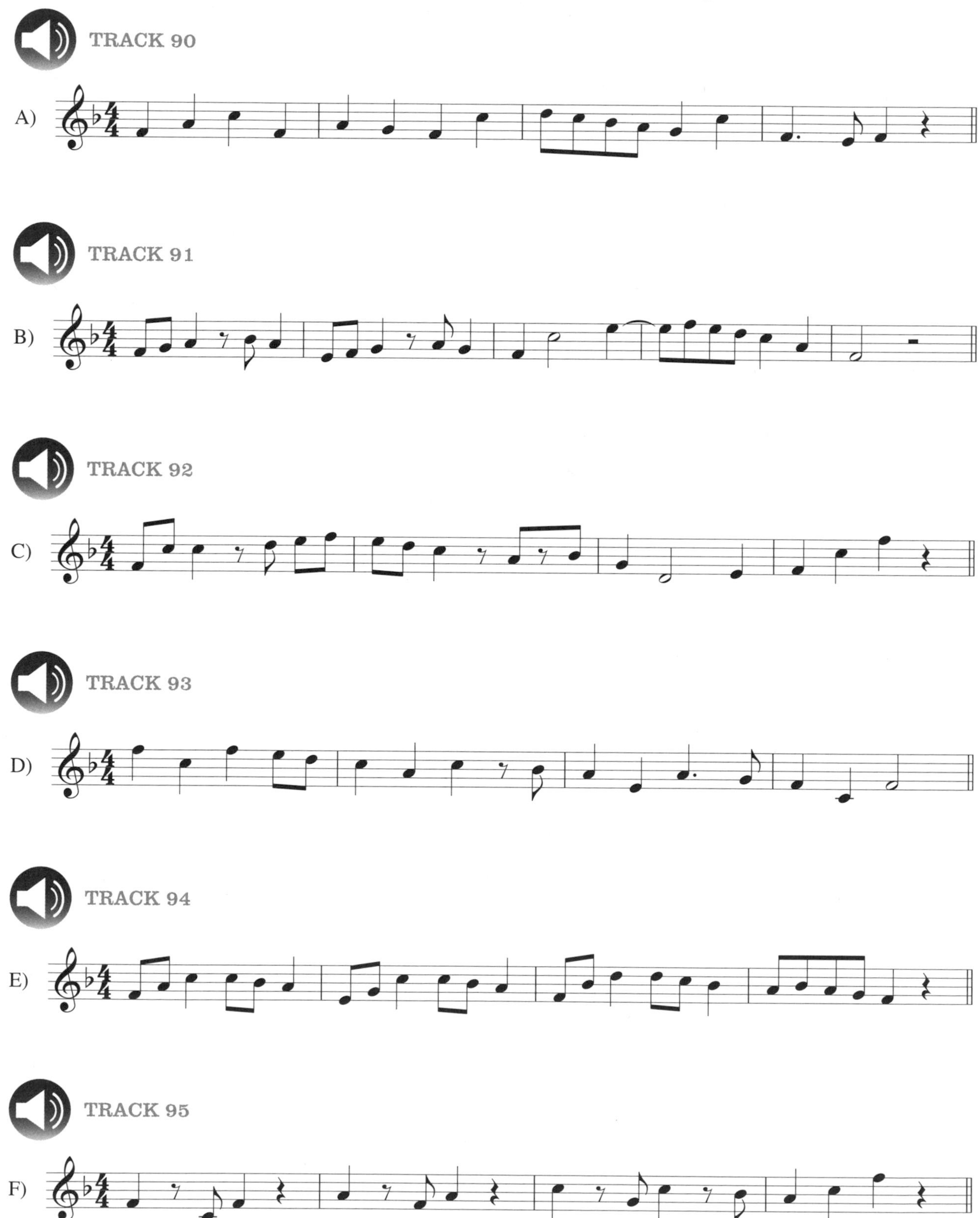

Key of D Minor

Observe how the notes in these melodies sound different when tonicizing D, the relative minor.

TRACK 96

A)

TRACK 97

B)

TRACK 98

C)

TRACK 99

D)

TRACK 100

E)

TRACK 101

F)

MELODIC DICTATION EXERCISES

In each of these exercises, the melody is played twice. Write it down on the music staff. The B♭ key signature has been added for you. (**Instructors:** See Appendix for notation of these exercises. Alternatively, these can be found on the accompanying audio.)

Key of F Major

TRACK 102

A) 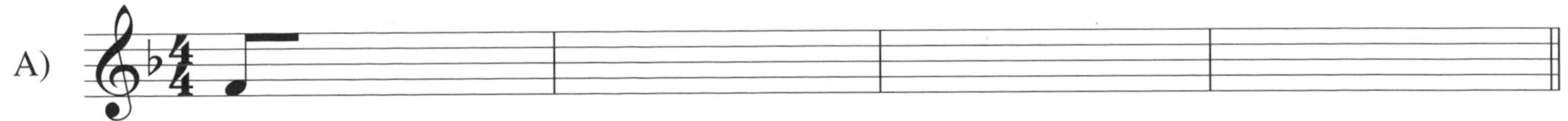

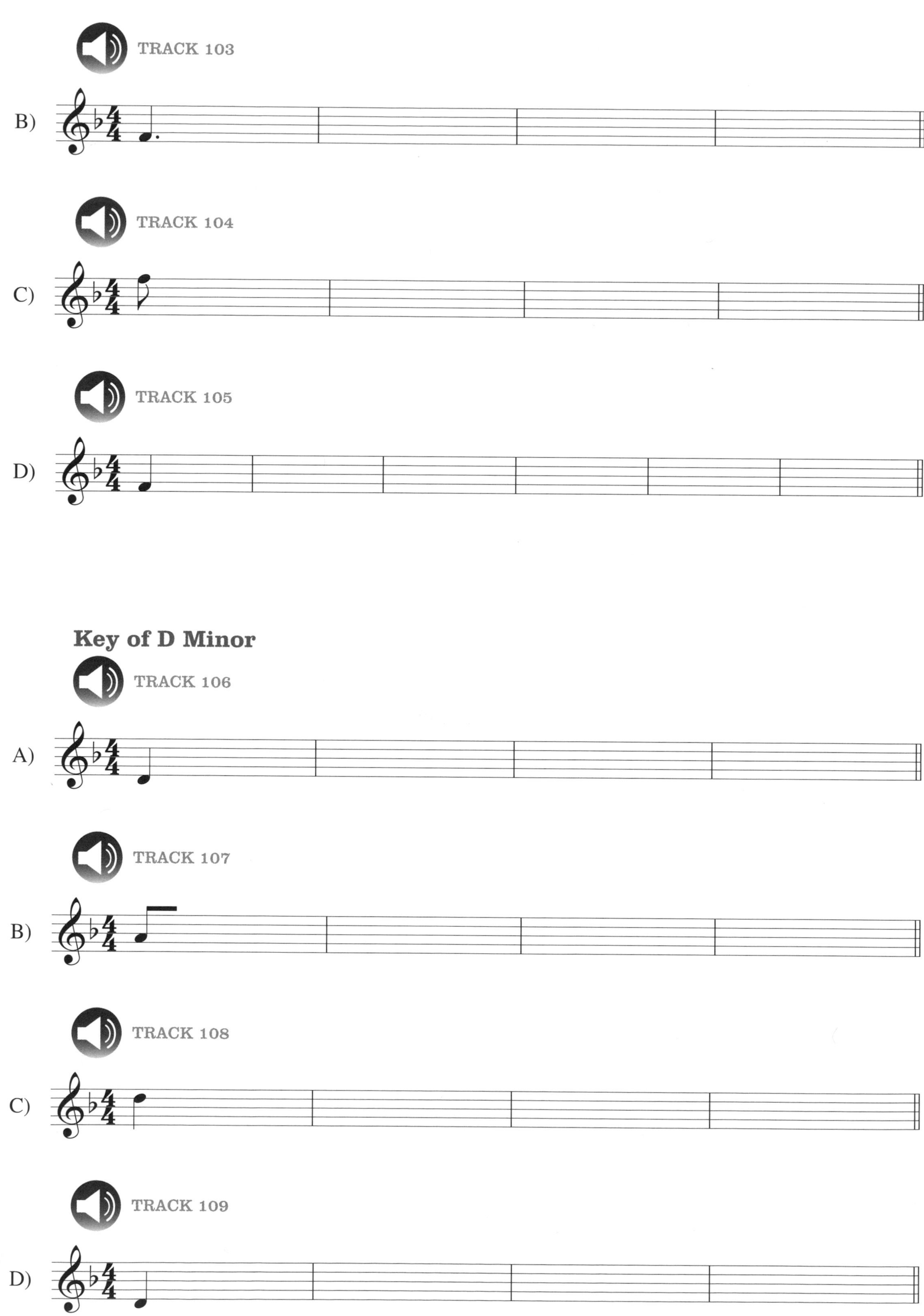
TRACK 103
B)
TRACK 104
C)
TRACK 105
D)
Key of D Minor
TRACK 106
A)
TRACK 107
B)
TRACK 108
C)
TRACK 109
D)

ECHO DRILLS

For these drills, listen to the phrase and then echo it back. (**Instructors:** See Appendix for notation of these exercises. Alternatively, these can be found on the accompanying audio.)

Rhythm Echoes

In these four exercises, you'll hear a one-bar rhythm followed by one bar of silence. Clap the rhythm back during the break.

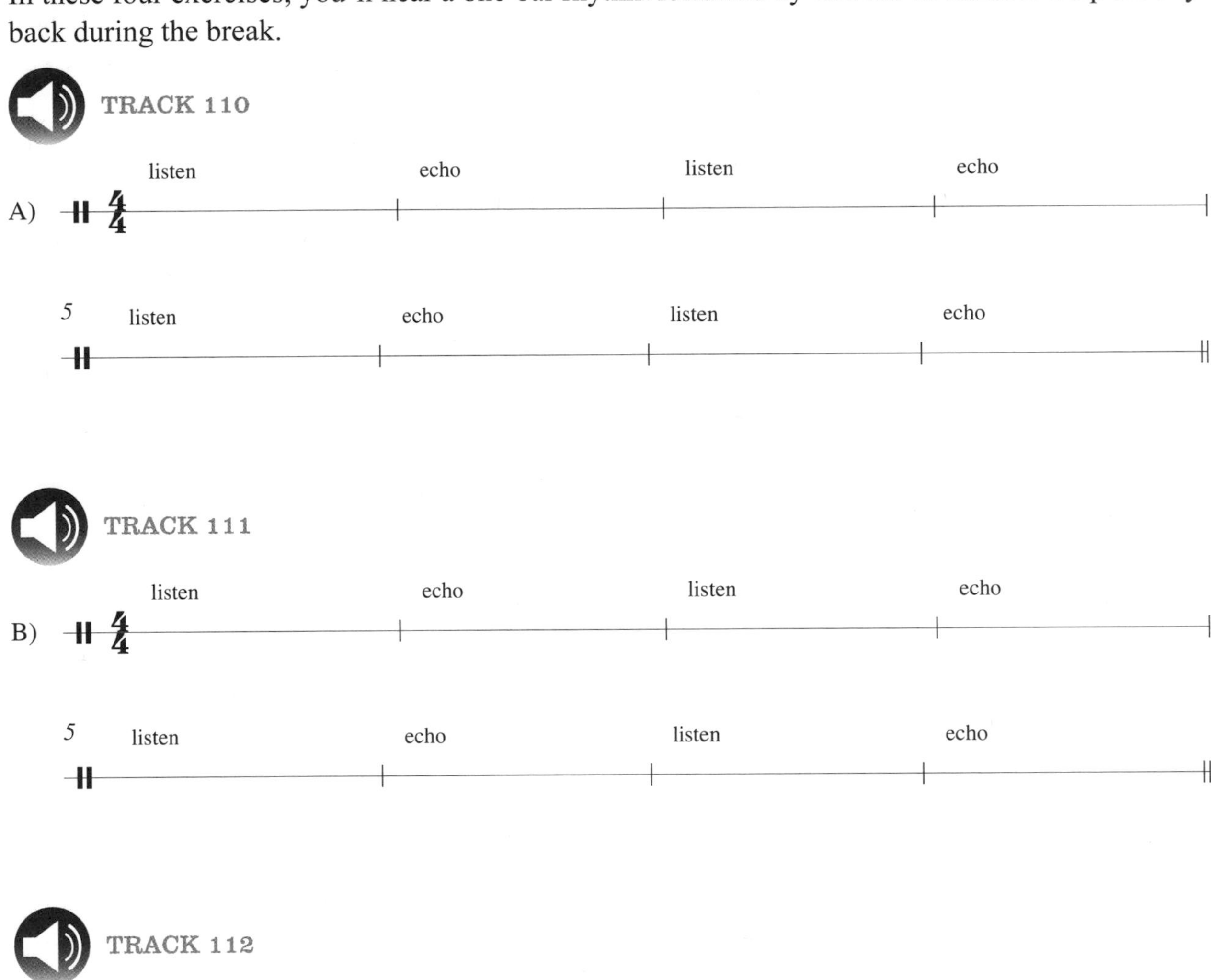

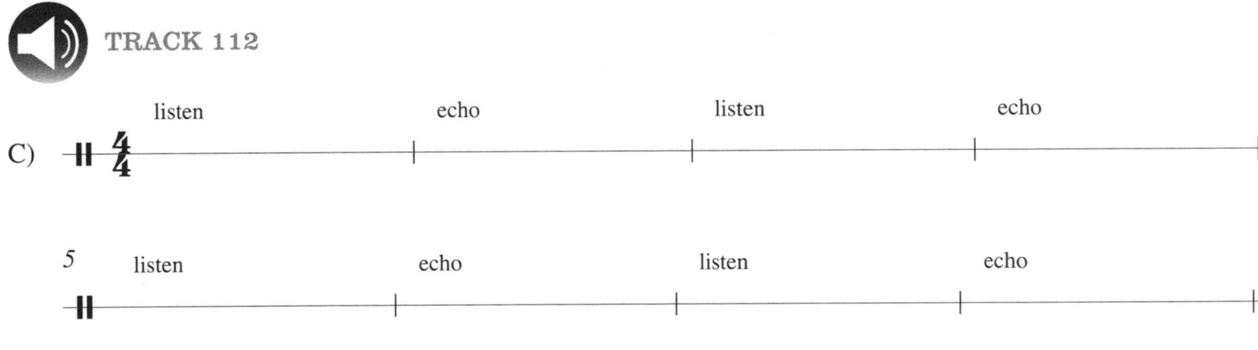

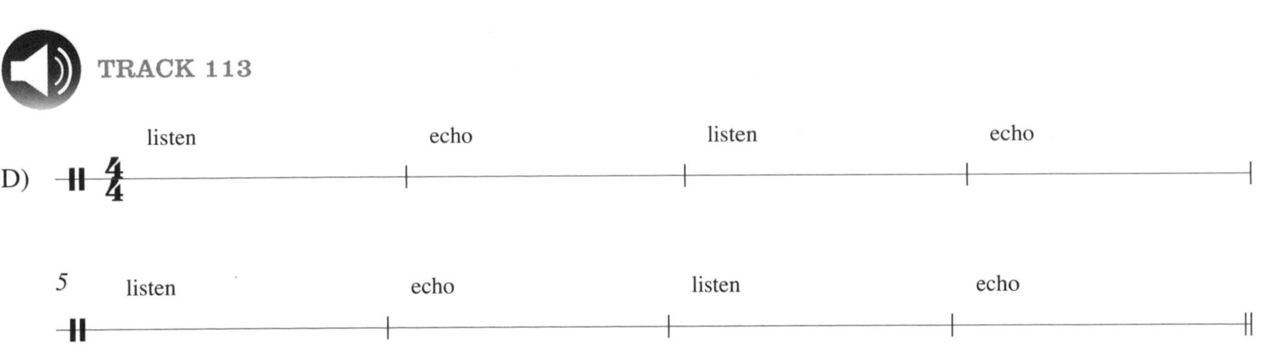

Melodic Echoes

In these four exercises, you'll hear a one-bar melody followed by one bar of silence. Sing the melody back during the break.

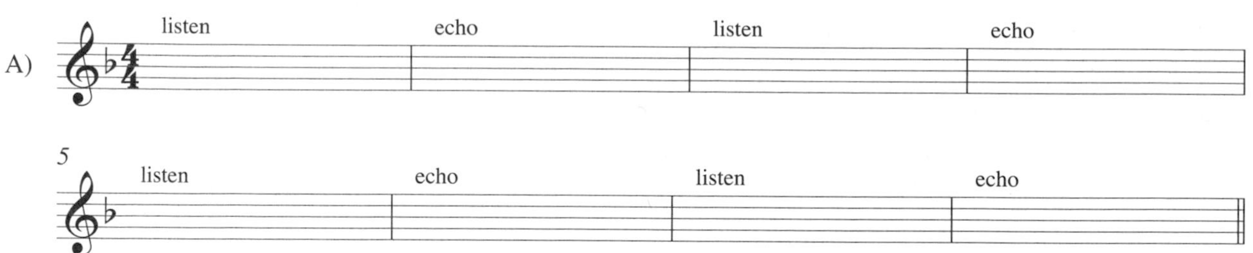

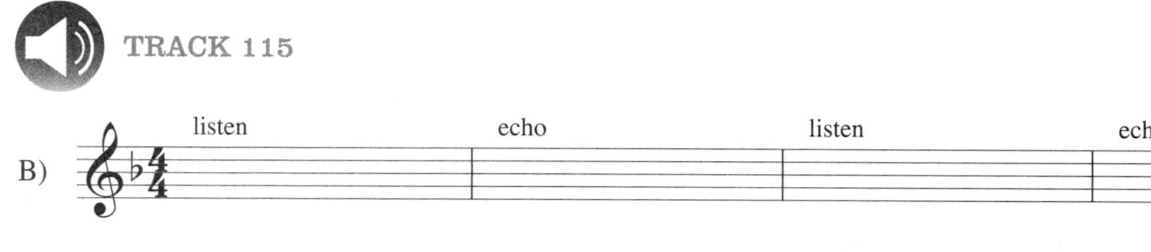

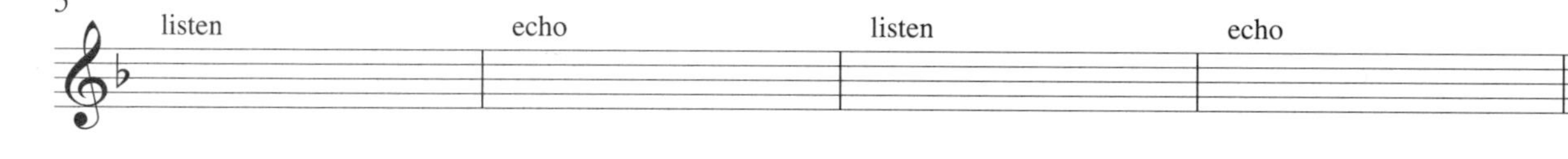

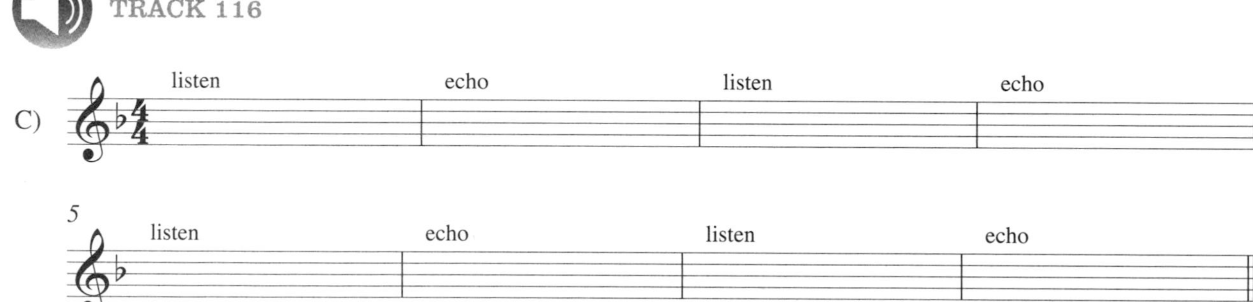

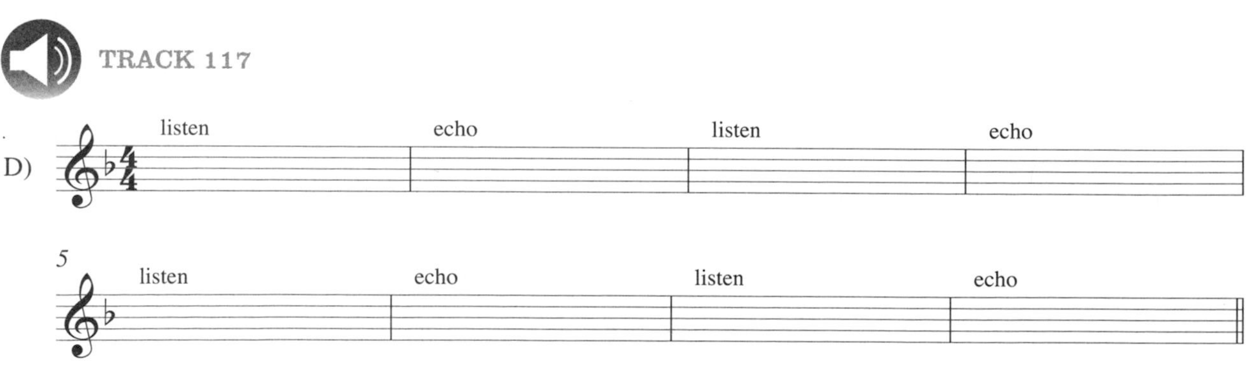

CHAPTER 6
EXERCISES IN D MAJOR AND B MINOR

In this chapter, we'll study the key of D major and its relative minor, B minor.

THE SCALES

To get the keys of D major and B minor, we add one more sharp. Let's see how this works.

D Major Scale

First, write out the letter names spanning from tonic to tonic:

D E F G A B C D

Looking at these notes on a piano keyboard and comparing them against the intervallic formula, we find two problems:

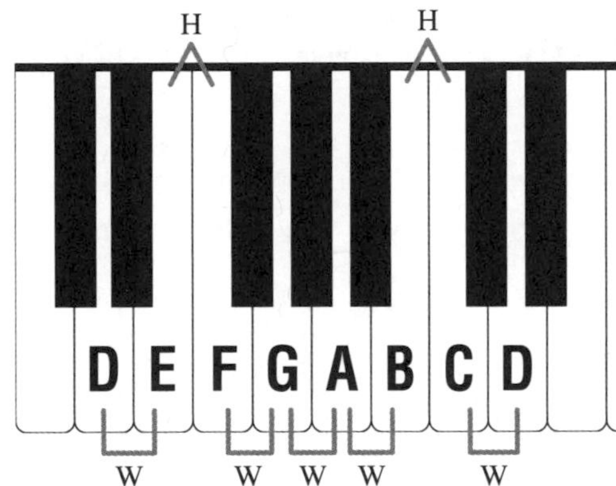

The F and C notes are out of sync with the formula. When we raise them to F# and C#, respectively, the proper configuration is restored.

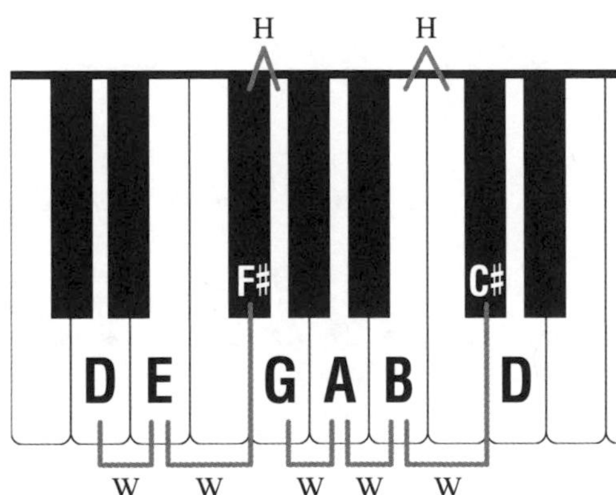

So, we now know that the D major scale is spelled D–E–F#–G–A–B–C#. And the key signature for D major is two sharps: F# and C#.

TRACK 118

B Minor Scale

B minor is the relative minor of D major, so its key signature also contains two sharps.

RHYTHM STUDY

We'll continue adding complexity to our rhythms in 4/4, and also look at a new meter (time signature), 3/4.

3/4 Time

In 3/4 time, the quarter note is counted as the beat, just as in 4/4, but there are only three beats per measure.

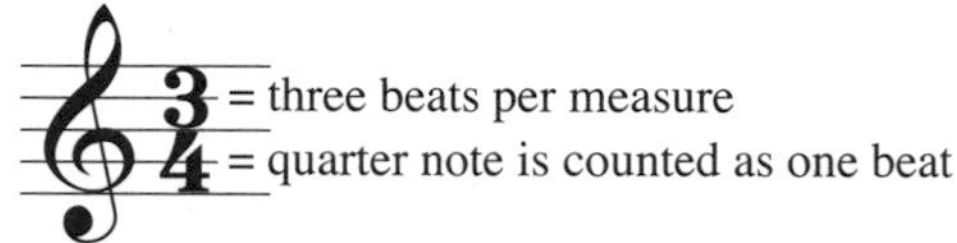

You've heard this meter in many waltzes, which are all in 3/4, but it's often encountered elsewhere. For example, "Happy Birthday" and "The Star-Spangled Banner" are both in 3/4.

Rhythmic Drills

Clap the following rhythms together as a class or in smaller groups.

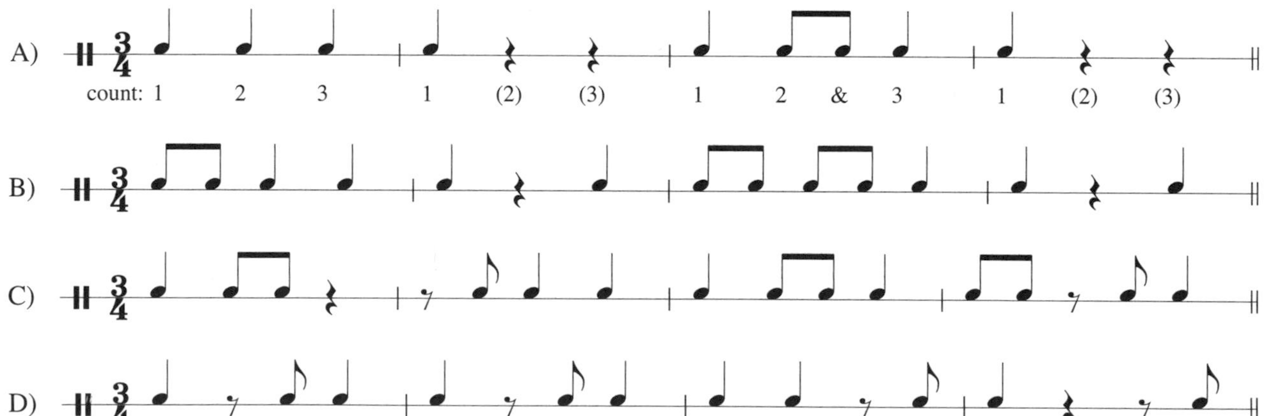

Rhythmic Dictation

Listen to the following rhythms and write them down. Each example will be played twice. Be sure to listen closely to the duration of each note.

A)

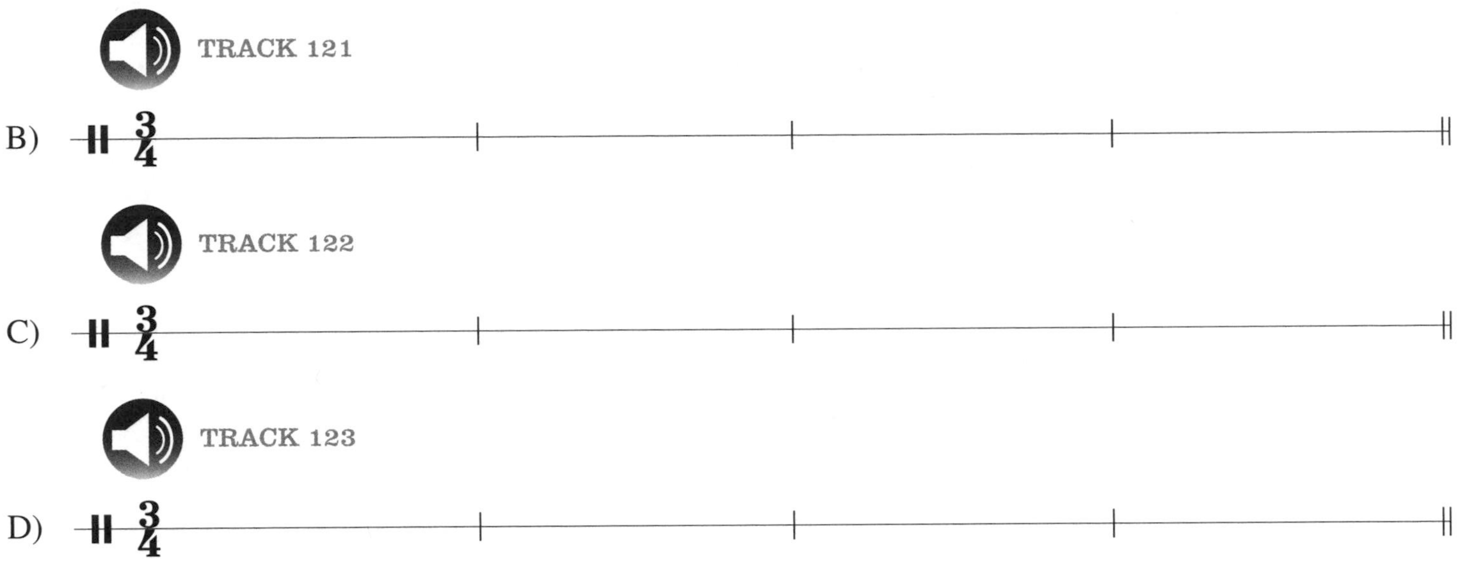

INTERVAL/CHORD STUDY

Rather than learning a new interval at this point, let's make further use of what we know already. We're going to look at arpeggios. An *arpeggio* is simply the notes of a chord played one at a time—as a melody—instead of all at once.

Triads

Before you can fashion an arpeggio, you need to know how to build a chord. For that, we go back to the major scale and a process called "stacking 3rds." If we take the tonic of our D major scale, for example, and stack a 3rd on it, we have D and F♯. The D is the tonic, or 1, E is the 2nd, or 2, and F♯ is the 3rd, or 3. Remember that a 3rd interval involves three letter names: D (1), E (2), and F♯ (3). Specifically, this is a major 3rd, because it contains four half steps.

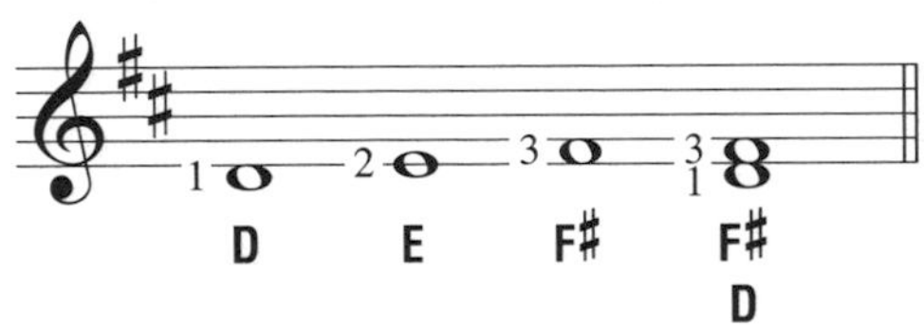

If we continue this process and stack another 3rd on top of the F♯, we'll add an A, because A is a 3rd above F♯. Technically, from F♯ to A is a minor 3rd, because it contains three half steps.

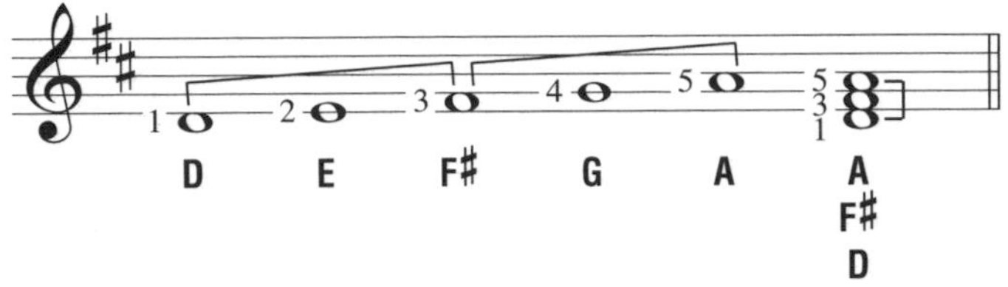

We've constructed a D major triad. It's called a *triad* because it contains three notes: a root, a 3rd, and a 5th (or 1, 3, and 5). The triad is the most common type of chord in music; almost all triads are built with a root, 3rd, and 5th. Since there are different types of 3rd and 5th intervals, there are different types of triads. Each is built upon a certain intervallic formula, just like scales are.

Major Triad

A major triad contains a root, a major 3rd, and a perfect 5th. A D major triad (the chord symbol is simply "D") is spelled D–F♯–A.

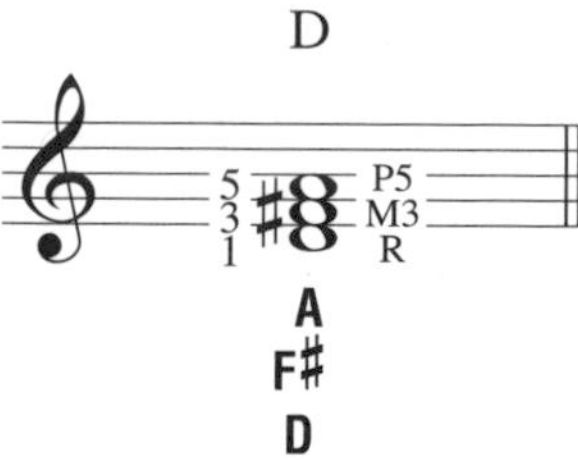

Minor Triad

A minor triad contains a root, a *minor* 3rd, and a perfect 5th. A D minor triad (Dm) is spelled D–F–A.

TRACK 125

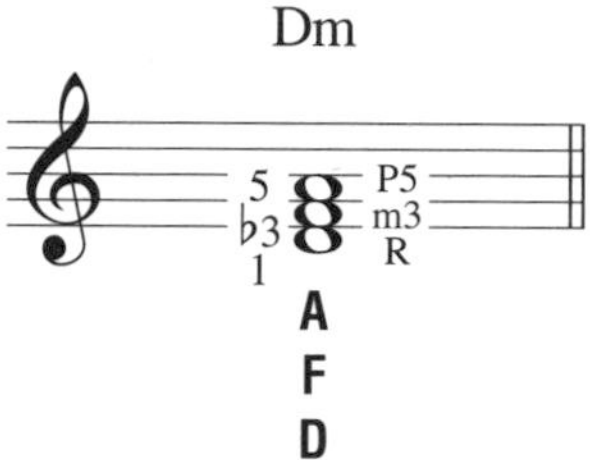

Augmented Triad

An augmented triad contains a root, a major 3rd, and an *augmented* 5th. A D augmented triad (D+) is spelled D–F♯–A♯.

TRACK 126

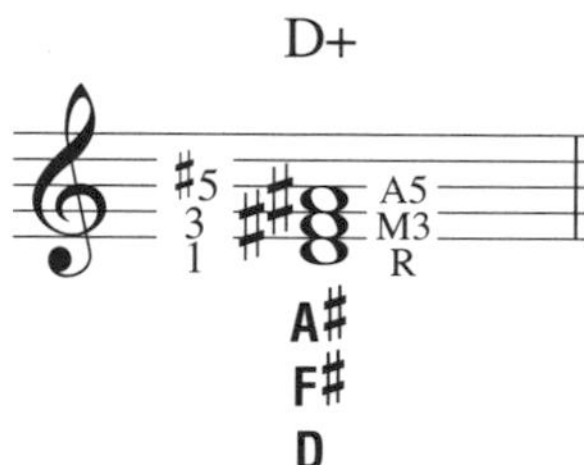

Diminished Triad

A diminished triad contains a root, a minor 3rd, and a diminished 5th. A D diminished triad (D°) is spelled D–F–A♭.

TRACK 127

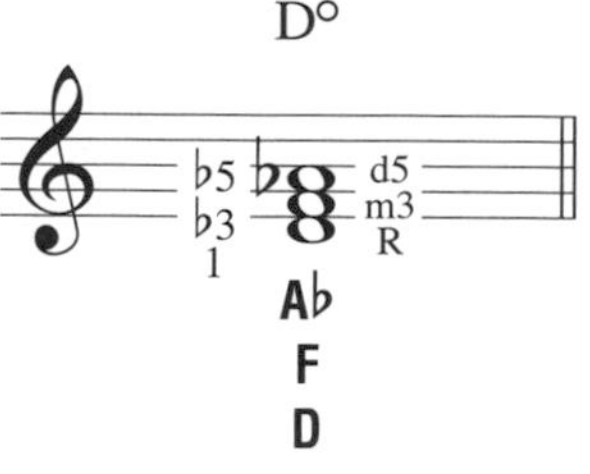

HARMONIZING THE MAJOR SCALE

Stacking 3rds for every note of the D major scale, we get three different types of triads: three major triads, three minor triads, and a diminished triad.

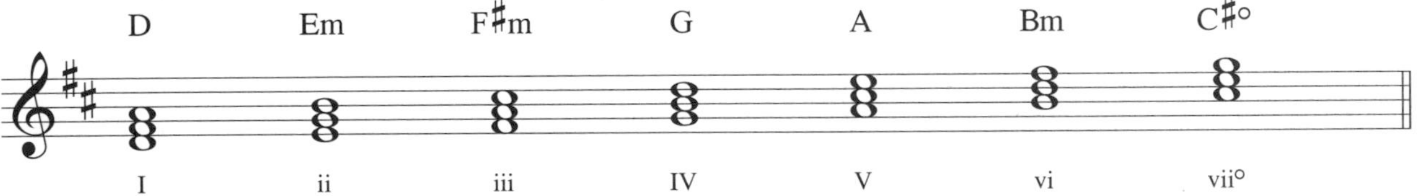

The Roman numerals identify the function of the chord within the key: uppercase for major chords and lowercase for minor chords. (The "vii°" symbol indicates a diminished chord.) Just like the major scale's intervallic formula of W-W-H-W-W-W-H, this arrangement of chord qualities is also a formula shared by every harmonized major scale:

I (major) ii (minor) iii (minor) IV (major) V (major) vi (minor) vii° (diminished)

Notice that the augmented triad is not present. An augmented chord never appears as a *diatonic* chord (diatonic means "within the key") and is found only as a *non-diatonic* chord.

TRIAD DICTATION

Let's work on recognizing these triads aurally. Listen to the following chords and determine whether they are major, minor, augmented, or diminished. They'll all be played with a D root note at this time.

A) ___

B) ___

C) ___

D) ___

E) ___

F) ___

G) ___

H) ___

SIGHT-SINGING EXERCISES

Now let's try our hand at singing some of these arpeggios. For now, we're going to concentrate on the I, IV, and V chords of the key. Before we get started, though, let's cover one more concept: *inversion*.

Root Position

A chord is said to be inverted when a note other than the root is on the bottom. In other words, this D major chord is in *root position* because its root, D, is on the bottom. It's arranged, from low to high, 1–3–5 (or root–3rd–5th).

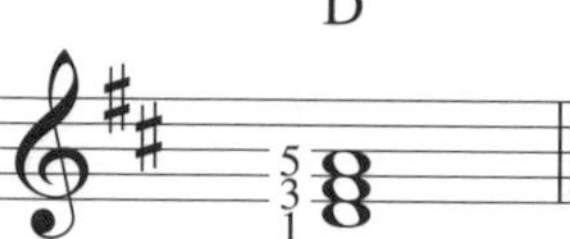

First Inversion

However, if we transfer that D note up an octave, we're left with the 3rd, F#, on the bottom, and the chord is now arranged, from low to high, 3–5–1 (3rd–5th–root). This arrangement is called *first inversion.*

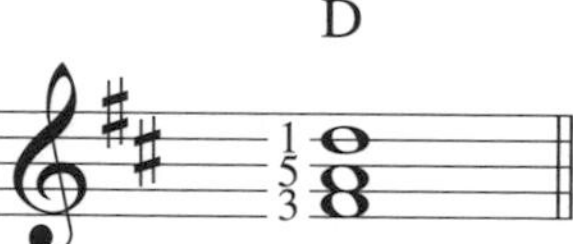

Second Inversion

If we repeat the process again, moving the lowest note (the 3rd) up an octave, we're left with the 5th, A, on the bottom, with an arrangement of 5–1–3. This is called *second inversion.*

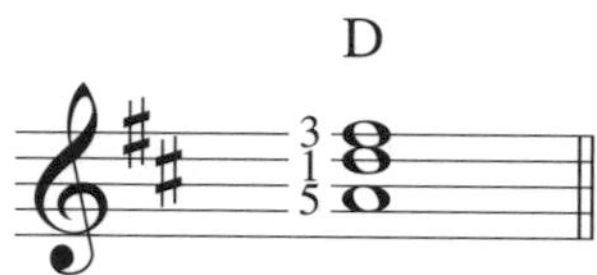

Repeating the process again brings us back to root position an octave higher than when we started.

Inversions are important because they allow for smoother voice-leading when changing chords and/or arpeggios. A pianist could play the I (D), IV (G), and V (A) chords in the key of D, like this:

TRACK 130

However, she could play some of them in inversion and not have to move around so much, resulting in a sleeker sound.

TRACK 131

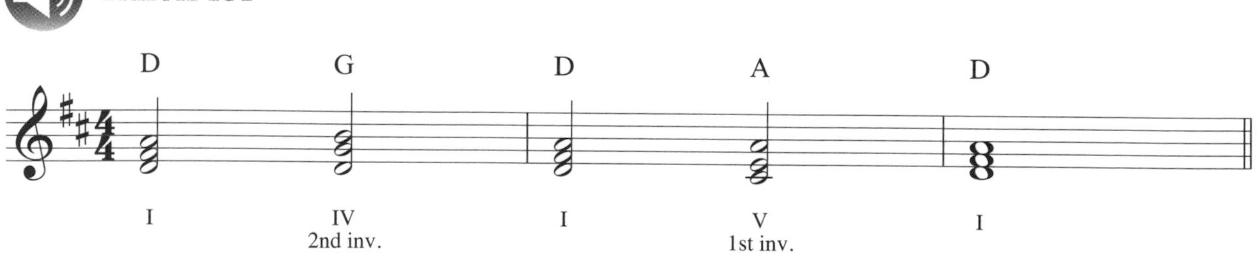

It's the same chord progression, but it sounds smoother and less disjointed. Similarly, we'll employ inversions when singing through these arpeggios; it would be difficult—and would sound rather bumpy—to sing root-position voicings for each chord.

Key of D Major

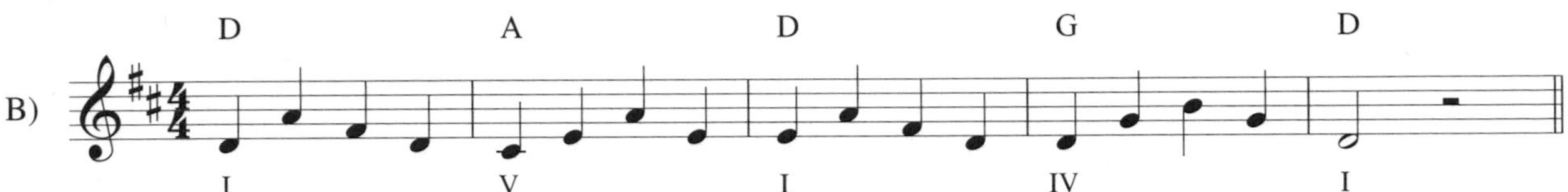

TRACK 135

Key of B Minor

B minor is the relative of D major (see page 13). When we harmonize the B minor scale, the following triads result:

TRACK 136

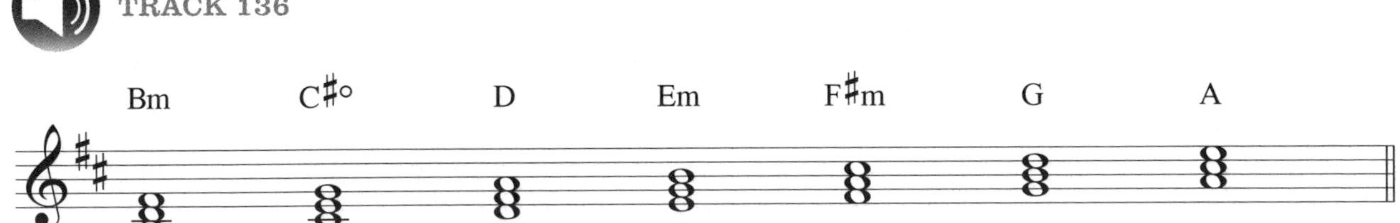

These are the same triads we built on the D major scale (see page 47), but now we're treating B minor as the tonic chord, so the Roman numerals reflect this. (In Chapter 16, we'll look at the harmonic and melodic minor scales, which make use of certain non-diatonic tones to allow for a more satisfying sense of resolution.)

So, the i, iv, and v chords in B minor are Bm (i), Em (iv), and F♯m (v). Let's sing through a few arpeggio exercises to outline them.

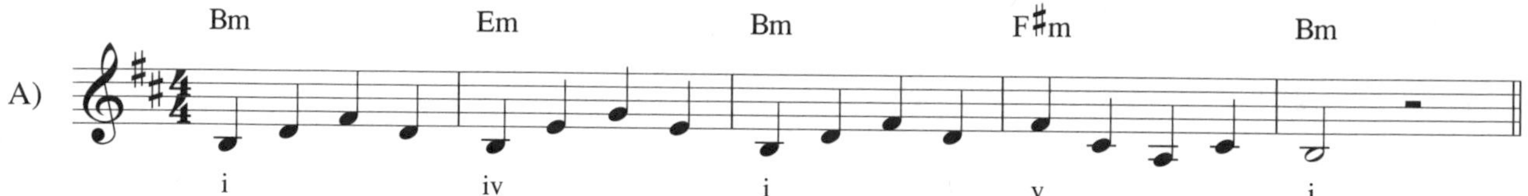

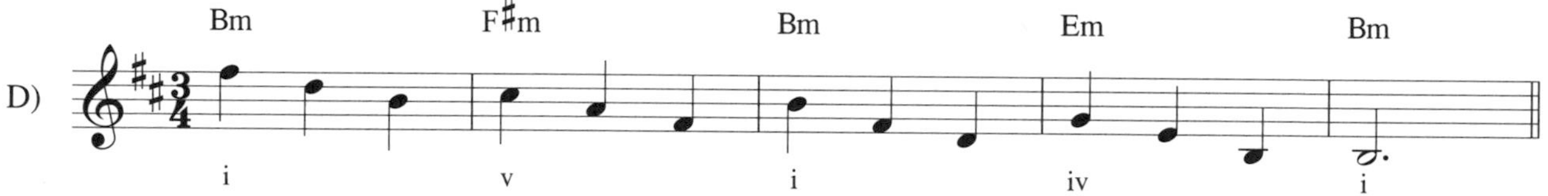

MELODIC DICTATION EXERCISES

In these exercises, you'll hear the instructor play a melody twice, and you'll write it down by ear. Remember to listen for the arpeggios and not just the individual notes. (**Instructors:** See Appendix for notation of these exercises. Alternatively, these can be found on the accompanying audio.)

Key of D Major

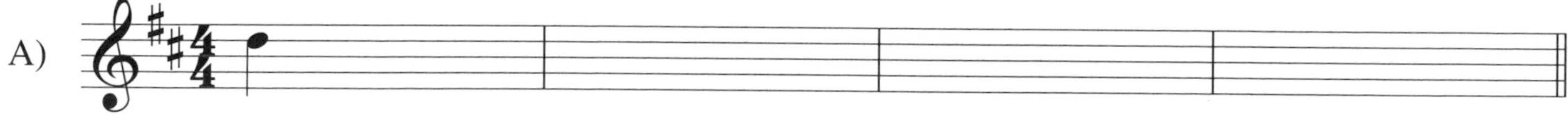

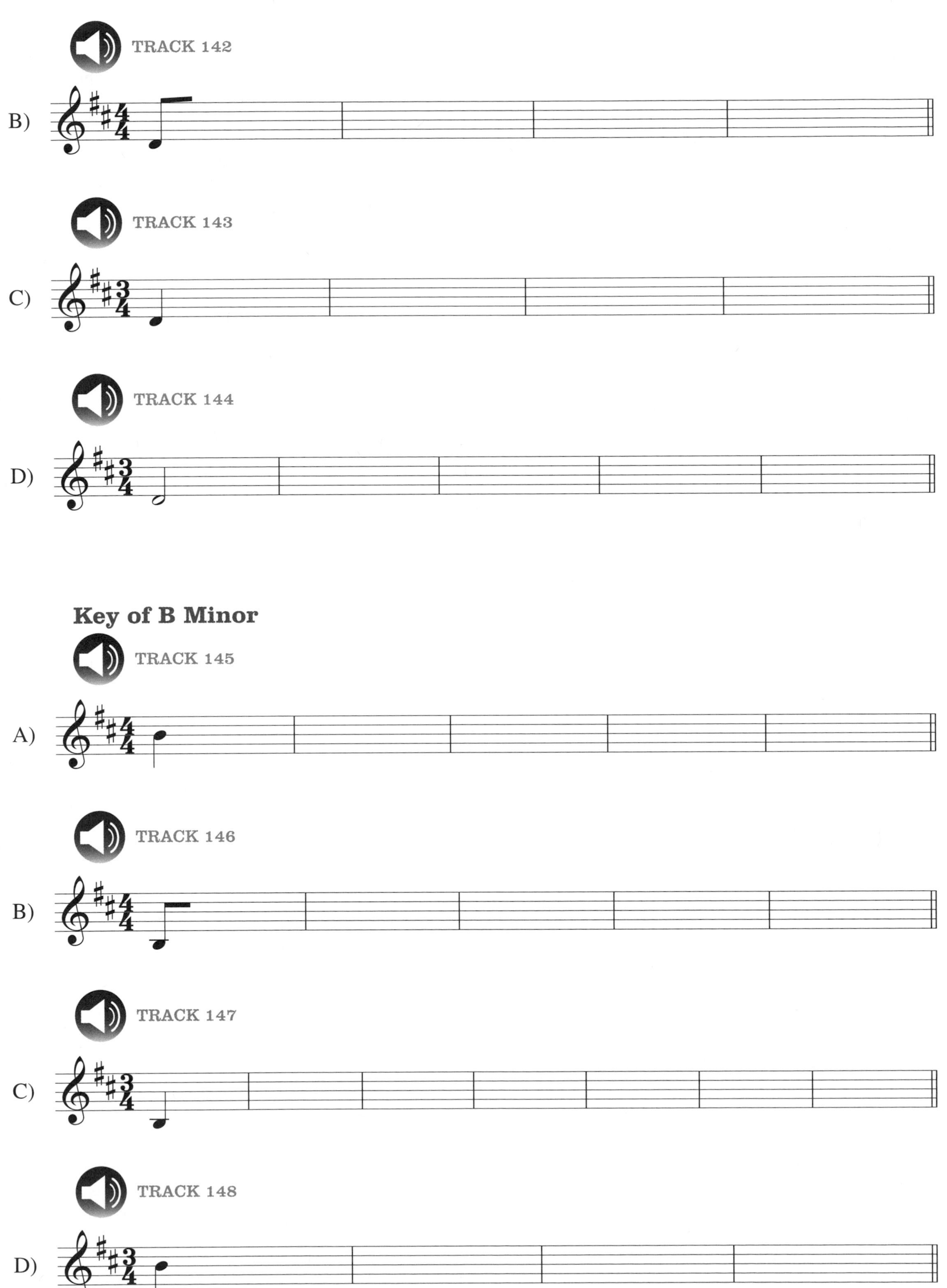
TRACK 142
B)
TRACK 143
C)
TRACK 144
D)
Key of B Minor
TRACK 145
A)
TRACK 146
B)
TRACK 147
C)
TRACK 148
D)

ECHO DRILLS

For these drills, listen to the phrase and then echo it back. (**Instructors:** See Appendix for notation of these exercises. Alternatively, these can be found on the accompanying audio.)

Rhythm Echoes

In these four exercises, you'll hear a one-bar rhythm followed by one bar of silence. Clap the rhythm back during the break.

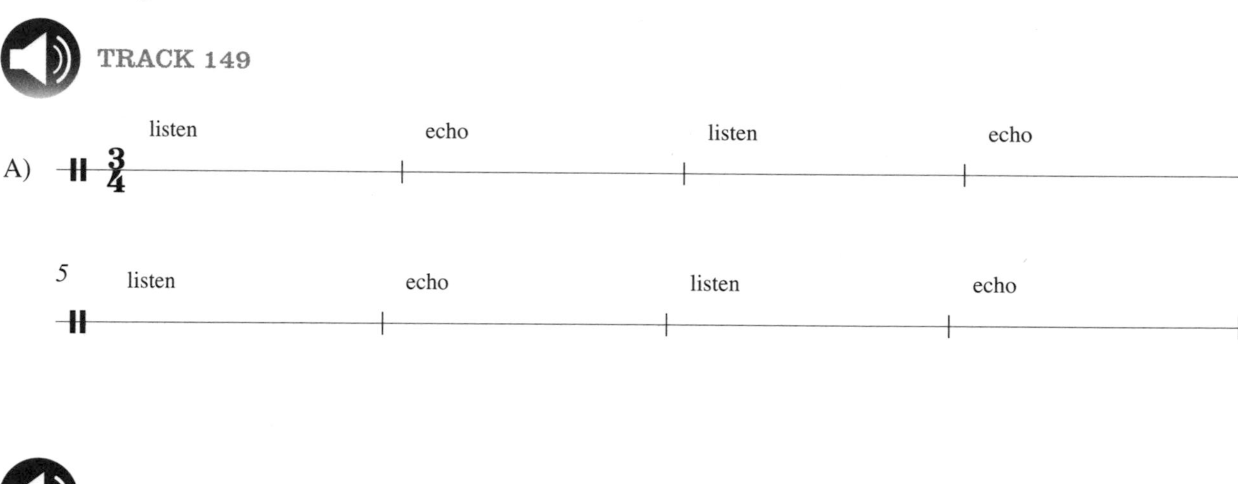

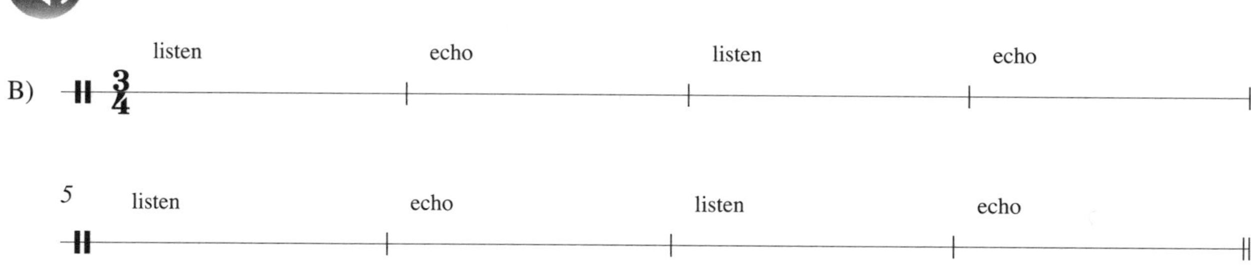

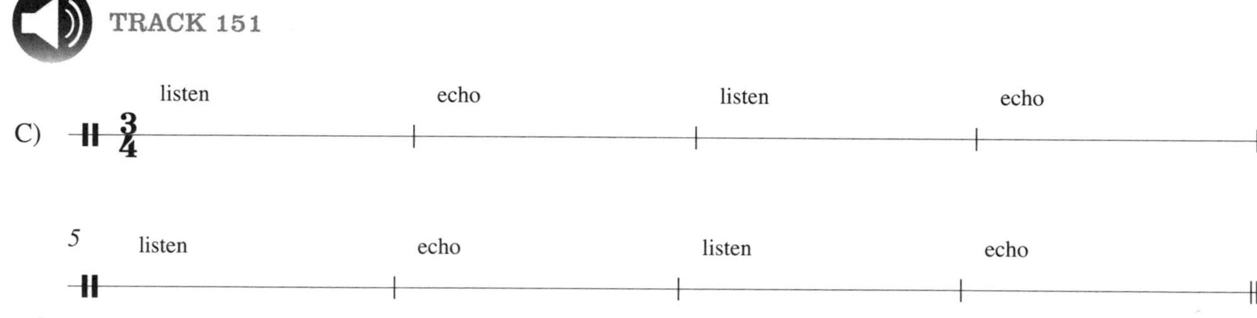

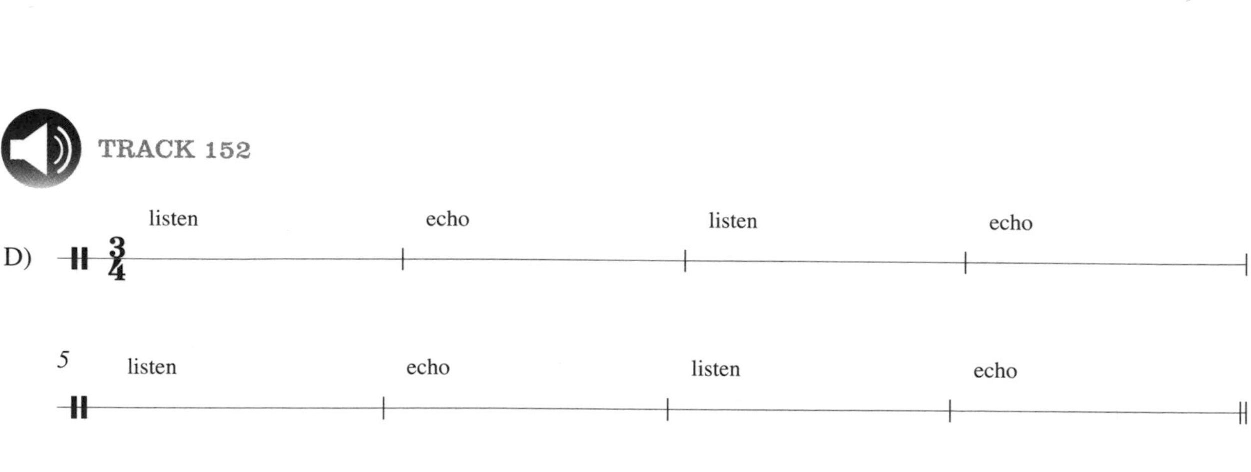

Melodic Echoes

In these four exercises, you'll hear a one-bar melody followed by one bar of silence. Sing the melody back during the break.

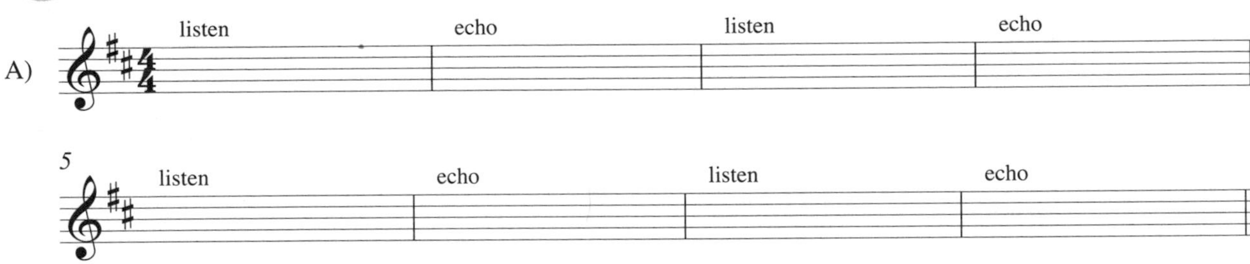

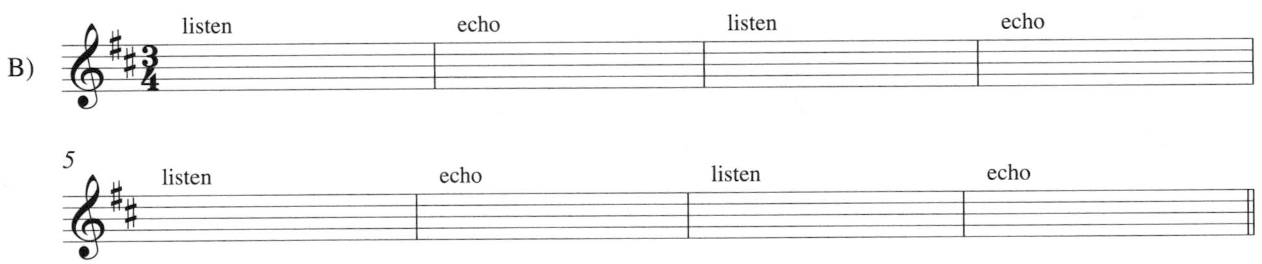

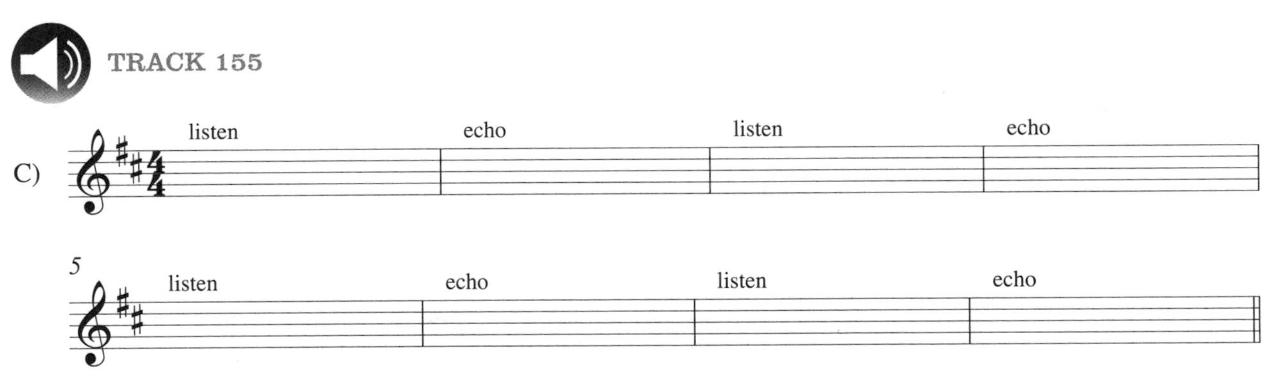

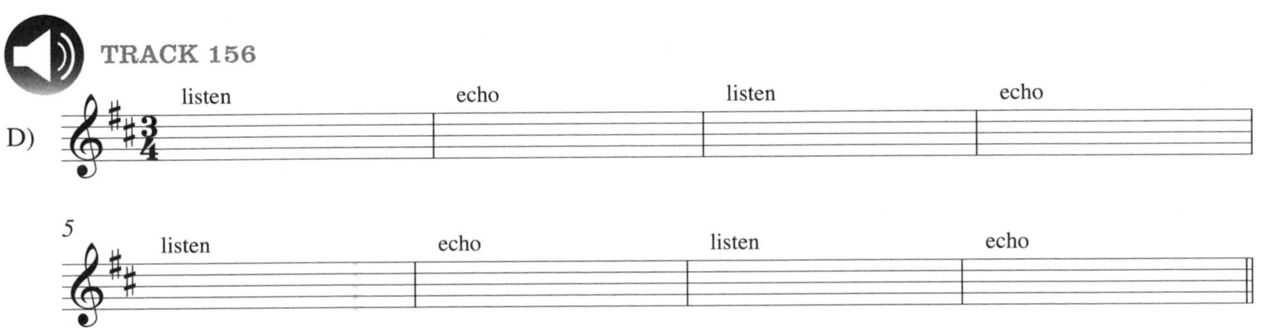

CHAPTER 7
EXERCISES IN B♭ MAJOR AND G MINOR

Now let's look at the keys of B♭ major and its relative minor, G minor.

THE SCALES

We add another flat, for a total of two flats, to get the keys of B♭ major or G minor. Let's see how this works.

B♭ Major Scale

First, as we know, we need to write out the letter names spanning from tonic to tonic:

B♭ C D E F G A B♭

Looking at these notes on a piano keyboard and comparing them against the intervallic formula, we find a problem:

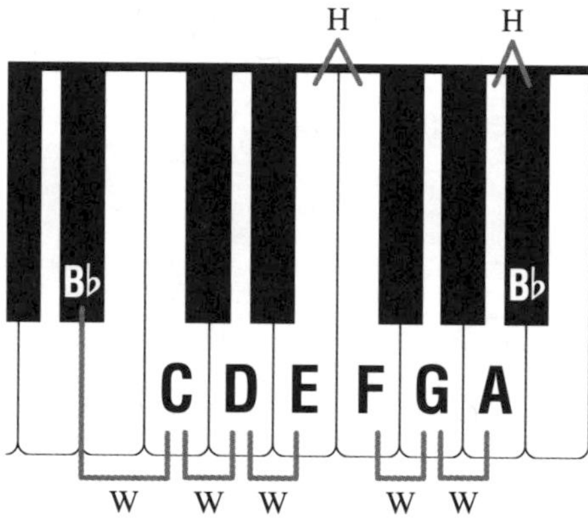

We have W-W-W-H-W-W-H instead of W-W-H-W-W-W-H. By lowering E to E♭, the formula is corrected.

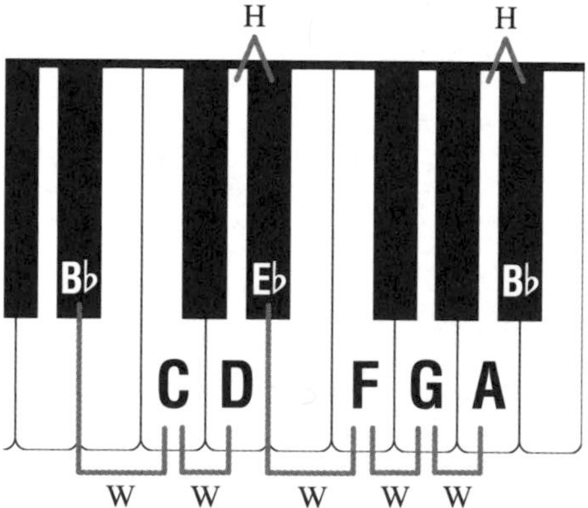

Thus, the B♭ major scale is spelled B♭–C–D–E♭–F–G–A, and the key signature for B♭ major is two flats: B♭ and E♭.

TRACK 157

G Minor Scale

G minor is the relative minor of B♭ major, so its key signature also contains two flats.

RHYTHM STUDY

In this chapter, we add a bit more complexity by using more *syncopation*—i.e., stressing the weak beats. Generally speaking, beats 1 and 3 in a 4/4 meter are accented slightly. In addition, the downbeats are more accented than the upbeats—i.e., the "and" in between the beats. By stressing beats 2 or 4 and/or the upbeats, syncopation is created.

Non-syncopated

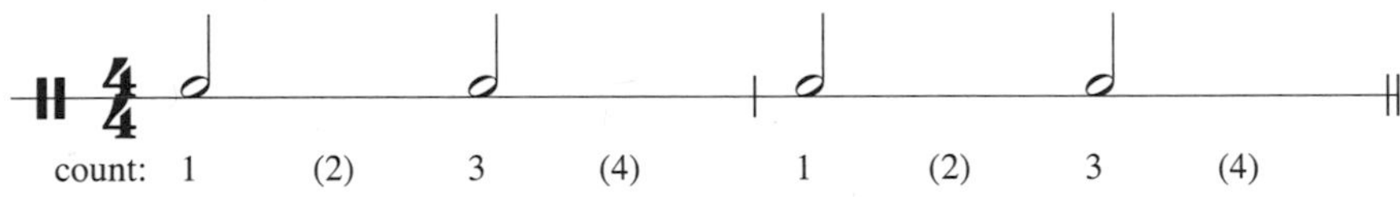

Syncopated

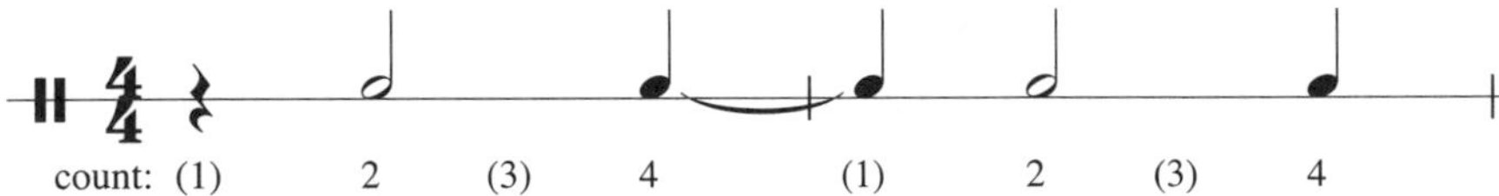

Rhythmic Drills

Clap the following rhythms together as a class or in smaller groups.

RHYTHMIC DICTATION

Listen to the following rhythms and write them down. Each example will be played twice. Be sure to listen closely to the duration of each note.

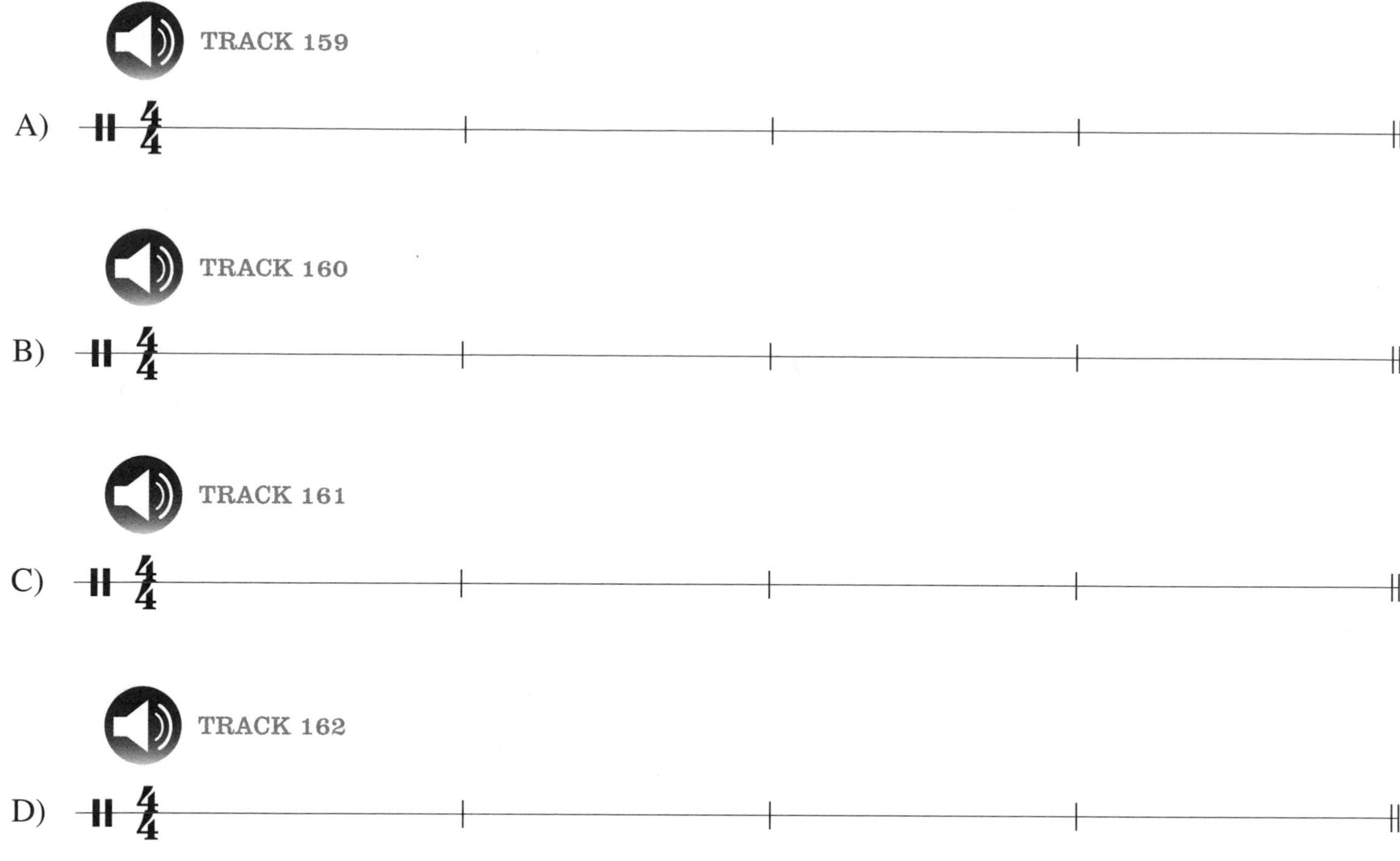

INTERVAL STUDY

In Chapter 5, we learned the perfect 4th and perfect 5th. Let's add the "imperfect" versions of those intervals to our study.

Diminished and Augmented 4ths and 5ths

A *diminished* interval is one half step smaller than its companion perfect one. (This is the same relationship as minor to major intervals when talking about 2nds or 3rds.) An *augmented* interval is one half step larger than its companion perfect one.

- From C to F is a perfect 4th, so C to F♯ (one half step more) is an augmented 4th.
- From C to G is a perfect 5th, so C to G♯ (one half step more) is an augmented 5th.
- From C to G is a perfect 5th, so C to G♭ (one half step less) is a diminished 5th.

Generally, we don't encounter diminished 4ths (from C to F♭, for example). That would equal four half steps, which is almost always spelled (and heard) as a major 3rd.

Remember! A 4th interval **must** have four letter names involved, and a 5th **must** have five! From C to F♯ (augmented 4th) and from C to G♭ (diminished 5th) will sound the same because they both span six half steps, but they're named differently, depending on how they're spelled.

This interval of six half steps goes by another name as well: the *tritone*. This is because it spans three whole steps (sometimes called whole *tones*). The tritone divides the octave in half (there are 12 notes in an octave) and creates a strong reaction in the listener. Its sound is one of dissonance and unrest; it very much wants to resolve.

Listen now to the sound of a tritone—i.e., an augmented 4th (from C to F♯) or a diminished 5th (from C to G♭)—as compared to the other perfect intervals.

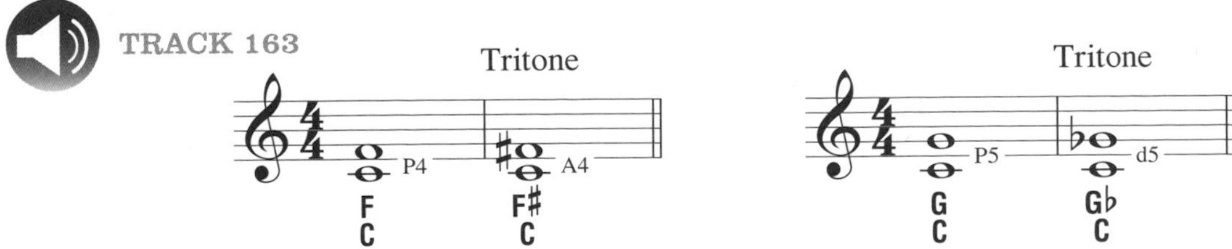

In the Middle Ages, people found the sound of a tritone so disturbing they dubbed it *diabolus in musica* ("the devil in music") and avoided it assiduously. For the past several hundred years, however, it's been a central part of tonal music.

Now compare the sound of an augmented 5th, from C to G♯, with the sound of a perfect 5th.

Interval Dictation

Identify the following intervals as tritones (TT) or augmented 5ths (A5). Each interval will be played twice, either melodically or harmonically.

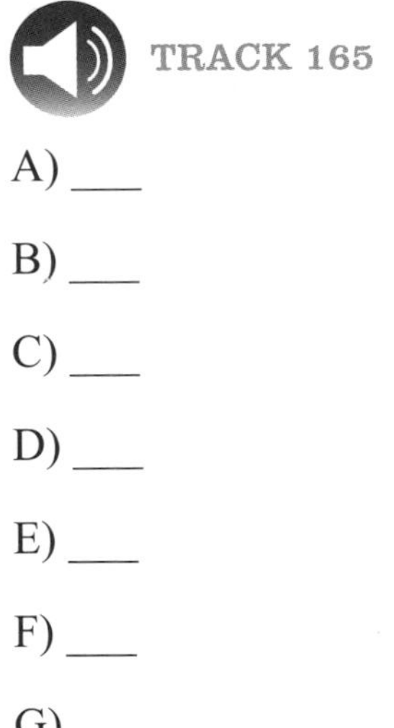

Accidentals and Courtesy Accidentals

An *accidental* is a temporary flat or sharp that applies to a note throughout the measure. In the subsequent measure, the note reverts back to its standard form, as shown in the key signature. However, it's common to add a *courtesy accidental*—usually only if the note is heard again in the same octave—to remind the performer of this. A *natural symbol* (♮) is used to cancel a flat or sharp.

SIGHT-SINGING EXERCISES

These examples feature all the intervals we've looked at thus far, including our newly learned augmented/diminished 4ths and 5ths. Note that the augmented 5th interval does not occur within a major scale, so we use an accidental to notate it.

Key of B♭ Major

Remember the key signature, which tells you that all the B and E notes are to be sung as B♭ and E♭, respectively.

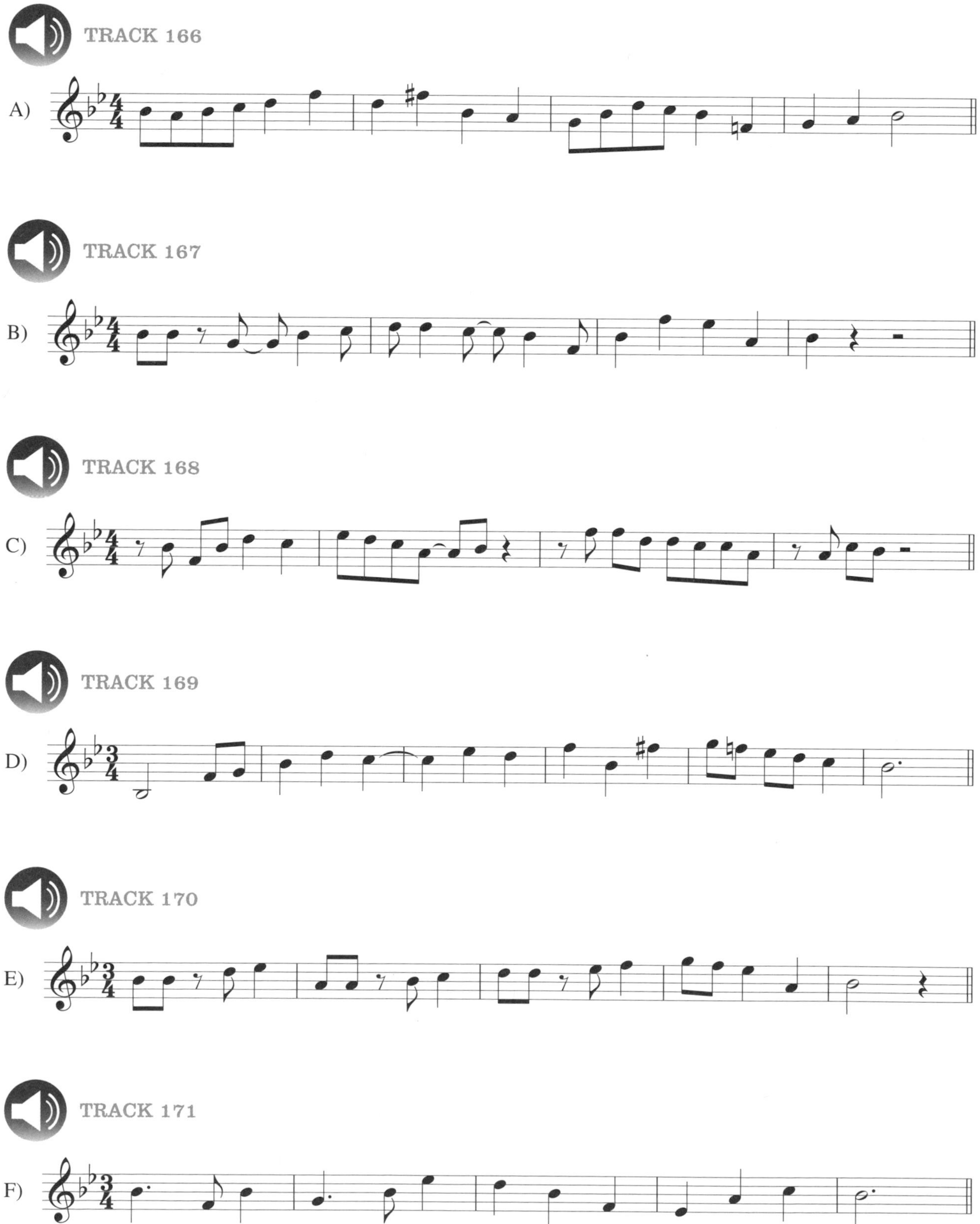

Key of G Minor

TRACK 172

A)

TRACK 173

B)

TRACK 174

C)

TRACK 175

D)

TRACK 176

E)

TRACK 177

F)

MELODIC DICTATION EXERCISES

In these exercises, you'll hear the instructor play a melody twice. Write it down by ear. The rhythms are getting a little trickier here, so pay close attention to the difference between a sustained note and a rest. (**Instructors:** See Appendix for notation of these exercises. Alternatively, these can be found on the accompanying audio.)

Key of B♭ Major

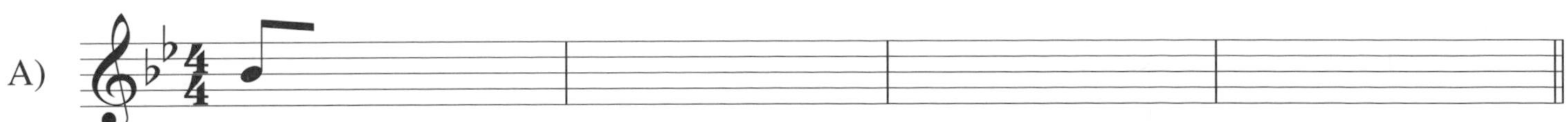

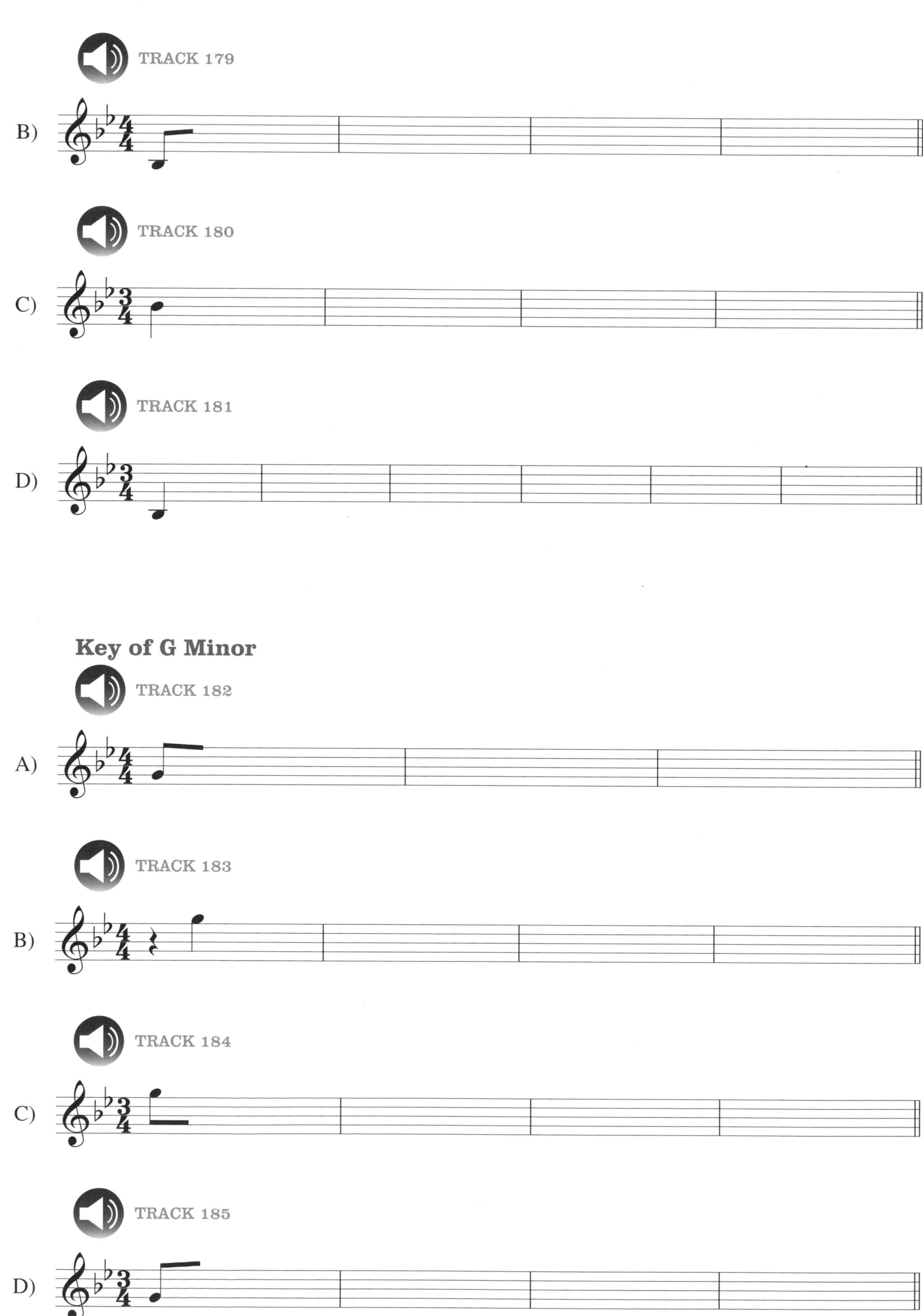
TRACK 179
B)
TRACK 180
C)
TRACK 181
D)
Key of G Minor
TRACK 182
A)
TRACK 183
B)
TRACK 184
C)
TRACK 185
D)

ECHO DRILLS

For these drills, listen to the phrase and then echo it back. (**Instructors:** See Appendix for notation of these exercises. Alternatively, these can be found on the accompanying audio.)

Rhythm Echoes

In these four exercises, you'll hear a one-bar rhythm followed by one bar of silence. Clap the rhythm back during the break.

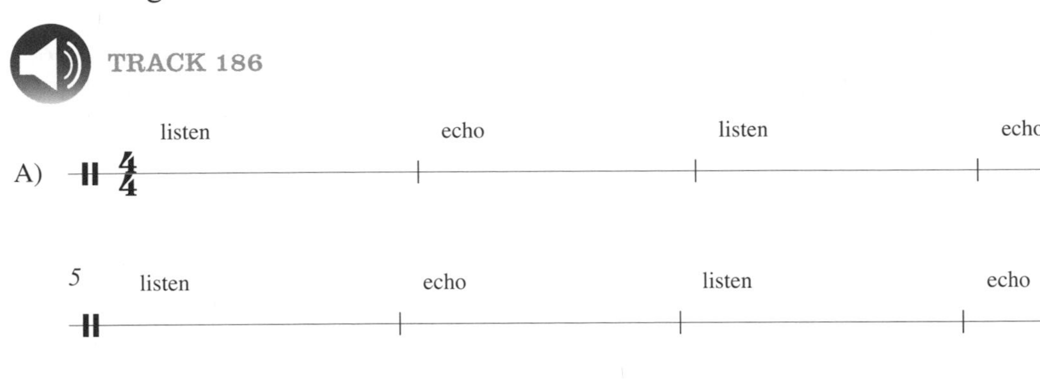

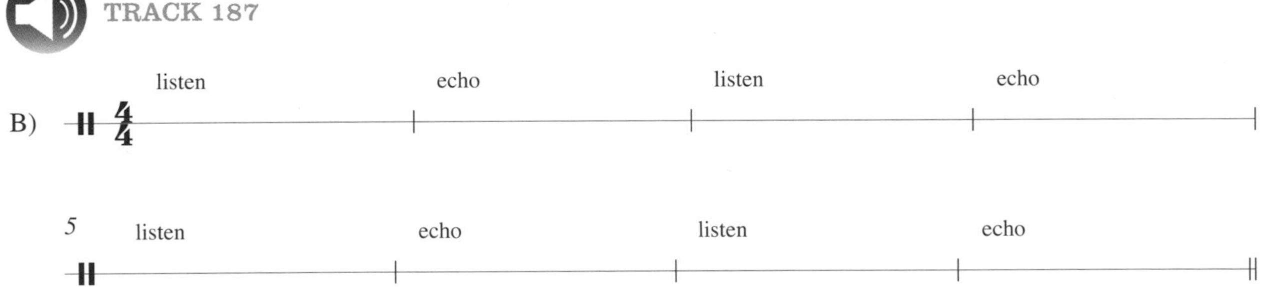

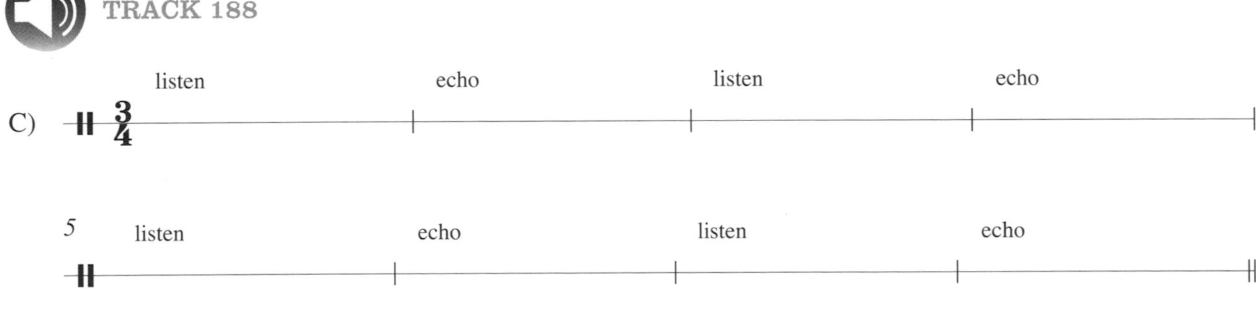

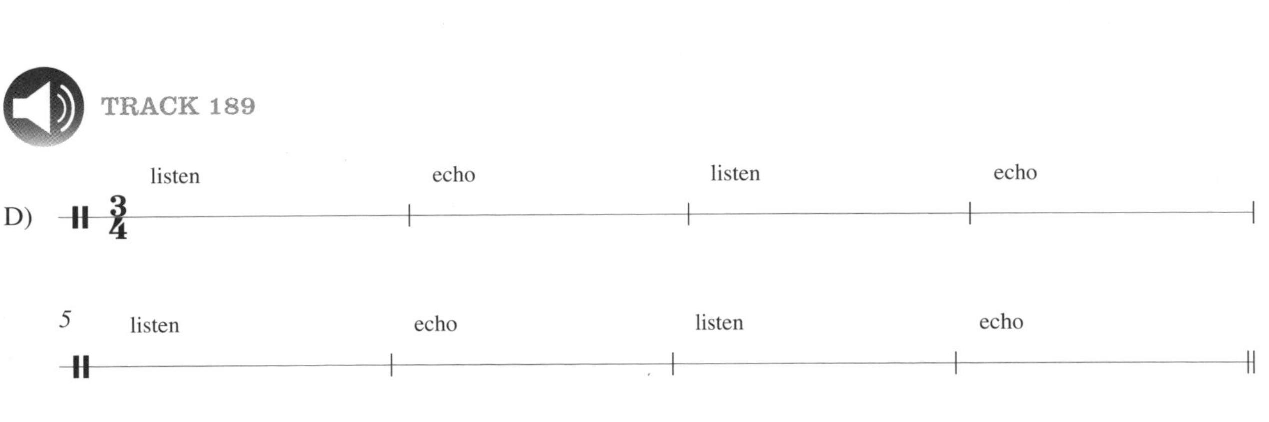

Melodic Echoes

In these four exercises, you'll hear a one-bar melody followed by one bar of silence. Sing the melody back during the break.

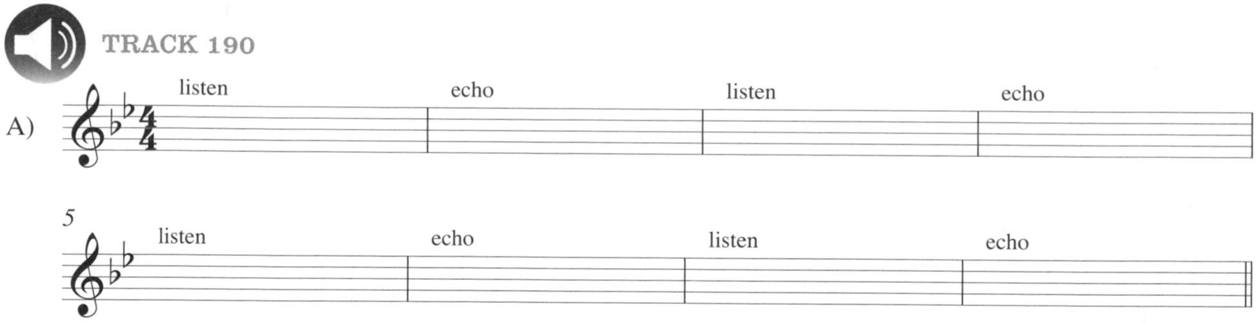

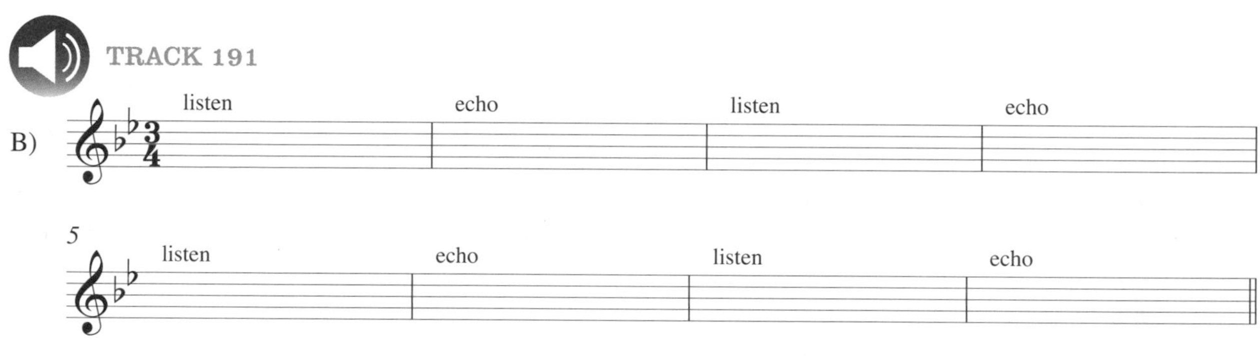

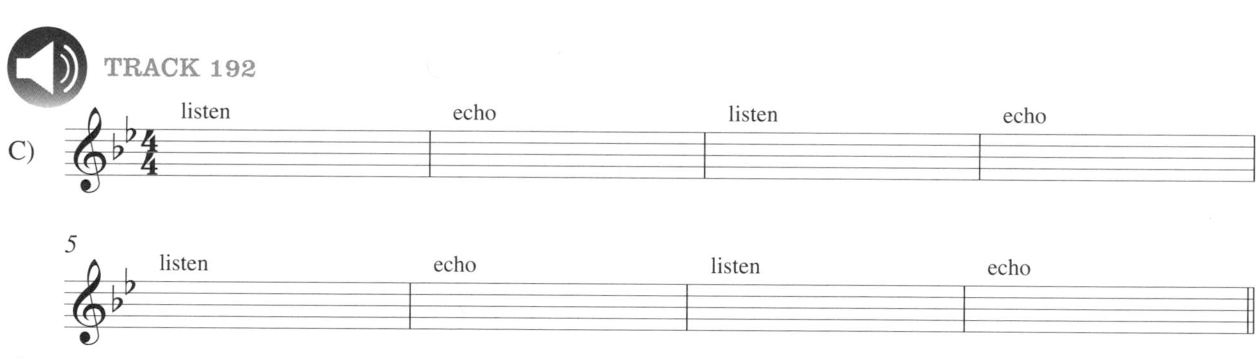

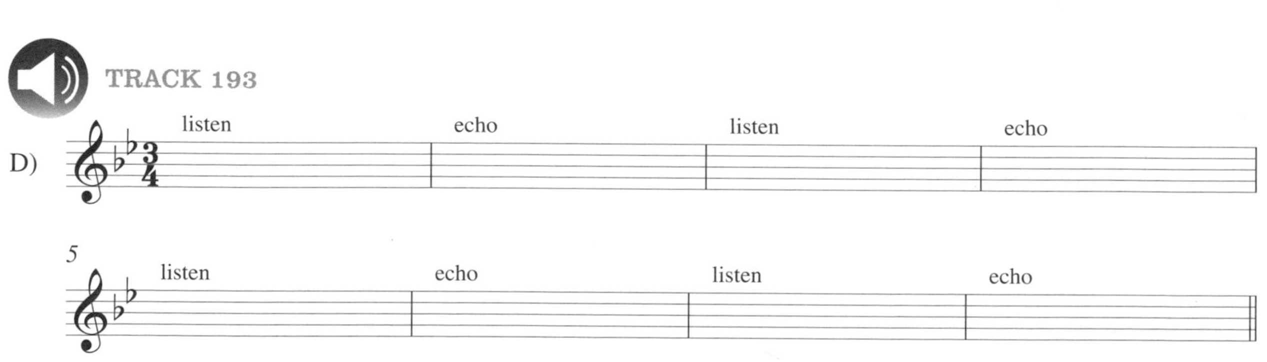

CHAPTER 8

EXERCISES IN A MAJOR AND F♯ MINOR

Now let's move on to A major and its relative minor, F♯ minor.

THE SCALES

We're going to add another sharp, for a total of three sharps, to get the keys of A major and F♯ minor. Let's see how this works.

A Major Scale

First, write out the letter names spanning from tonic to tonic:

A B C D E F G A

After examining these notes on the piano keyboard, we realize alterations are required to maintain the intervallic formula. In this case, raise the notes C, F, and G a half step each.

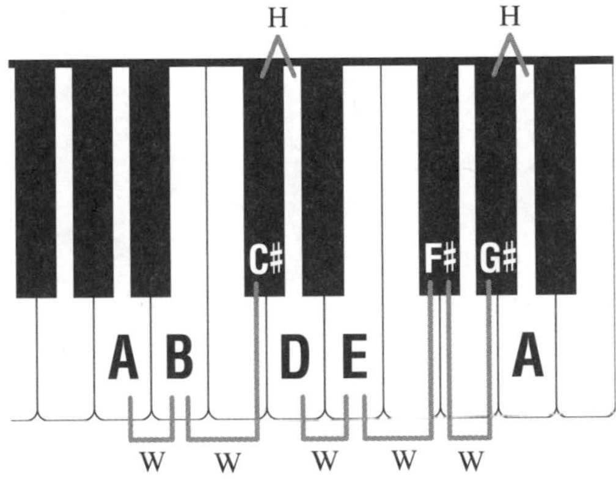

The A major scale, then, is spelled A–B–C♯–D–E–F♯–G♯. And the key signature for A major is three sharps: F♯, C♯, and G♯.

TRACK 194

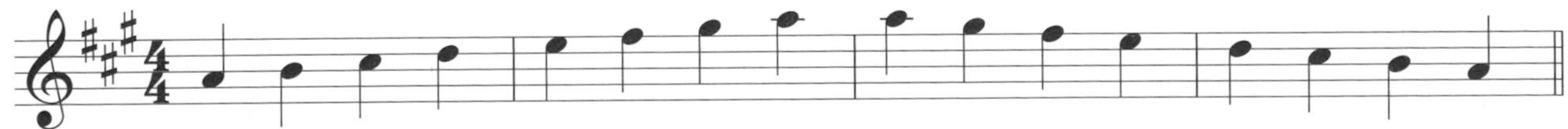

F♯ Minor Scale

F♯ minor is the relative minor of A major, so its key signature also contains three sharps.

TRACK 195

RHYTHM STUDY

Let's look at a new meter (time signature): 6/8. In 6/8 time, there are six beats in a measure, but the *eighth* note is counted as the beat—not the quarter note.

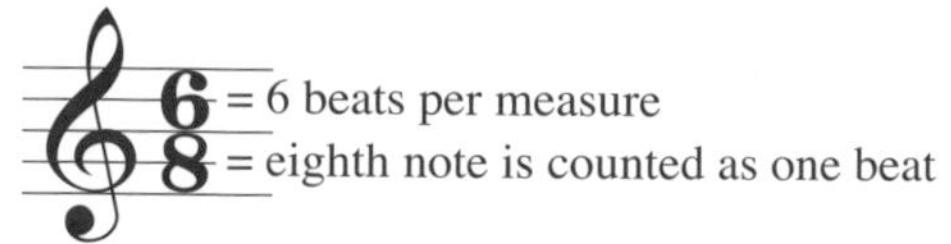

So you may ask, "What's the difference between 6/8 and 3/4? Since 3/4 has three quarter notes in each measure, then both meters have six eighth notes in each measure." And this is correct. The difference is with the accented beats.

Whereas 3/4 is counted "**1** and **2** and **3** and"—with a slight accent on each quarter note—6/8 is counted as two groups of three eighth notes: **1** 2 3 **4** 5 6. This puts a slight accent on beats 1 and 4. (Remember that the eighth note is counted as the beat.) Alternatively, you could say that a dotted-quarter note (equal to three eighth notes) gets the pulse. So, although the meters both have the same number of eighth notes in each measure, they sound and feel different because of the accents.

Alternatively, instead of counting 6/8 as **1** 2 3 **4** 5 6, some prefer to count it as "**1** and a, **2** and a," which is a little less wordy and also suggests the dotted-quarter-note pulse.

Rhythmic Drills

Clap the following rhythms together as a class or in smaller groups.

Rhythmic Dictation

Listen to the following rhythms and write them down. Each example will be played twice.

A)

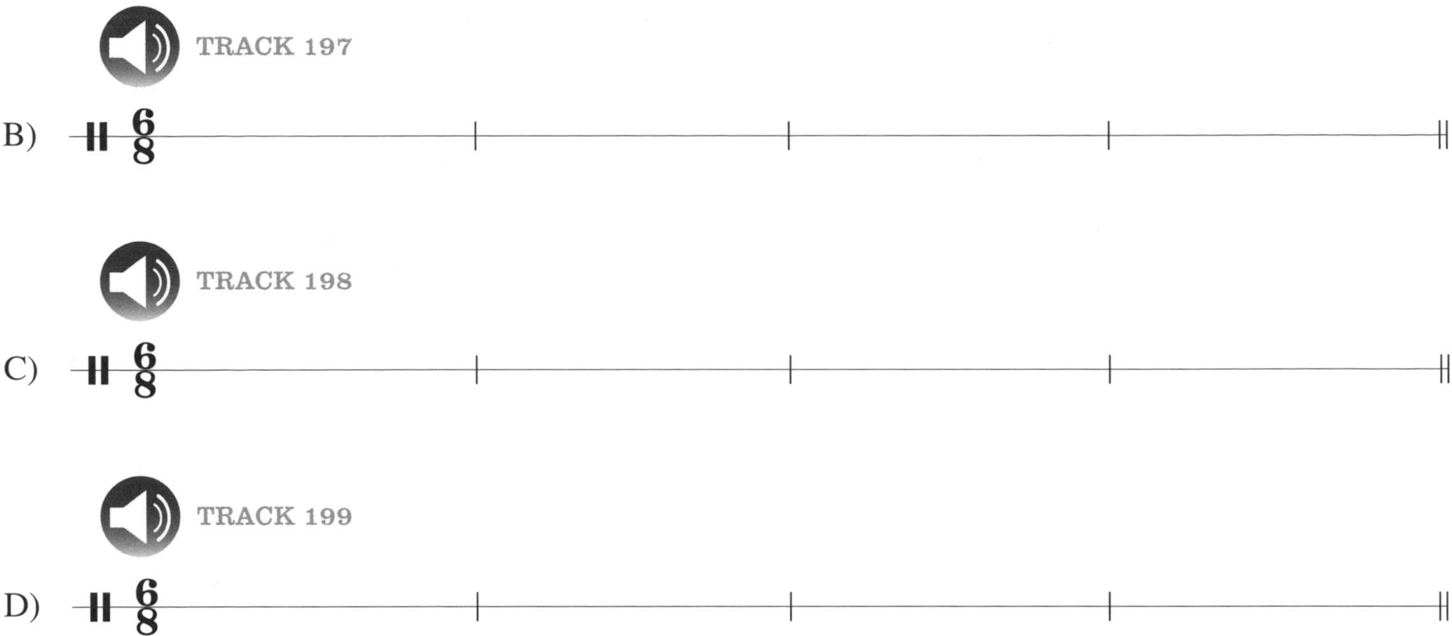

INTERVAL STUDY

The next interval in line is the 6th. A 6th involves six note names, such as from C up to A: C (1)–D (2)–E (3)–F (4)–G (5)–A (6). And just as with 2nds and 3rds, we can have major and minor 6ths. Again, the major 6th is one half step larger than the minor 6th.

- Major 6th = nine half steps (or four and a half steps)
- Minor 6th = eight half steps (or four steps)

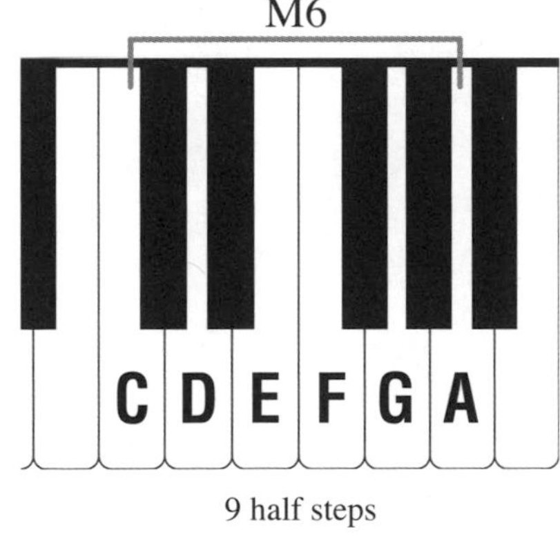

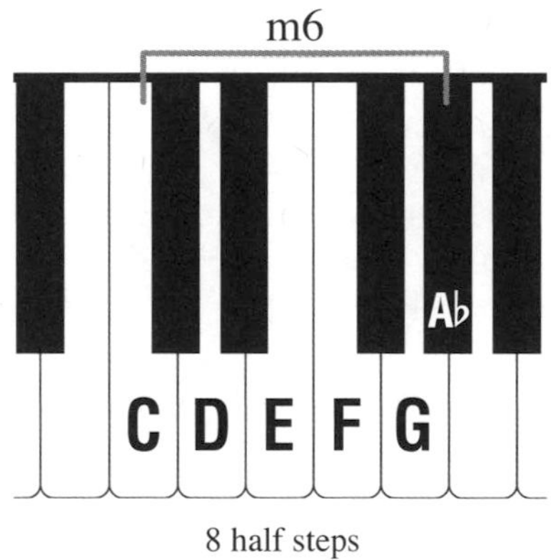

Enharmonic Reminder

In Chapter 7, we studied the augmented 5th, another interval that contains eight half steps. From C to G♯ is an example of this interval. However, remembering our rule of interval quantity, the letter name used will determine whether it's an augmented 5th or a minor 6th interval. They'll sound the same to the ear, because they're both eight half steps, but a 5th interval has to contain five letter names, and a 6th has to contain six letter names. So from C to A♭ is a minor 6th, but from C to G♯ is augmented 5th.

Inverted Intervals

The 6th interval is fairly wide, but it still sounds harmonious. This is because a 6th is also an inverted 3rd. Think about it. The note C with an A above it is a major 6th. But if that A note is moved down an octave, the A is on the bottom and the C is above it. This results in a minor 3rd (three half steps).

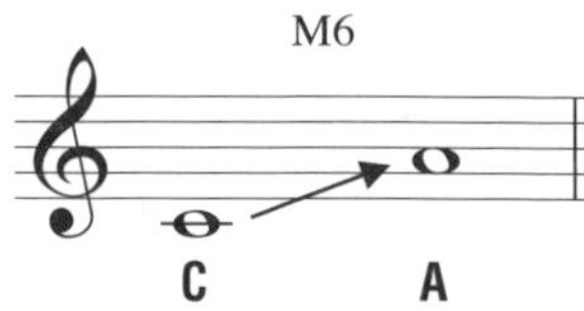

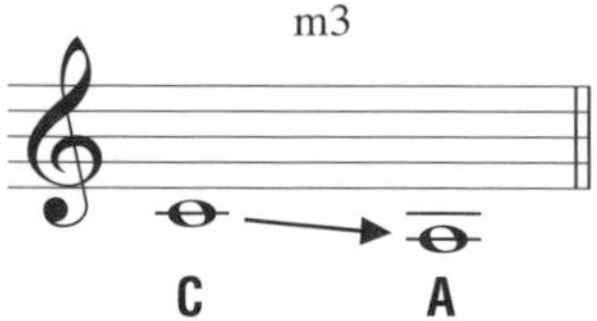

Memorize this rule: *When a major interval is inverted, a minor interval results—and vice versa.*

From C up to E, for example, is a major 3rd. Drop the E note down an octave (or raise the C note up an octave), and you'll end up with E up to C, which is a *minor* 6th.

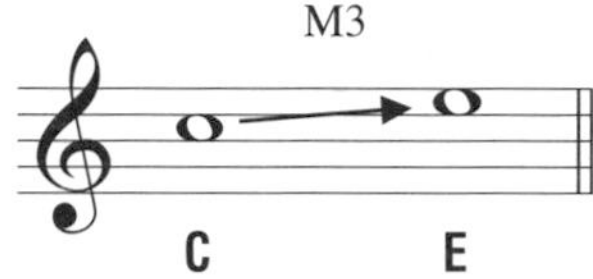

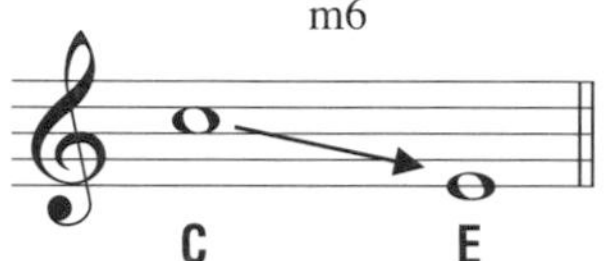

Perfect intervals, however, stay perfect when inverted. For example, from C up to F is a perfect 4th. If you invert that, you have C down to F, which is a perfect 5th.

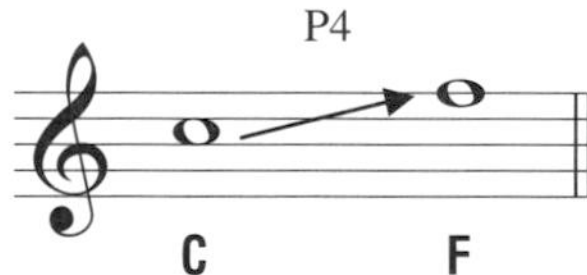

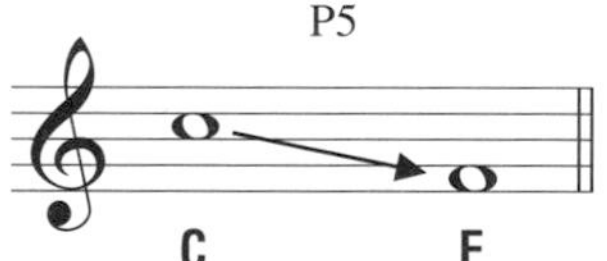

So, in summary:

- 6th intervals become 3rds when inverted, and vice versa.
- 4th intervals become 5ths when inverted, and vice versa.
- Minor intervals become major when inverted, and vice versa.
- Perfect intervals stay perfect when inverted.

Listen to the sound of a major 6th, from C to A.

Here's the sound of a minor 6th, from C to A♭.

Interval Dictation

Listen to the following intervals and determine if they are major 6ths or minor 6ths.

SIGHT-SINGING EXERCISES

These examples will feature all the intervals we've looked at thus far: 2nds through 6ths.

> ### Bass Clef
> The following exercises appear in bass clef. Sing them in whichever octave is comfortable for you; the point is not to expand your vocal range, but rather to practice reading in another common clef. It will take a bit of adjustment at first, but will become easier fairly quickly. Should you need a refresher on the notes, refer to page 6 in Chapter 1.

Key of A Major

Watch out for the examples in 6/8 time!

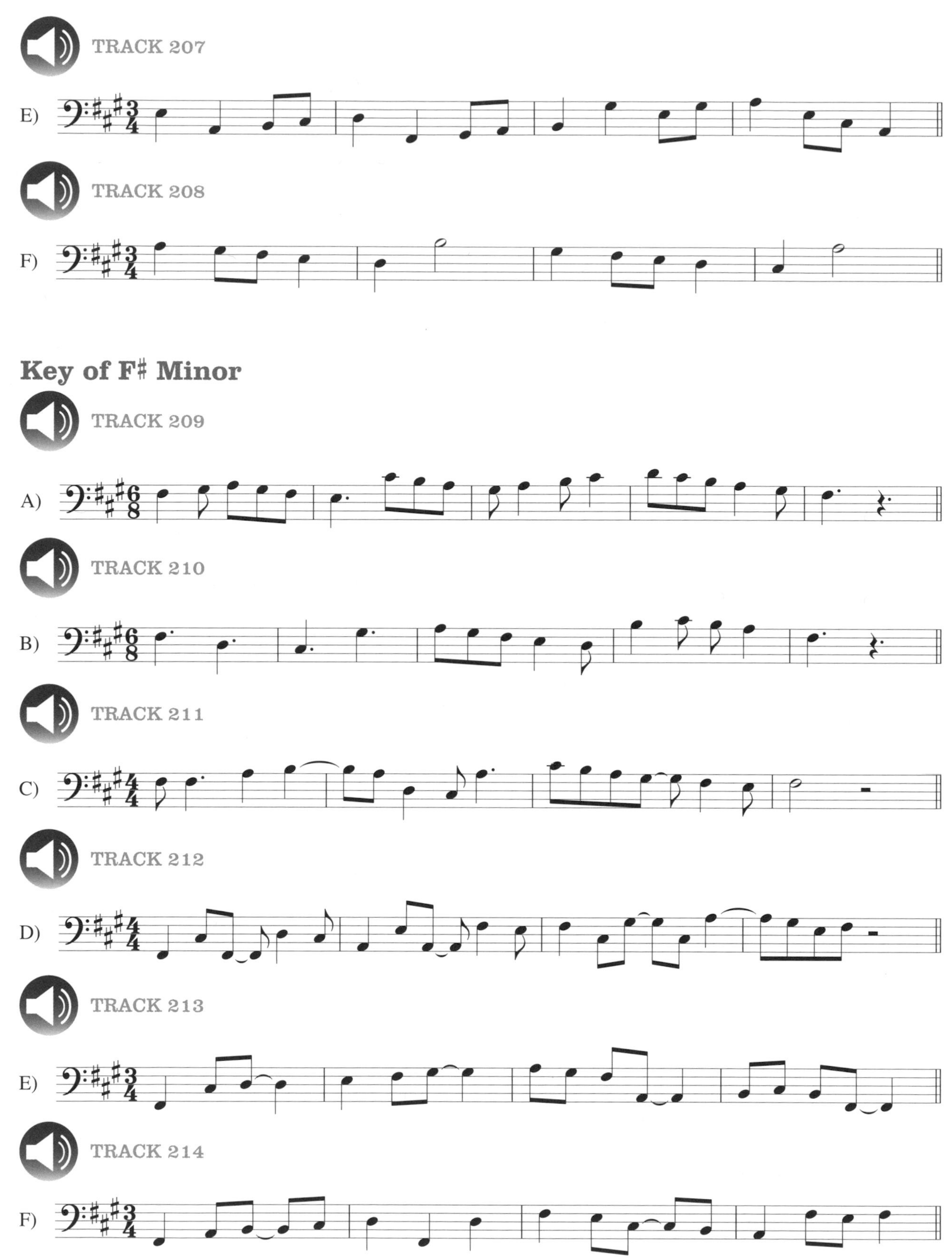

MELODIC DICTATION EXERCISES

In these exercises, you'll hear the instructor play a melody twice. Write it down by ear. (**Instructors:** See Appendix for notation of these exercises. Alternatively, these can be found on the accompanying audio.)

Key of A Major

TRACK 215

A)

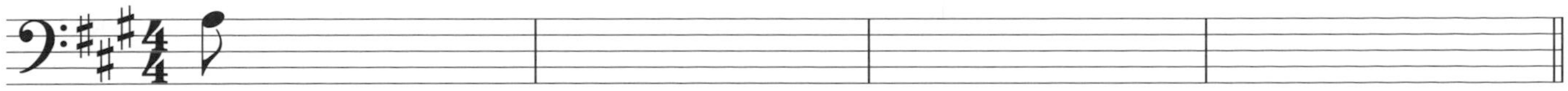

TRACK 216

B)

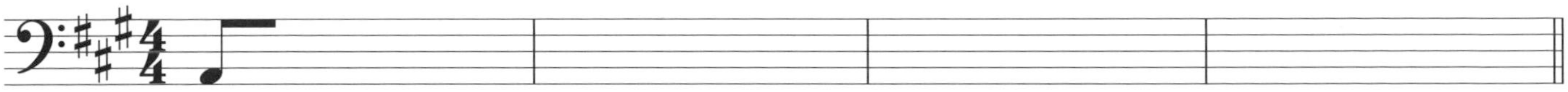

TRACK 217

C)

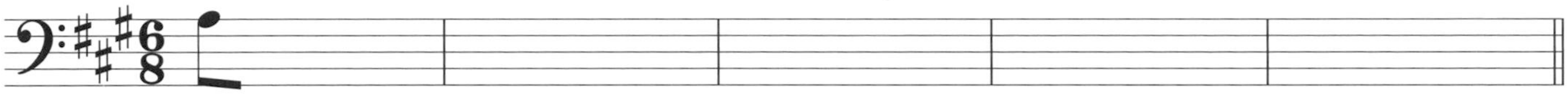

TRACK 218

D)

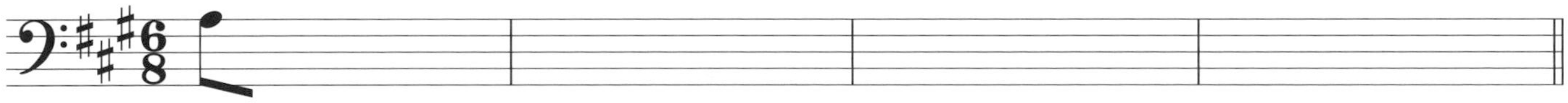

Key of F♯ Minor

TRACK 219

A)

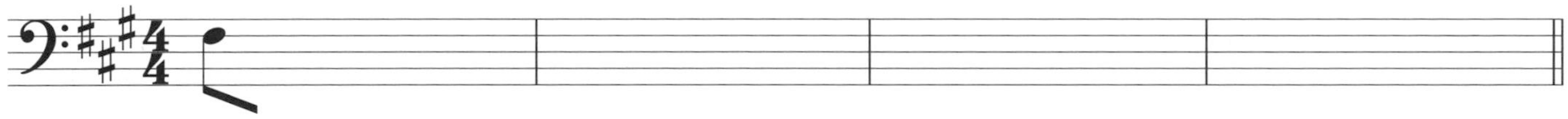

TRACK 219

B)

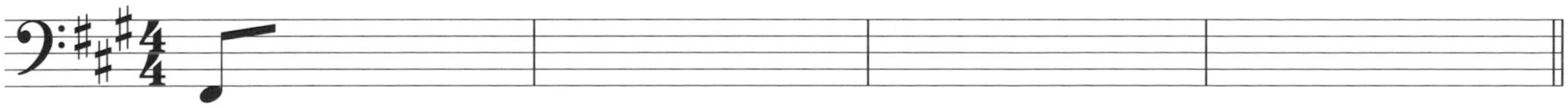

TRACK 221

C)

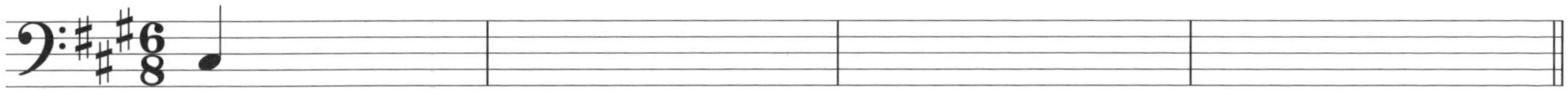

TRACK 222

D)

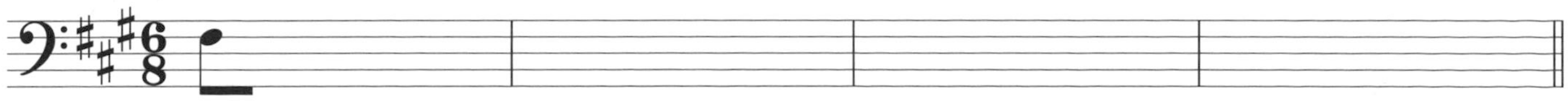

ECHO DRILLS

For these drills, listen to the phrase and then echo it back. (**Instructors:** See Appendix for notation of these exercises. Alternatively, these can be found on the accompanying audio.)

Rhythm Echoes

We'll step up the difficulty a bit. These four exercises are in 6/8, but you're going to echo two-bar phrases instead of one-bar phrases.

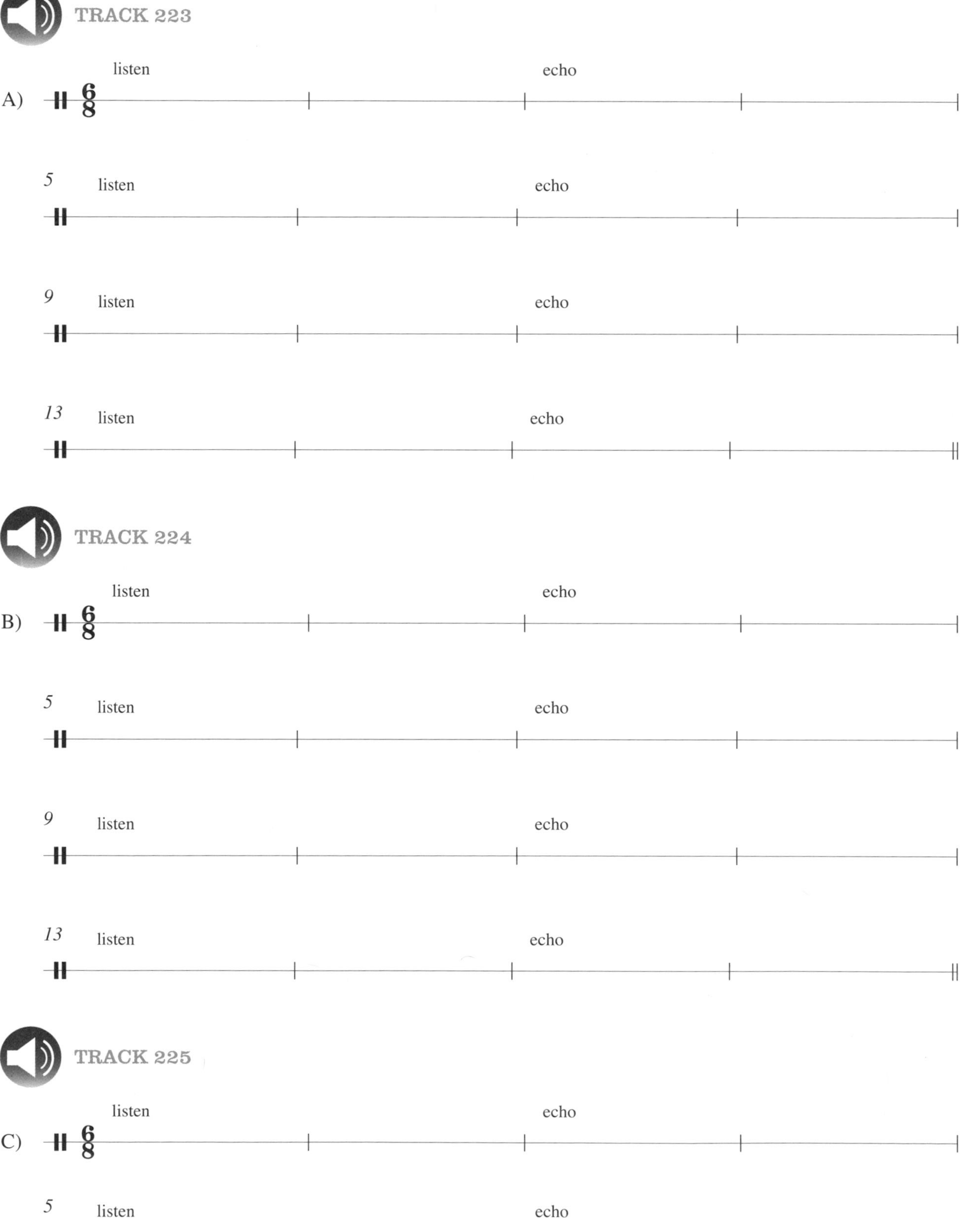

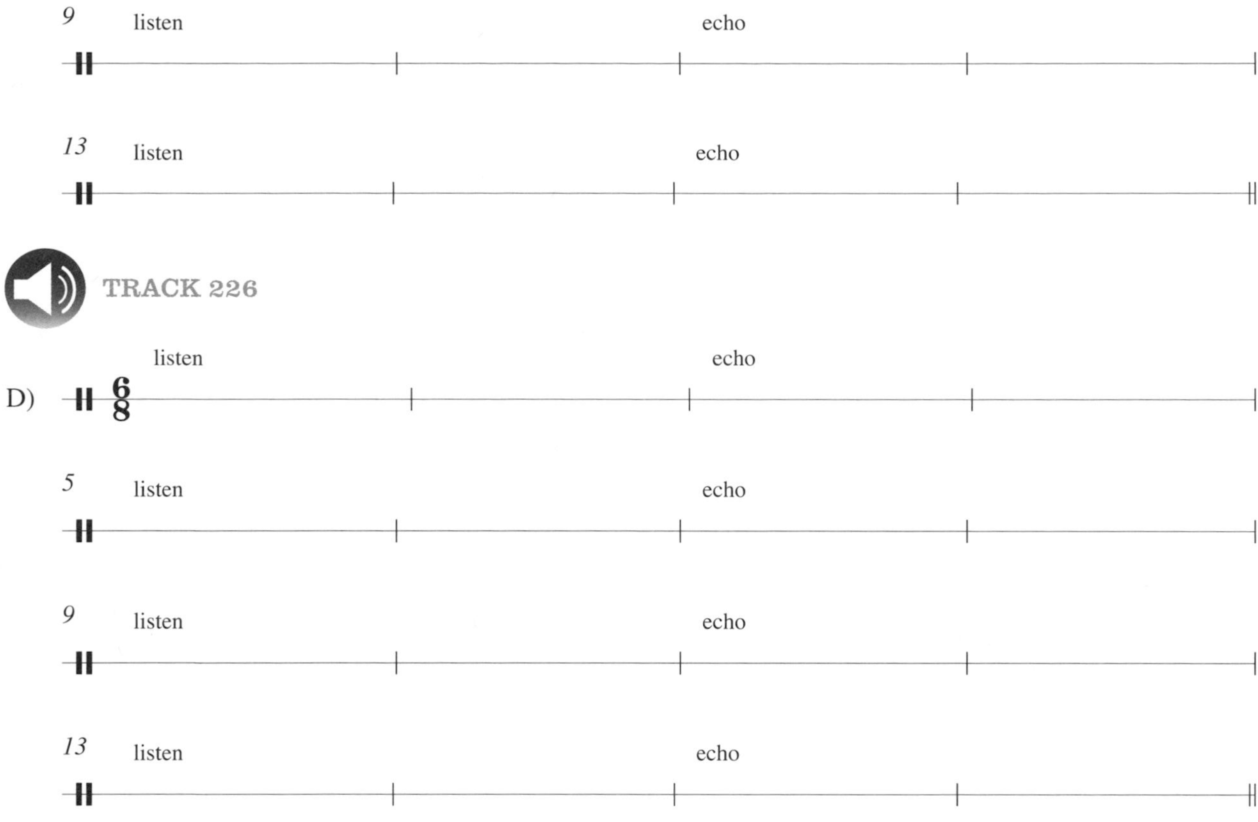

Melodic Echoes

In these four exercises, you'll hear a two-bar melody followed by two bars of silence. Sing the melody back during the break.

TRACK 228

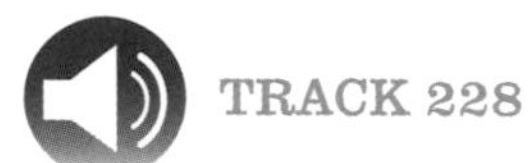

B)

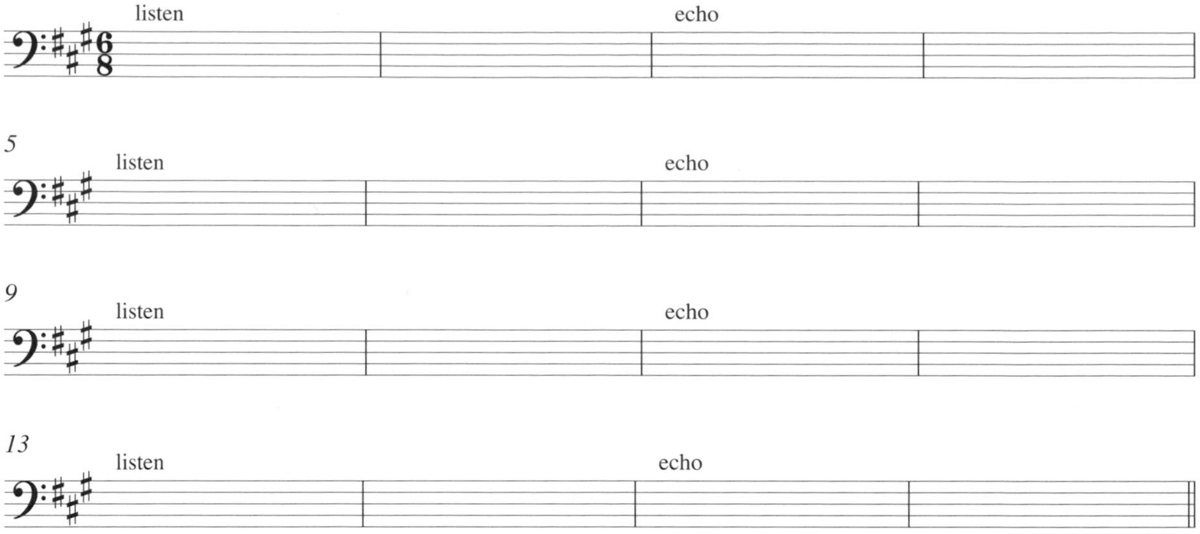
listen
echo
5
listen
echo
9
listen
echo
13
listen
echo

TRACK 229

C)

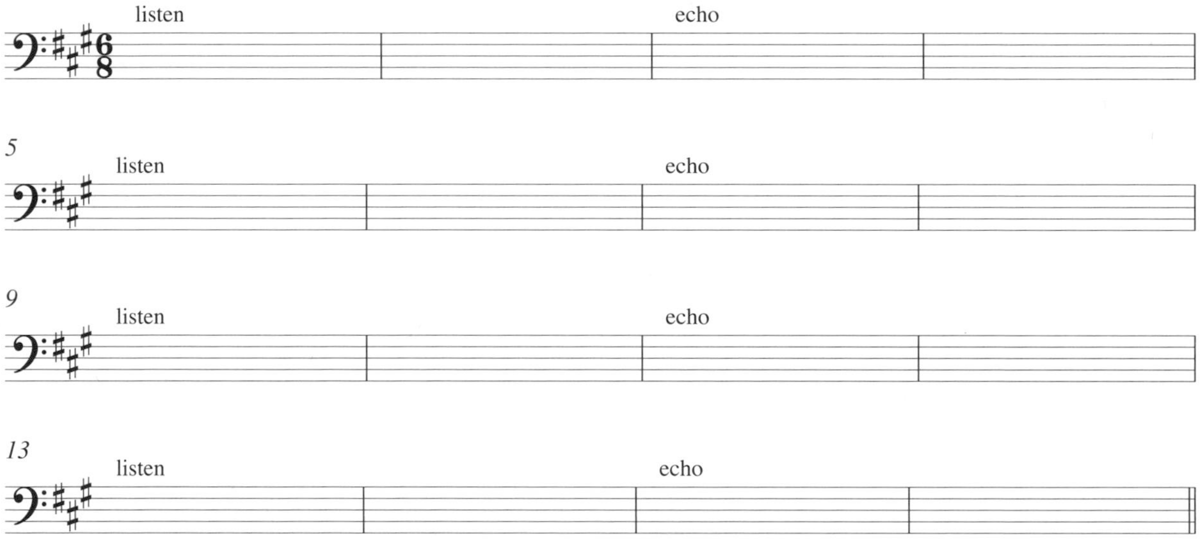
listen
echo
5
listen
echo
9
listen
echo
13
listen
echo

TRACK 230

D)

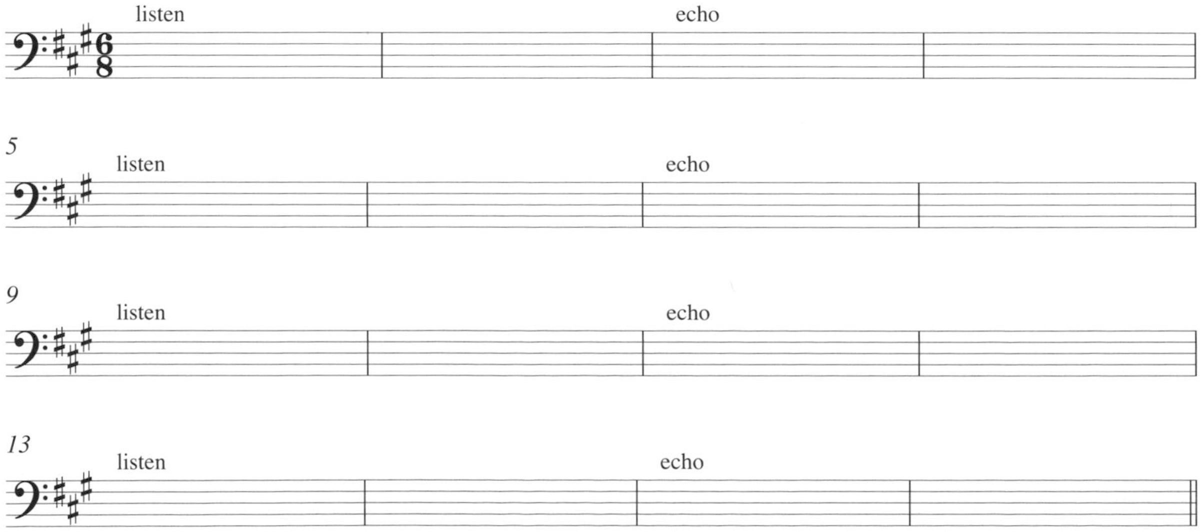
listen
echo
5
listen
echo
9
listen
echo
13
listen
echo

CHAPTER 9

EXERCISES IN E♭ MAJOR AND C MINOR

Further around the flat side we travel, this time to the keys of E♭ major and its relative minor, C minor.

THE SCALES

In this chapter, we have a total of three flats to get the keys of E♭ major and C minor. Let's see how this works.

E♭ Major Scale

First, write out the letter names spanning from tonic to tonic:

E♭ F G A B C D E♭

After examining these notes on the piano keyboard, we realize we need to make alterations to maintain the intervallic formula. In this case, lower the notes A and B a half step each.

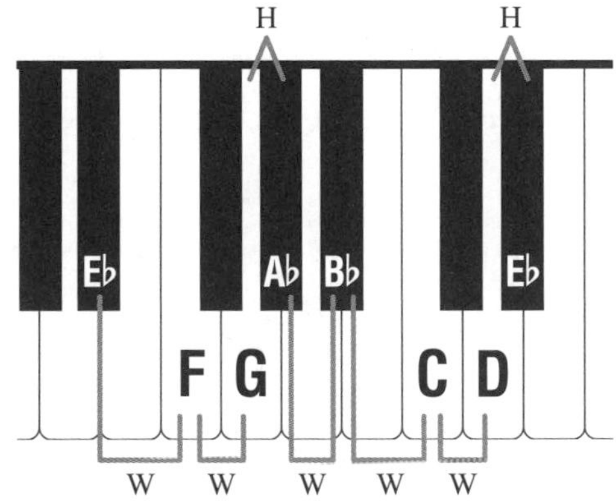

We see that the E♭ major scale is spelled E♭–F–G–A♭–B♭–C–D. And the key signature for E♭ major is three flats: B♭, E♭, and A♭.

C Minor Scale

C minor is the relative minor of E♭ major, so its key signature also contains three flats.

RHYTHM STUDY

The new meter we looked studied in Chapter 8, 6/8, is known as a *compound meter*. A compound meter is one in which each beat or pulse is divided into three equal parts. Remember that we count 6/8 as "**1** 2 3 **4** 5 6" or "**1** and a **2** and a." A simple meter is one in which each beat is divided into half, such as 4/4, which is counted "**1** and **2** and **3** and **4** and."

More specifically, 4/4 is simple quadruple meter, because each beat or pulse is divided in half (simple), and there are four pulses per measure (quadruple). Likewise, 6/8 is compound duple meter, because each pulse is divided into three (compound), and there are two pulses per measure.

12/8 Time

Like 6/8 meter, 12/8 is a compound meter, so each pulse is divided in three. It's like 6/8, but each measure is twice as long. It's counted "**1** 2 3 **4** 5 6 **7** 8 9 **10** 11 12" or, more often, "**1** and a **2** and a **3** and a **4** and a."

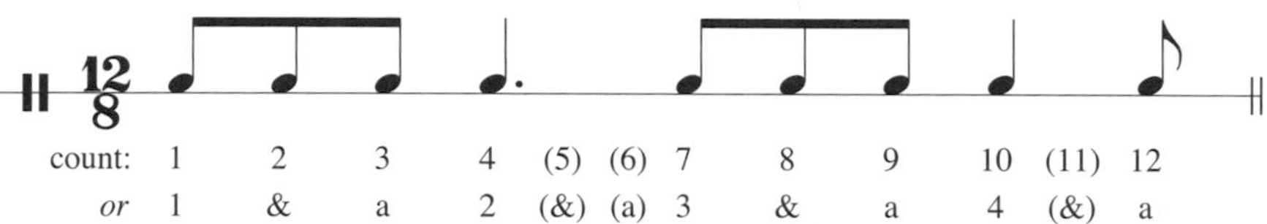

Rhythmic Drills

Clap the following rhythms together as a class or in smaller groups.

Rhythmic Dictation

Listen to the following rhythms and write them down. Each example will be played twice.

C) 12/8

D) 12/8

INTERVAL STUDY

The 7th is the next interval in line. It involves seven note names; for example, from C up to B: C (1)–D (2)–E (3)–F (4)–G (5)–A (6)–B (7). As with 2nds, 3rds, and 6ths, there are major and minor 7ths. Again, the major 7th is one half step larger than the minor 7th.

- Major 7th = 11 half steps (or five-and-a-half steps)
- Minor 7th = 10 half steps (or five steps)

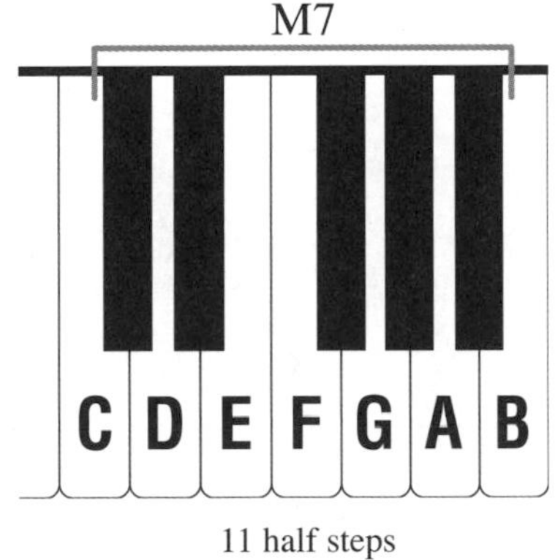

11 half steps

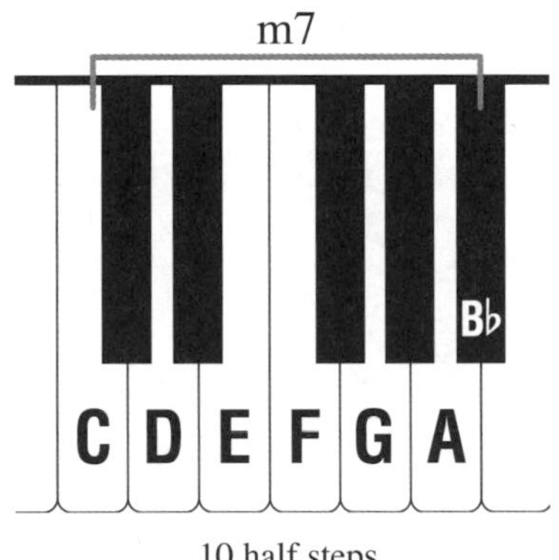

10 half steps

More Enharmonic Intervals

We've seen examples of several enharmonic intervals already, most notably the tritone, which can go by the name of an augmented 4th or a diminished 5th. There's also the augmented 5th, which sounds the same as the minor 6th. In both instances, an augmented interval is one half step larger than a perfect interval, and a diminished interval is one half step smaller than a perfect one.

- P4 = five half steps (C to F), but A4 = six half steps (C to F♯)
- P5 = seven half steps (C to G), but A5 = eight half steps (C to G♯), and d5 = six half steps (C to G♭)

Regarding augmented intervals, there are further examples that result in enharmonic-sounding intervals. In both 2nds and 6ths, for example, there is an augmented interval that's one half step greater than a major interval. For example, from C to D is a major 2nd, but from C to D♯ is an *augmented* 2nd. This is the distance of three half steps, which sounds the same as a minor 3rd. Since only two letter names are used (C and D♯), we have to call it a 2nd.

Similarly, an augmented 6th is one half step larger than a major 6th. From C to A is a major 6th, but from C to A♯ is an augmented 6th. This sounds the same as a minor 7th, because they're both ten half steps, but since only six letter names are used, it is called an augmented 6th.

TRACK 237

Listen to the sound of a major 7th, from C to B.

TRACK 238

Here's the sound of a minor 7th, from C to B♭.

Interval Dictation

Listen to the following intervals and determine whether they are major 7th or minor 7th intervals.

TRACK 239

A) ___

B) ___

C) ___

D) ___

E) ___

F) ___

G) ___

H) ___

SIGHT-SINGING EXERCISES

These examples include all the intervals we've looked at thus far: 2nds through 7ths.

Key of E♭ Major

TRACK 240

TRACK 241

TRACK 242

TRACK 243

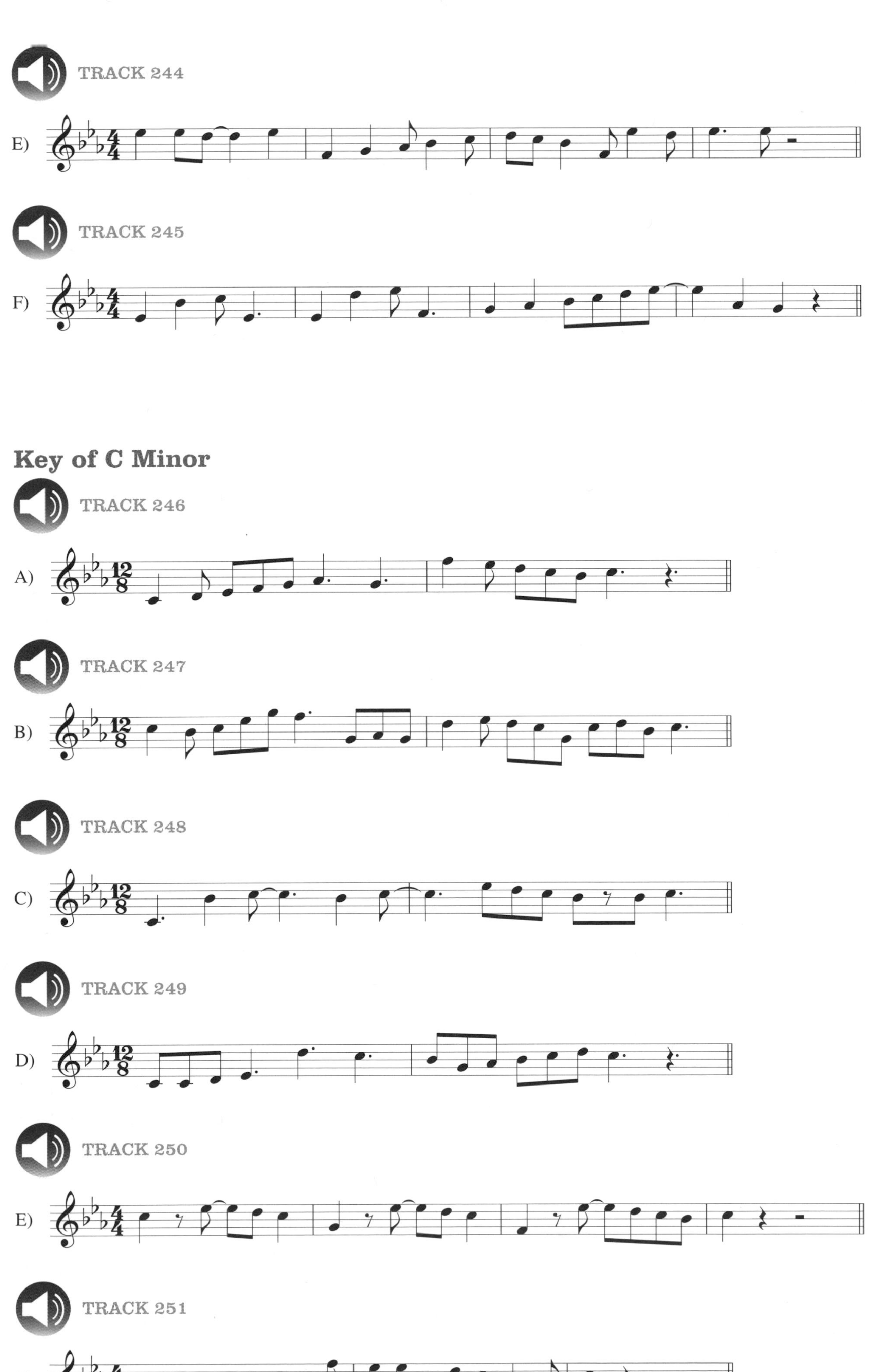
TRACK 244
E)
TRACK 245
F)
Key of C Minor
TRACK 246
A)
TRACK 247
B)
TRACK 248
C)
TRACK 249
D)
TRACK 250
E)
TRACK 251
F)

MELODIC DICTATION EXERCISES

In these exercises, you'll hear the instructor play a melody twice, and you'll write it down by ear. (**Instructors:** See Appendix for notation of these exercises. Alternatively, these can be found on the accompanying audio.)

Key of E♭ Major

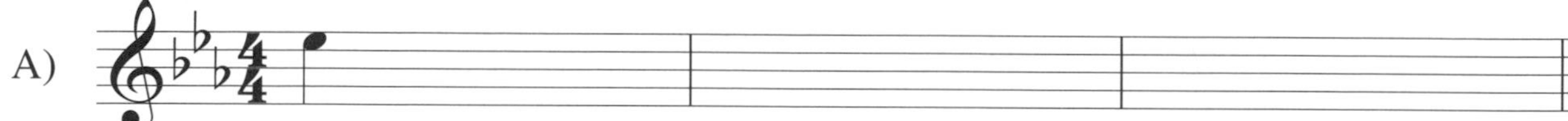

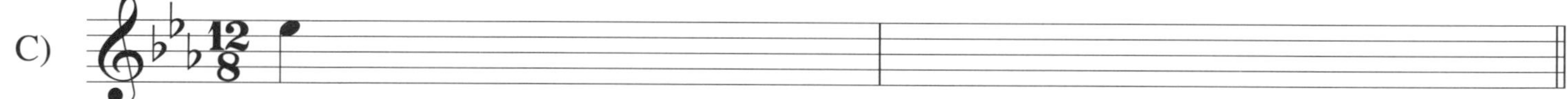

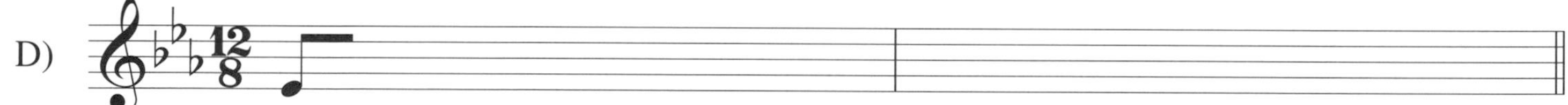

Key of C Minor

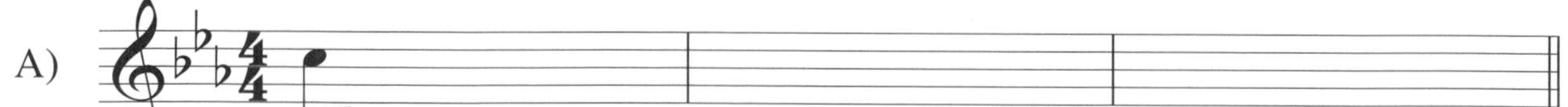

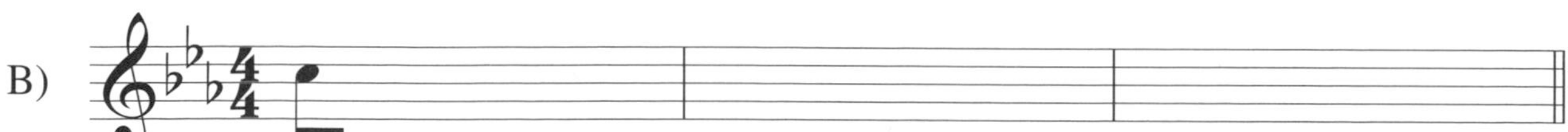

ECHO DRILLS

For these drills, listen to the phrase and then echo it back. (**Instructors:** See Appendix for notation of these exercises. Alternatively, these can be found on the accompanying audio.)

Rhythm Echoes

In these four exercises, you'll hear one-measure phrases in 12/8. Listen to the rhythms and clap them back during the breaks.

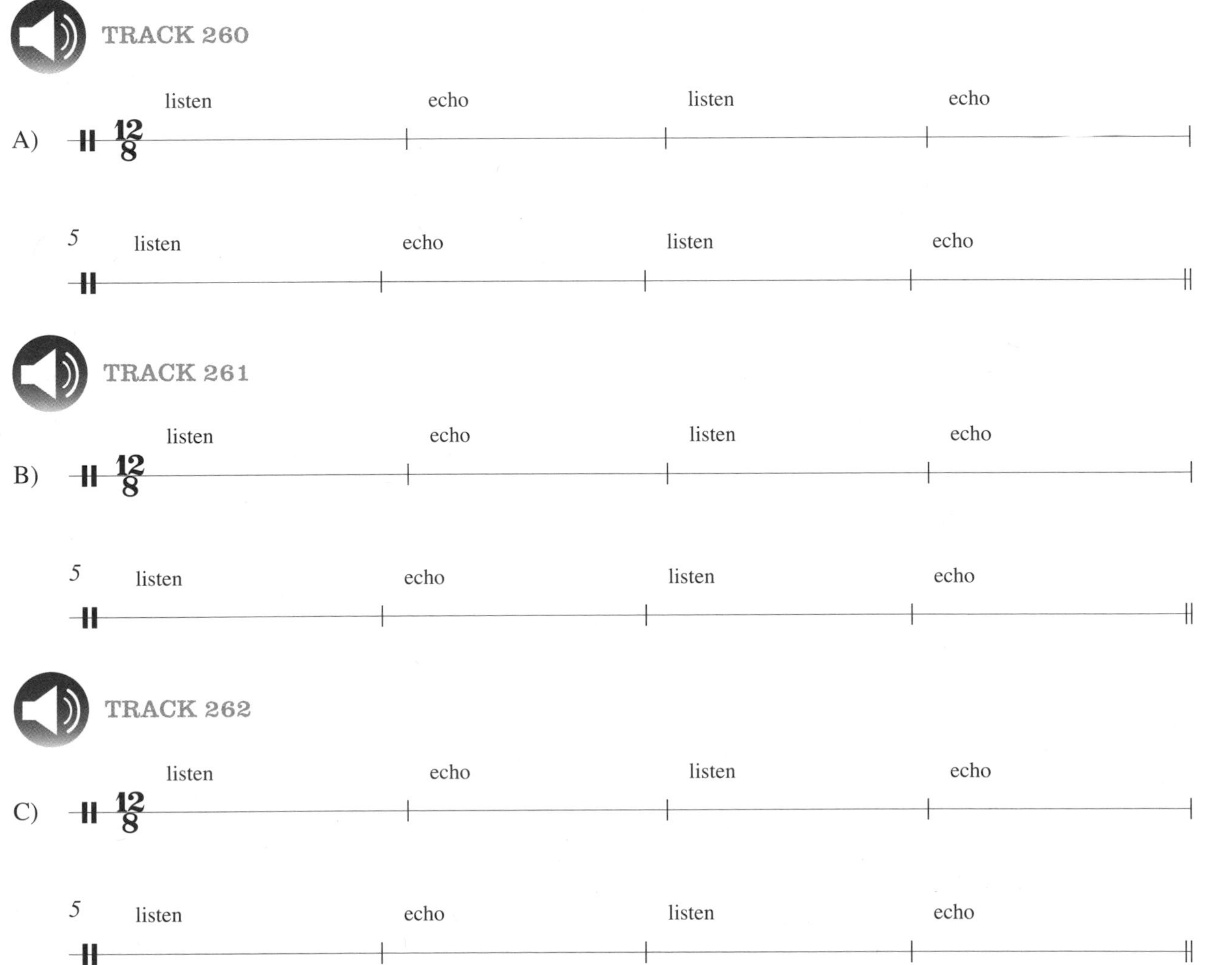

TRACK 263

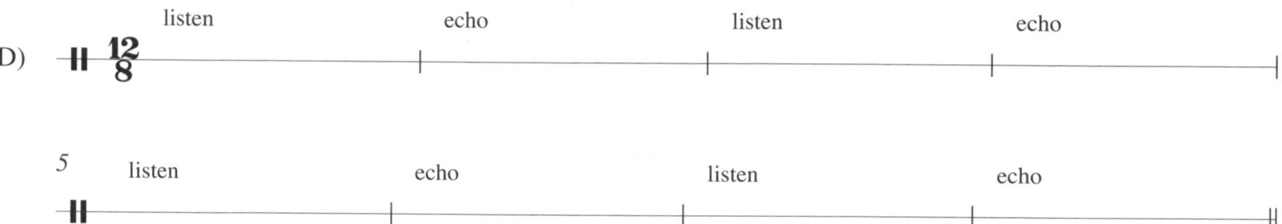

Melodic Echoes

In these four exercise, you'll hear a one-bar melody followed by one bar of silence. Sing the melody back during the break.

TRACK 264

A) listen echo listen echo

5 listen echo listen echo

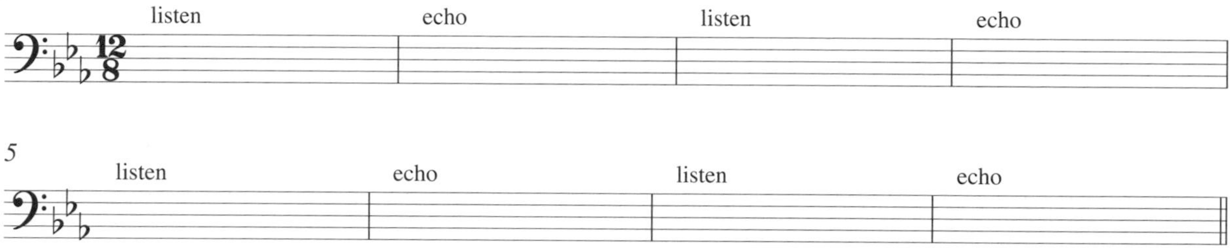

TRACK 265

B) listen echo listen echo

5 listen echo listen echo

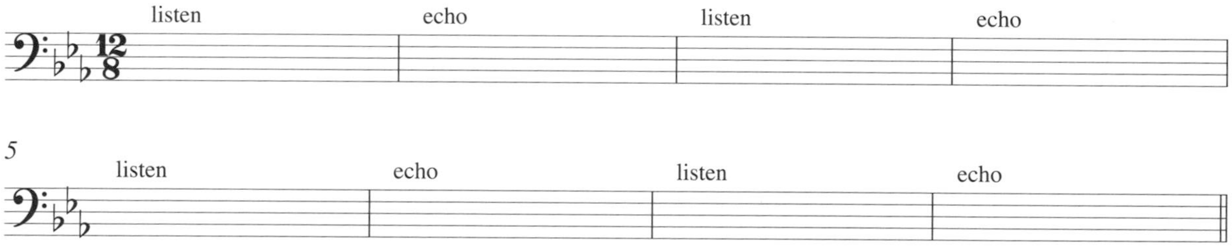

TRACK 266

C) listen echo listen echo

5 listen echo listen echo

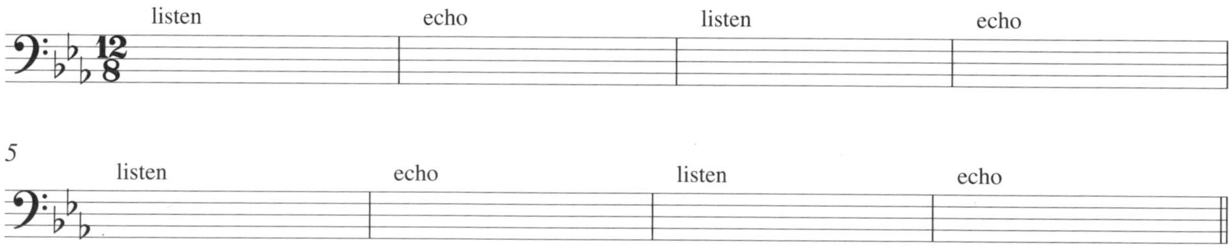

TRACK 267

D) listen echo listen echo

5 listen echo listen echo

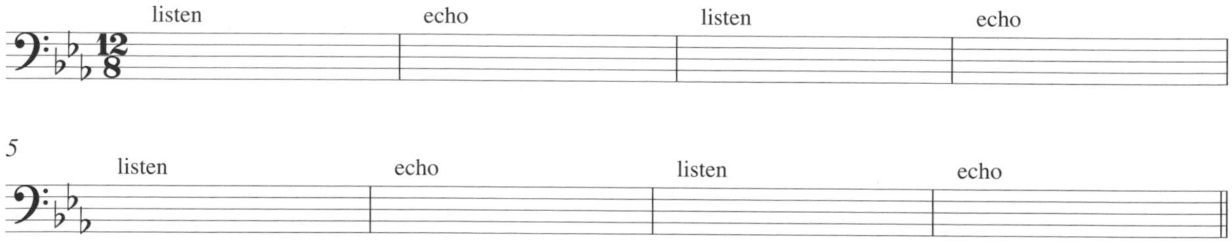

CHAPTER 10

EXERCISES IN E MAJOR AND C♯ MINOR

In this chapter, we'll study the keys of E major and its relative minor, C♯ minor.

THE SCALES

The keys of E major and C♯ minor contain a total of four sharps. Let's see how this works.

E Major Scale

First, write out the letter names spanning from tonic to tonic:

E F G A B C D E

After examining these notes on the piano keyboard, it's obvious we need to make alterations to achieve the intervallic formula. In this case, we raise the notes F, G, C, and D a half step each.

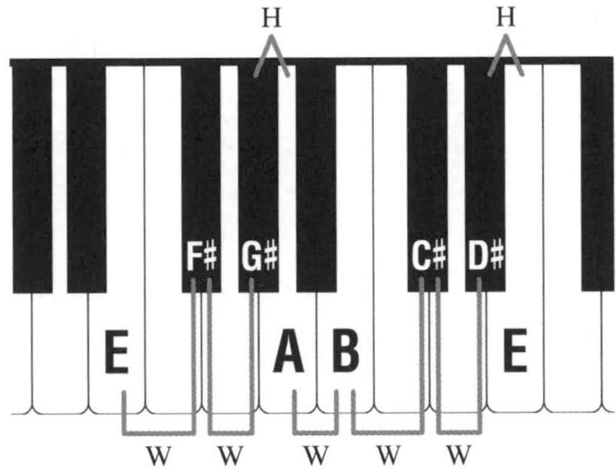

Therefore, we now know that the E major scale is spelled E–F♯–G♯–A–B–C♯–D♯, and the key signature for E major is four sharps: F♯, C♯, G♯, and D♯.

C♯ Minor Scale

C♯ minor is the relative minor of E major, so its key signature also contains four sharps.

TRACK 269

A Bit More on Key Signatures and the Leading Tone

You may have noticed: flats or sharps for a certain key signature are not listed in alphabetical order. They are listed according to the order they accumulate with each key. For example, G major has one sharp in its key signature, which is F#. Every new sharp we add contains the sharps from the previous sharp keys plus one more. D major contains two sharps: F# (the one from G major) and a new one, C#. The next sharp key is A major, which has three sharps: F#, C#, and the new one, G#. And so on. When the key signature is written at the beginning of the staff, the sharps are listed in this cumulative order.

Check out the Circle of Fifths diagram in the Appendix (page 149) for a visual representation of how this works. Consequently, every new sharp added around the sharp side is always the *leading tone* of the new key. What's the leading tone? It's scale degree 7 in a major scale, always a half step from the tonic (remember W-W-H-W-W-W-**H**). In the key of C, the note B is the leading tone. Since that's already a half step from C, we don't need a sharp. But in the key of G, we had to add a sharp to the F note to create a half step from the tonic. And that's the case with each new sharp key going around the circle.

RHYTHM STUDY

In this chapter, we'll concentrate on compound meters (6/8 and 12/8), increasing the difficulty by adding more syncopation. It's important that you tap the dotted-quarter-note pulse (equivalent to three eighth notes) with your foot, or at least nod your head, with these examples. Otherwise, it's easy to lose your place in syncopated compound rhythms.

Rhythmic Drills

Clap the following rhythms together as a class or in smaller groups.

Rhythmic Dictation

Listen to the following rhythms and write them down. Each example will be played twice.

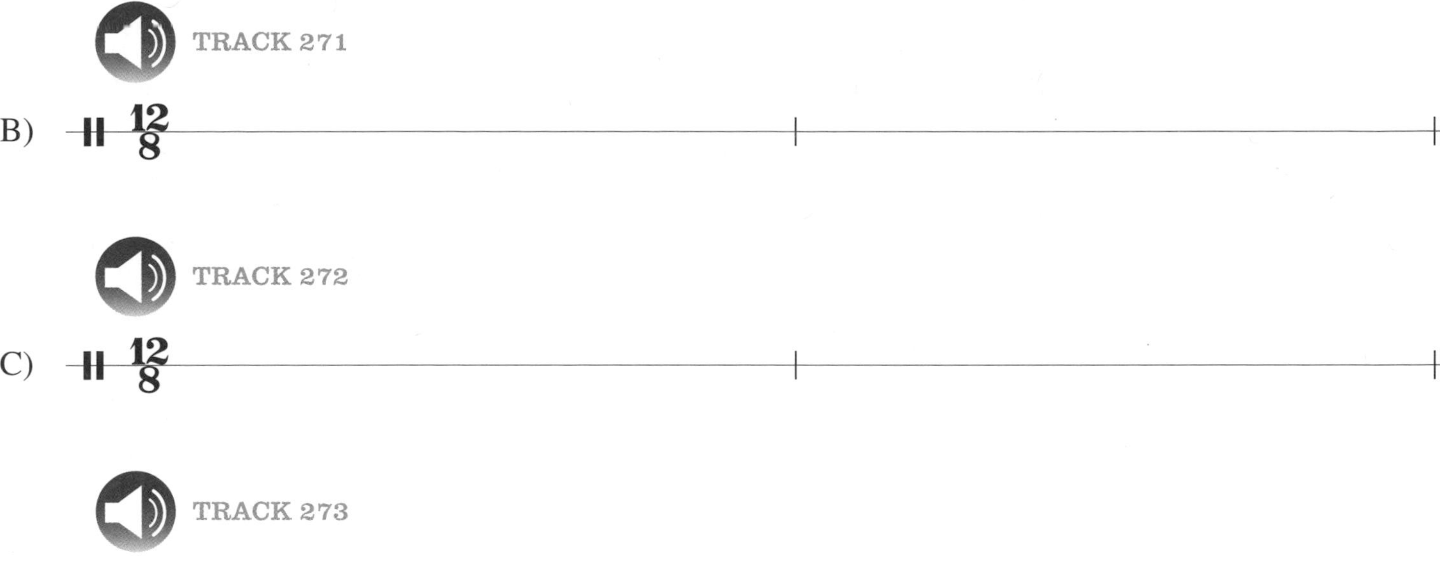

INTERVAL/TRIAD STUDY

We've come to the octave, which is simply the same note in a higher register, such as from C up to C: C (1)–D (2)–E (3)–F (4)–G (5)–A (6)–B (7)–C (8). The proper name for the octave is perfect octave, or P8. It contains 12 half steps.

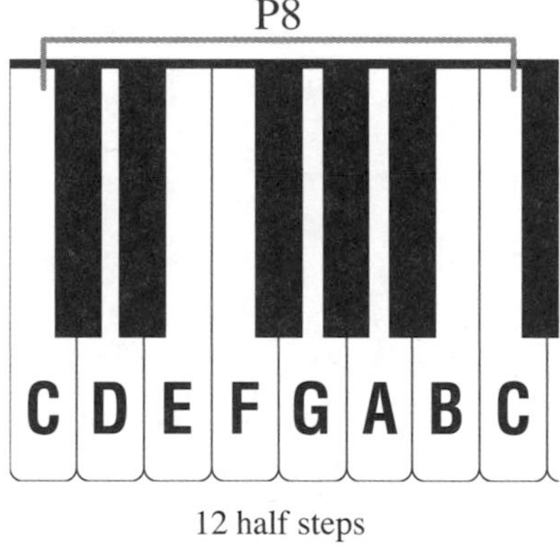

The octave is the only interval that stays exactly the same when inverted (turned upside down). Listen to the sound of a perfect octave, from C to C.

More Arpeggios

We've looked at arpeggios built from the I, IV, and V chords. In the current key of E major, this would be E, A, and B. In Chapter 6, we listened to determine whether a triad was major, minor, augmented, or diminished. This time, we'll listen to the three different major arpeggios in the key of E major to determine whether they are the I, IV, or V chord.

The 1-7 or "do-ti" Line

When listening to the following examples, it'll help to consider the *1-7*, or *do-ti line*. The syllables "do" (pronounced "doe," a female deer) and "ti" (pronounced "tea," a drink with jam and bread) are from the solfège system and are equivalent to the tonic and 7th degrees of a major scale, respectively. (See Appendix, page 149.) Since the tonic note of a scale is usually the easiest to recognize, it's a good note on which to concentrate when trying to determine which chord or arpeggio you're hearing.

The V chord is built on the 5th scale degree and therefore contains the 5th, 7th, and 2nd notes of the scale. (See Chapter 6 for more on this.) It does not contain the tonic. The IV chord contains the 4th, 6th, and 1st (tonic) notes of the key, so it does contain the tonic. The I chord contains the 1st (tonic), 3rd, and 5th notes of the key; obviously, it contains the tonic as well.

Key of C: I, IV, V chords

What does this mean? In the dictation exercises that follow, if you hear a major arpeggio but don't hear the tonic (or "1") of the key, then you know it's the V chord. If you do hear the tonic, then you know it's either the IV chord or the I chord. Again, the I chord will feel completely resolved, or "at home." The IV chord can be recognized as the chord from the "Amen" cadence. The IV chord is heard on the "ah-" syllable, and the I chord is heard on the "-men" syllable.

Triad Dictation

Listen to the following major triads from the key of E major and determine if they are the I (E), IV (A), or V (B) chords. Before the first example, you will hear the key tonicized with a I–IV–V–I progression. The examples will appear in either harmonic (chords) or melodic (arpeggios) fashion.

TRACK 276

A) ___

B) ___

C) ___

D) ___

E) ___

F) ___

G) ___

H) ___

SIGHT-SINGING EXERCISES

These examples include the octave, as well as the others, and the arpeggios we just worked on.

Key of E Major

TRACK 277

A)

TRACK 278

B)

TRACK 279

C)

TRACK 280

D)

TRACK 281

E)

TRACK 282

F)

Key of C♯ Minor

In Chapter 6, we also learned the chords of the harmonized minor scale, in which the i, iv, and v chords are all minor triads. In the key of C♯ minor, they look like this:

Key of C♯m: i, iv, v chords

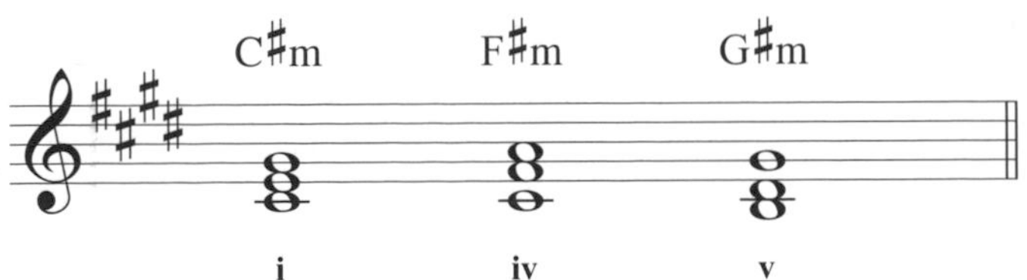

Now let's sing through some exercises that concentrate on those arpeggios, as well as our octave interval.

TRACK 283

A)

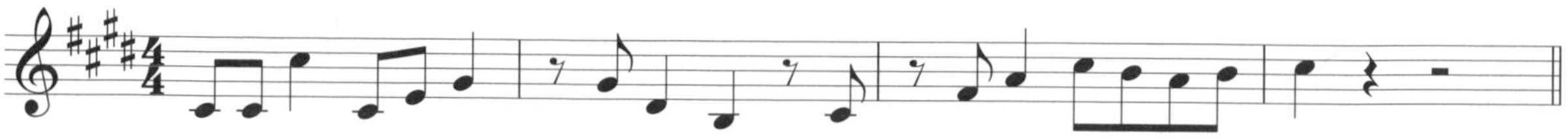

TRACK 284

B)

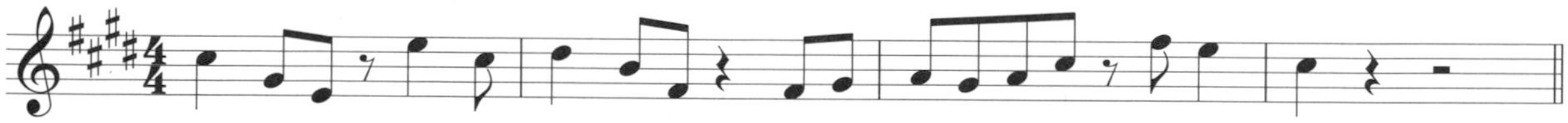

TRACK 285

C)

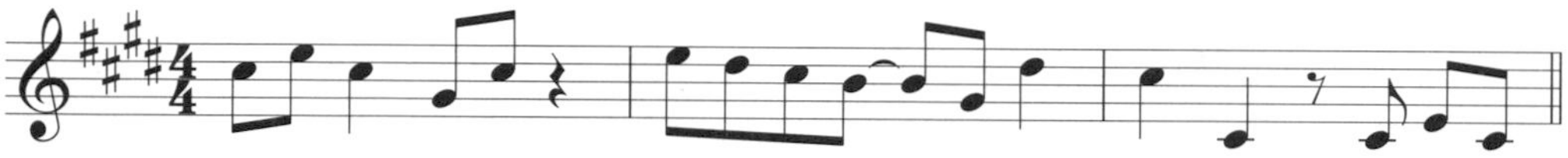

TRACK 286

D)

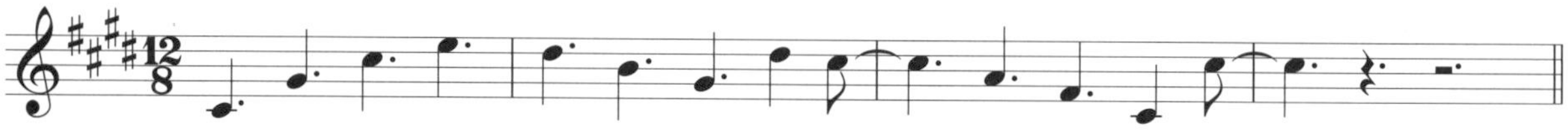

TRACK 287

E)

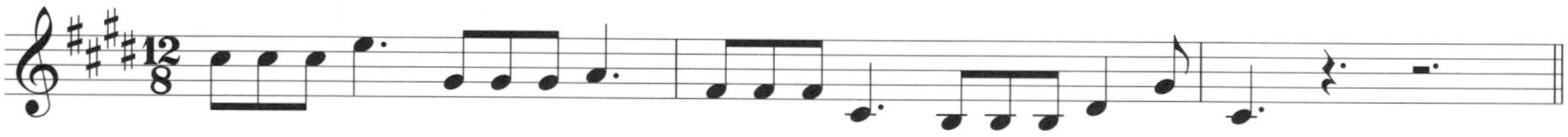

TRACK 288

F)

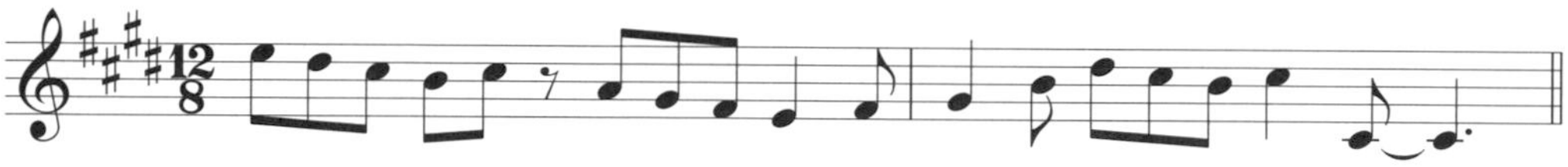

MELODIC DICTATION EXERCISES

In these exercises, you'll hear the instructor play a melody twice, and you'll write it down by ear. (**Instructors:** See Appendix for notation of these exercises. Alternatively, these can be found on the accompanying audio.)

Key of E Major

TRACK 289

A)

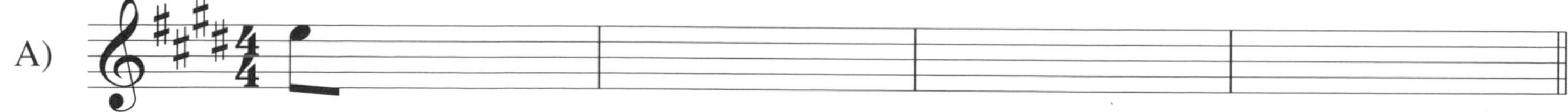

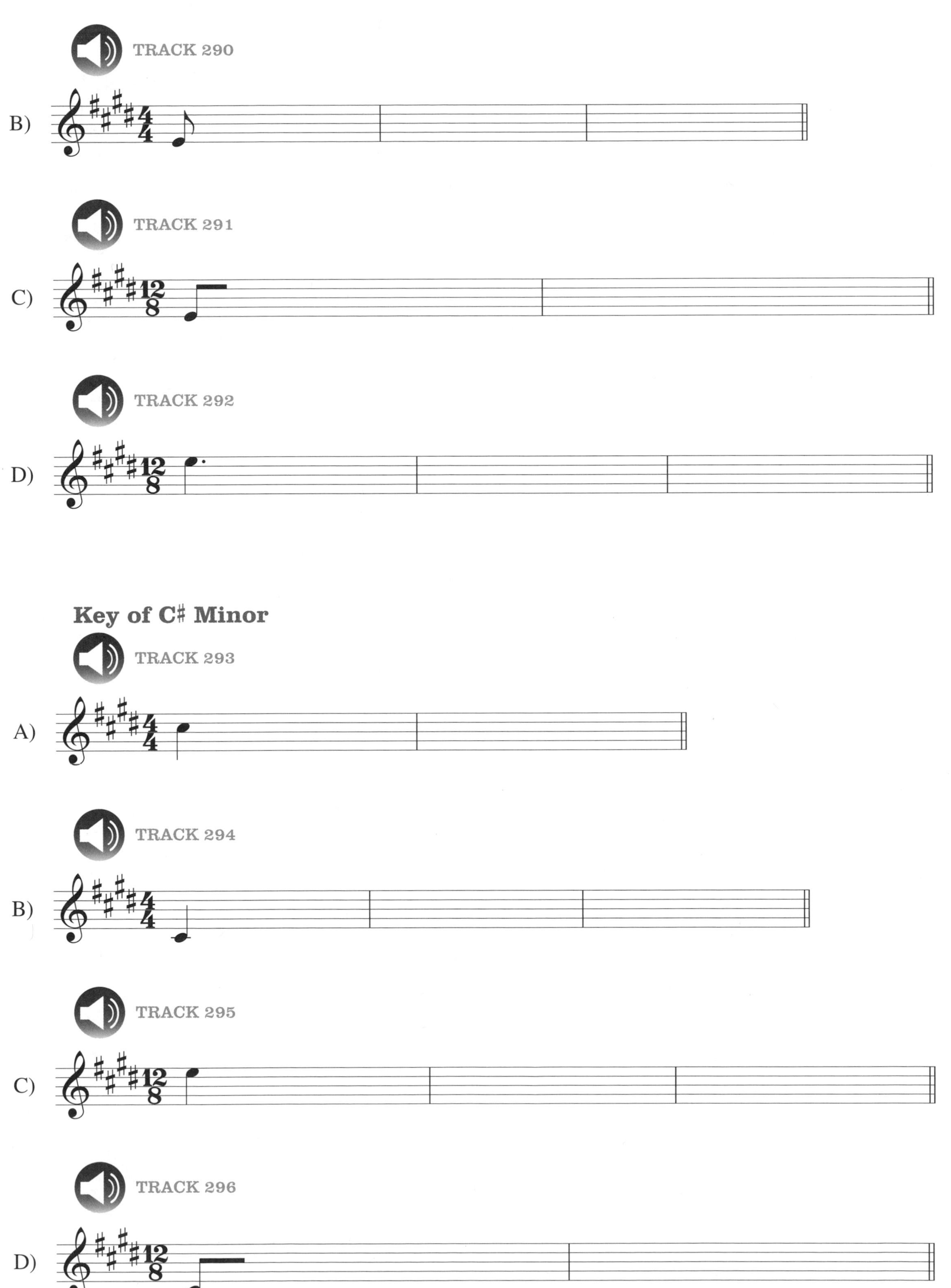
TRACK 290
B)
TRACK 291
C)
TRACK 292
D)
Key of C♯ Minor
TRACK 293
A)
TRACK 294
B)
TRACK 295
C)
TRACK 296
D)

ECHO DRILLS

For these drills, listen to the phrase and then echo it back. (**Instructors:** See Appendix for notation of these exercises. Alternatively, these can be found on the accompanying audio.)

Rhythm Echoes

These four exercises consist of *two-measure* phrases in 6/8. Clap the rhythms back during the breaks.

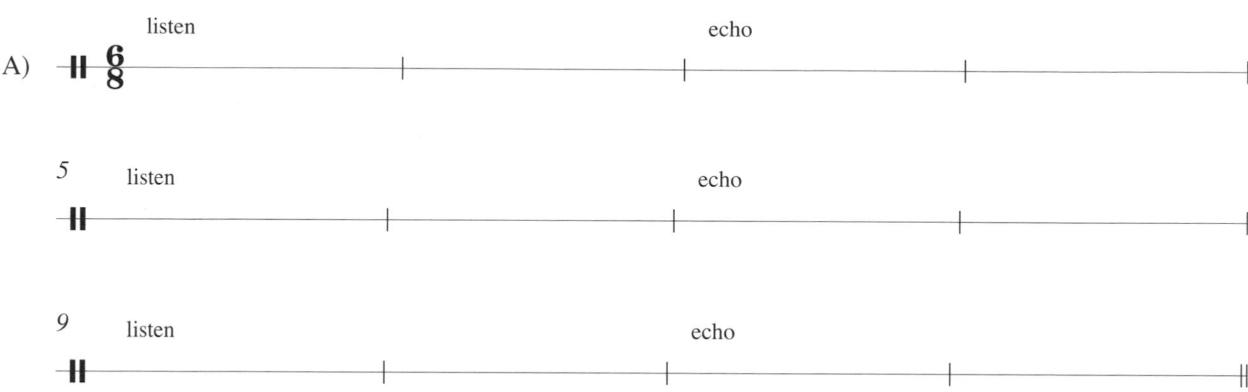

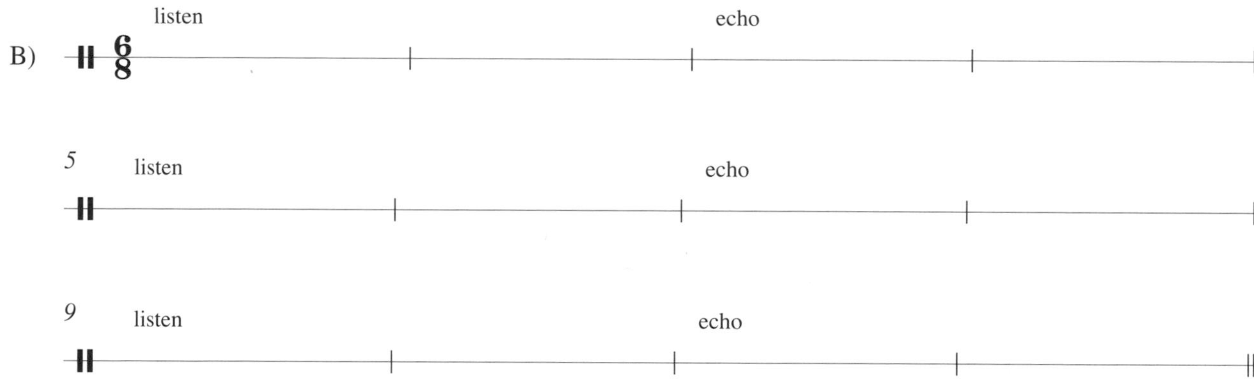

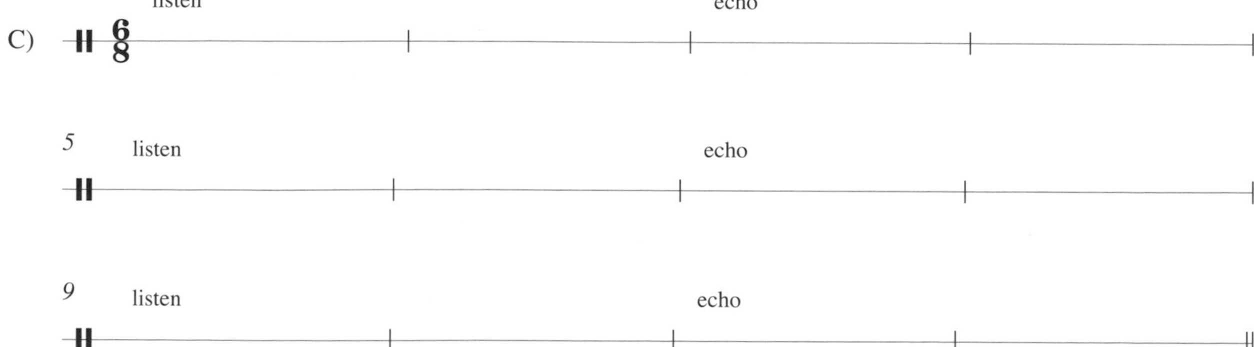

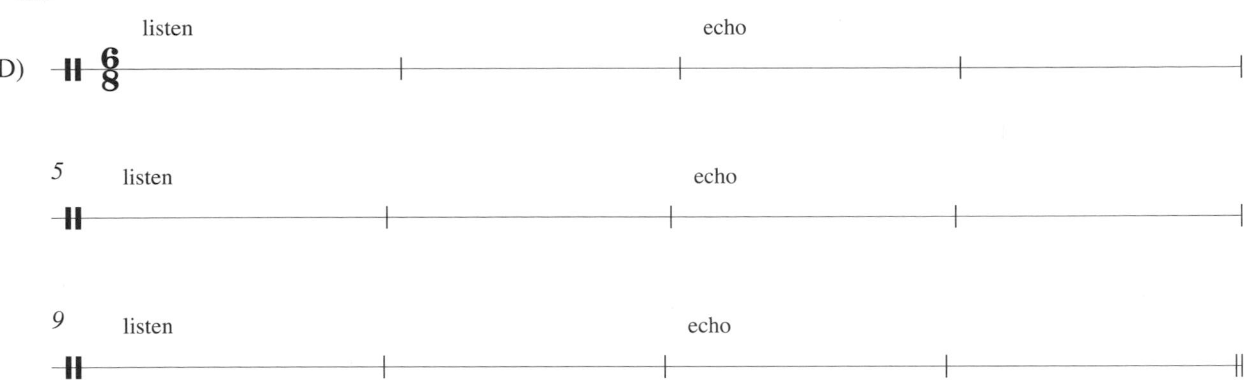

Melodic Echoes

In these four exercises, you'll hear a *two-bar* melody in 6/8 followed by two bars of silence. Sing the melody back during the breaks.

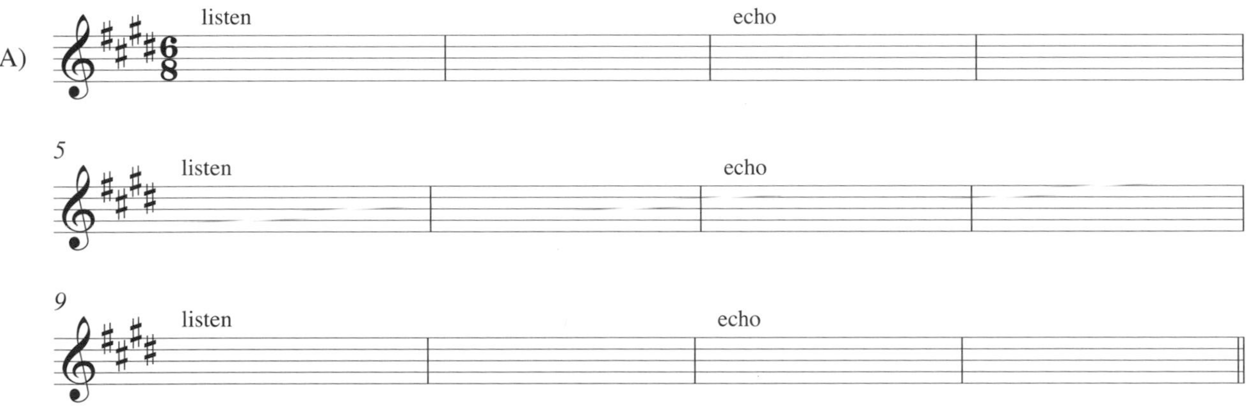

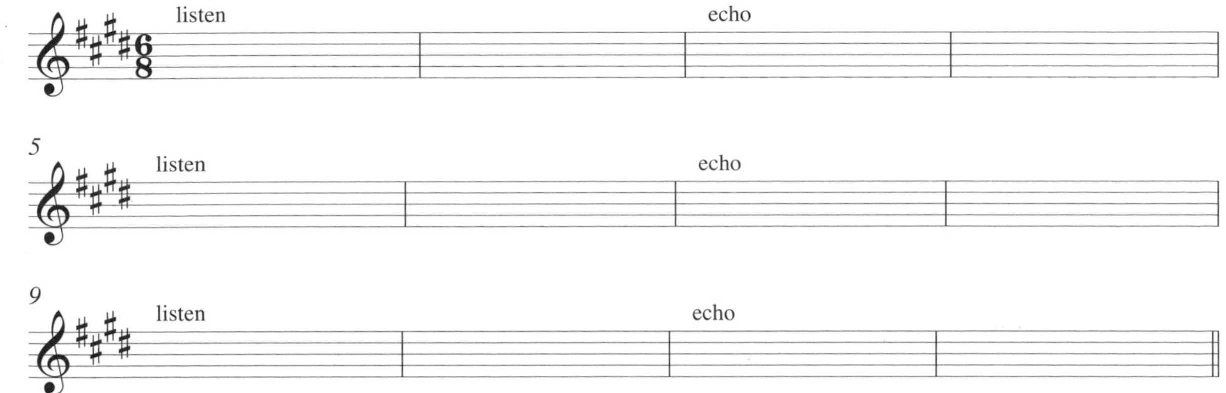

TRACK 303

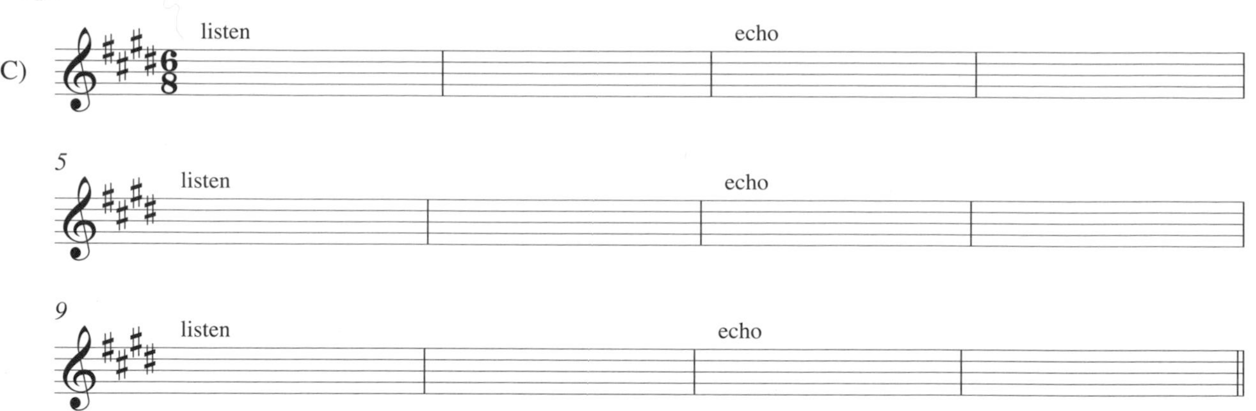
C)
listen
echo
5
listen
echo
9
listen
echo

TRACK 304

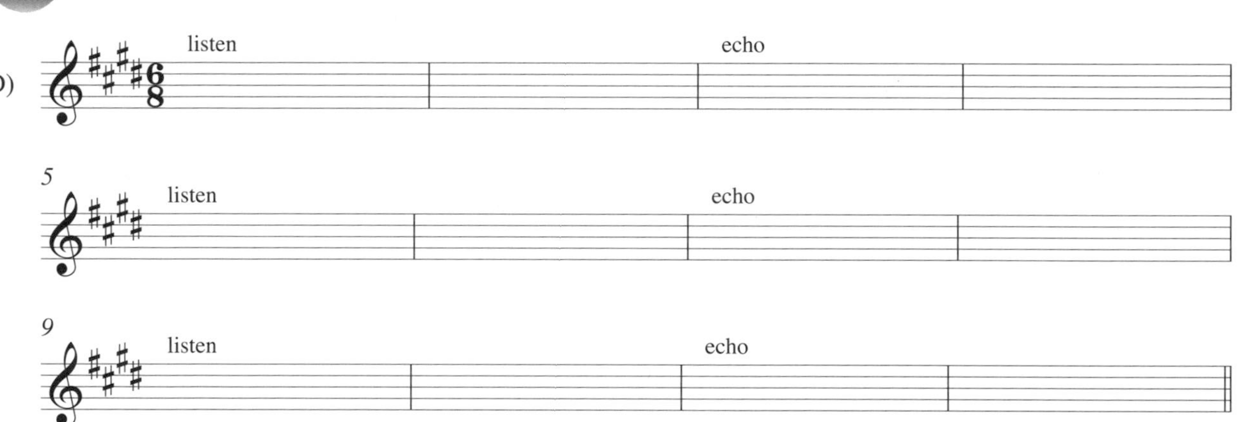
D)
listen
echo
5
listen
echo
9
listen
echo

CHAPTER 11

EXERCISES IN A♭ MAJOR AND F MINOR

In this chapter, we come to the keys of A♭ major and its relative minor, F minor.

THE SCALES

There are four flats in the keys of A♭ major and F minor. Let's see how this works.

A♭ Major Scale

First, write out the letter names spanning from tonic to tonic:

A♭ B C D E F G A♭

After examining these notes on the piano keyboard, we realize we need to make alterations to maintain the intervallic formula. In this case, lower the notes B, D, and E a half step each.

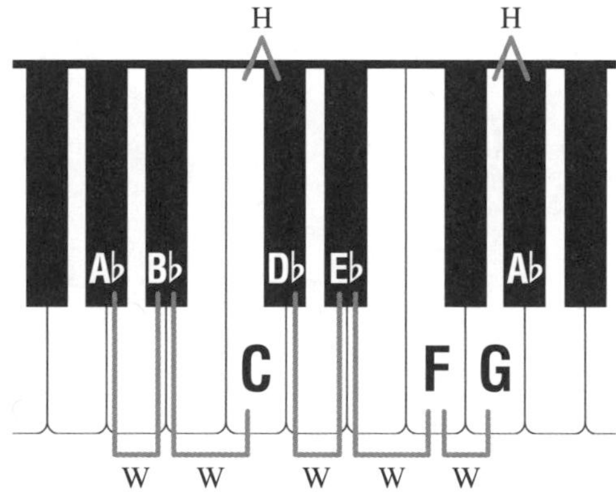

Thus, the A♭ major scale is spelled A♭–B♭–C–D♭–E♭–F–G, and the key signature for A♭ major is four flats: B♭, E♭, A♭, and D♭.

TRACK 305

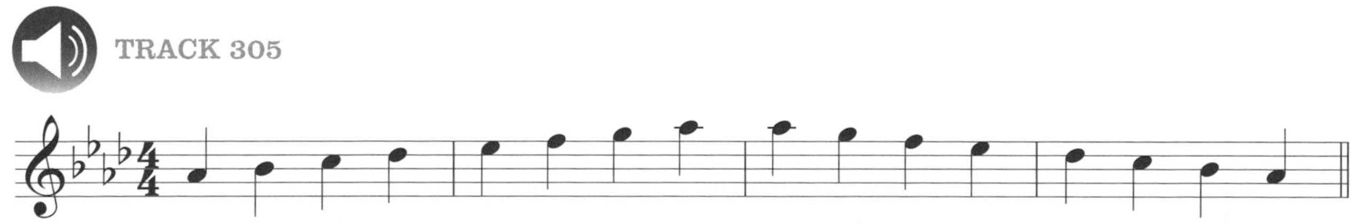

F Minor Scale

F minor is the relative minor of A♭ major, so its key signature also contains four flats.

TRACK 306

The Flat Side of the Circle

Refer again to the Circle of Fifths again in the Appendix (page 149). Note that flats are added in the same cumulative fashion as sharps. Each new key going around the circle has the same flats as the previous key and adds one more. On the sharp side, this new sharp is always the leading tone (the 7th degree); in the flat keys, the new flat is always the 4th degree of the scale. This makes sense when we look at the C major scale. The two natural half steps—from E to F and from B to C—in the musical alphabet fall exactly in the 3-4 and 7-8 (1) spots of the scale. That's why C major requires no sharps or flats in its key signature.

In F major, the first flat key, we lowered the B to B♭ so there would be a half step from the 3rd to 4th scale degrees. Every flat key behaves the same way. It needs the 4th degree to be flatted a half step. Once you've memorized the order of keys on the Circle of Fifths, the order of flats in a key signature is easier to remember than the sharp ones, because each key signature foretells what the next one will be. In other words, the key of F has one flat, which is B♭. B♭ also happens to be the next key along the circle on the flat side. The key of B♭ contains B♭ (obviously) and also E♭, which is the next key along the circle, and so on.

RHYTHM STUDY

We'll expand our rhythms here by looking at the triplet. Whereas a beat in simple meter (like 4/4, 3/4, etc.) is normally divided in half (eighth notes), a *triplet* divides the beat into three equal parts.

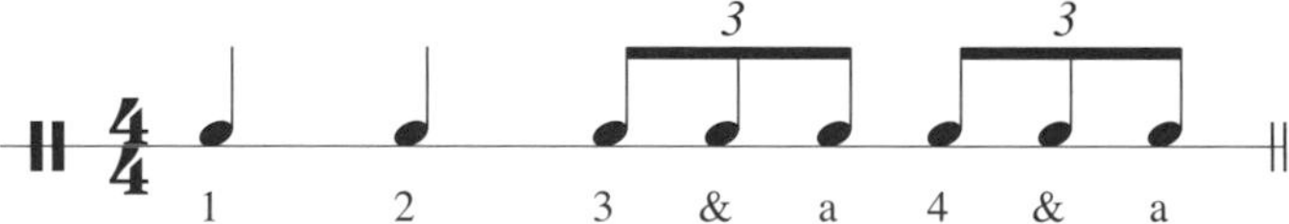

Previously, we've seen this with compound meters (6/8 and 12/8), but the difference here is that we'll be mixing triplets into simple meters. We'll learn to transition between dividing the beat in half and dividing the beat into three parts at different times. It will take a bit of getting used to at first, but soon it will begin to feel natural.

Rhythmic Drills

Clap the following rhythms together as a class or in smaller groups. Notice that when a triplet is incomplete—i.e., one or more of the divisions is a rest—a bracket is used to clearly show the rhythmic grouping.

Rhythmic Dictation

Listen to the following rhythms and write them down. Each example will be played twice.

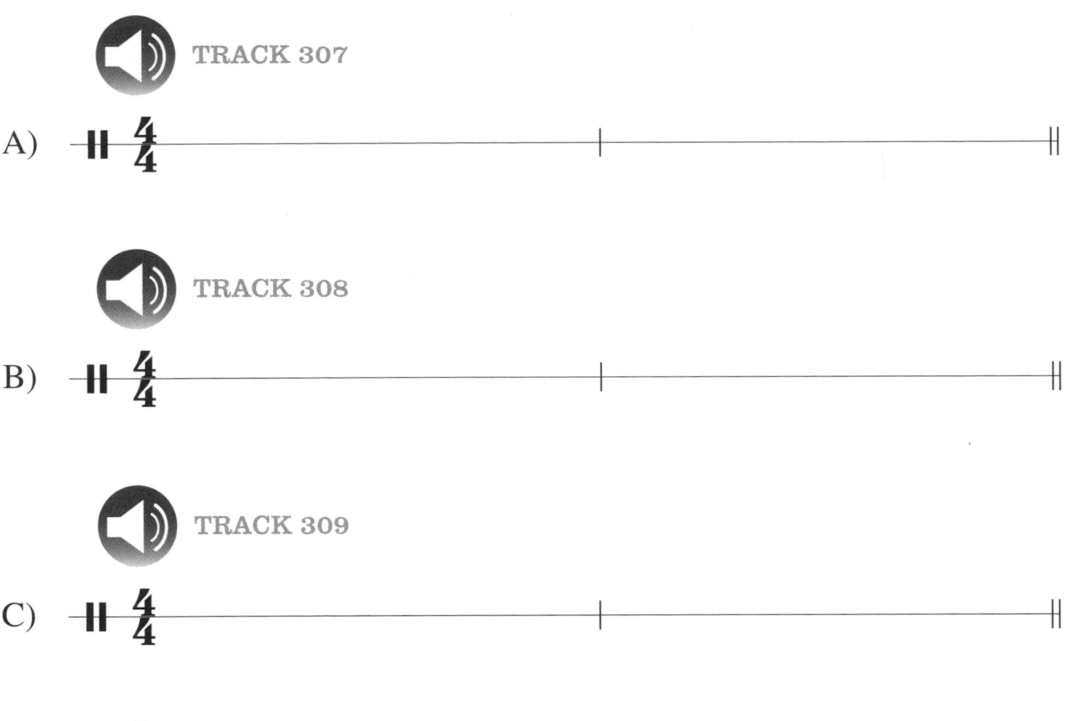

TRACK 310

TRIAD STUDY

Since we studied the octave in Chapter 10, let's now take a closer look at the other chords of a key. As we know, the I, IV, and V chords in a major key are all major. In A♭ major, these are A♭, D♭, and E♭, respectively.

Key of A♭: I, IV, V chords

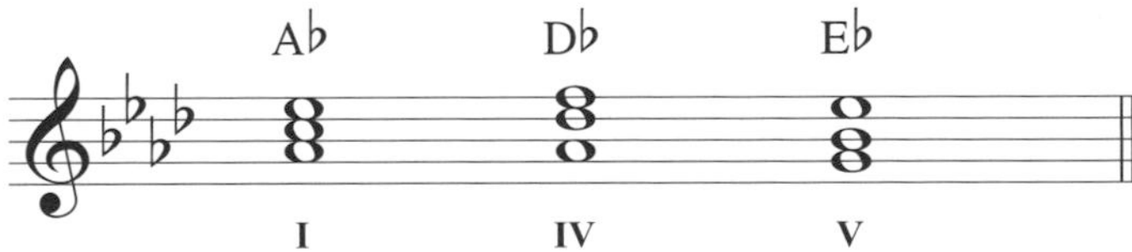

We also know that the ii, iii, and vi chords are minor triads. In the key of A♭, these are B♭m, Cm, and Fm, respectively. (Note that we're using inversions when showing these chord forms.)

Key of A♭: ii, iii, vi chords

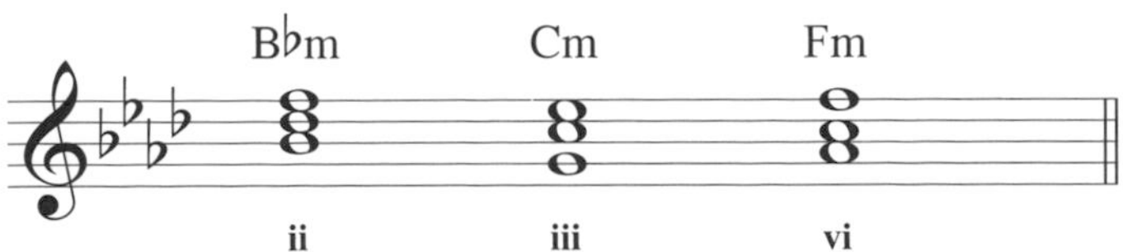

Regarding the "1-7 line" idea from the previous chapter, the vi chord is the only one of these triads that contains the 1st degree (tonic). The iii chord is the only one that contains the 7th degree. The ii chord contains neither of these degrees.

Key of A♭: ii, iii, vi chords

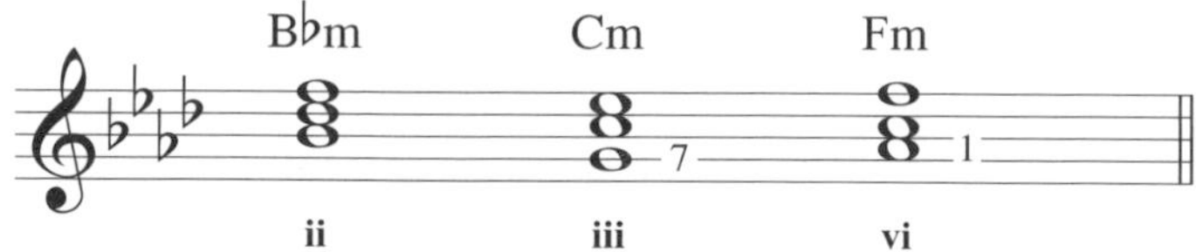

In the following exercises, if you hear the tonic, it's the vi chord. If you hear the 7th, it's the iii chord. If you hear neither of them, it's the ii chord. In the case of the ii chord, the 4th scale degree (D♭ in the key of A♭ major) is usually easy to pick out. Since it appears in the ii chord (as the minor 3rd of that chord), it can be used as an indicator that you're hearing the ii chord.

Eventually, of course, you'll recognize the sound of these without having to think in terms of the 1-7 line, but it can be helpful in the beginning to get you on the right track.

Triad Dictation

Listen to the following minor triads from the key of A♭ major and determine if they are the ii (B♭m), iii (Cm), or vi (Fm) chords. Before the first example, you will hear the key tonicized with a I–IV–V–I progression. The examples will appear in either harmonic (chords) or melodic (arpeggios) fashion.

TRACK 312

A) ___

B) ___

C) ___

D) ___

E) ___

F) ___

G) ___

H) ___

SIGHT-SINGING EXERCISES

The following examples feature all the intervals spanning the octave, as well as the minor arpeggios we just worked on.

Key of A♭ Major

TRACK 314

B)

TRACK 315

C)

TRACK 316

D)

TRACK 317

E)

TRACK 318

F)

Key of F Minor

In Chapter 6, we learned the chords of the harmonized minor scale, in which the i, iv, and v chords are all minor triads. The major chords in a minor key are built on the 3rd, 6th, and 7th degrees of the minor scale. In the key of F minor, these are A♭, D♭, and E♭, respectively:

TRACK 319

Key of Fm: III, VI, VII chords

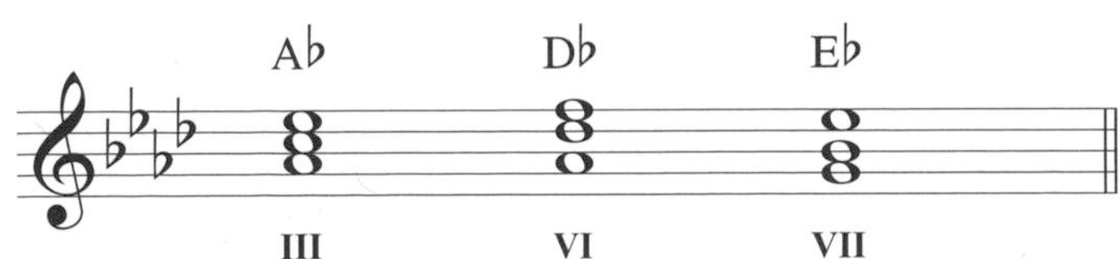

Now let's sing through some exercises in F minor that concentrate on the III, VI, and VII arpeggios, as well as intervals that span the octave.

TRACK 320

A)

TRACK 321

B)

TRACK 322

C)

TRACK 323

D)

TRACK 324

E)

TRACK 325

F)

MELODIC DICTATION EXERCISES

In these exercises, you'll hear the instructor play a melody twice, and you'll write it down by ear. (**Instructors:** See Appendix for notation of these exercises. Alternatively, these can be found on the accompanying audio.)

Key of A♭ Major

A)

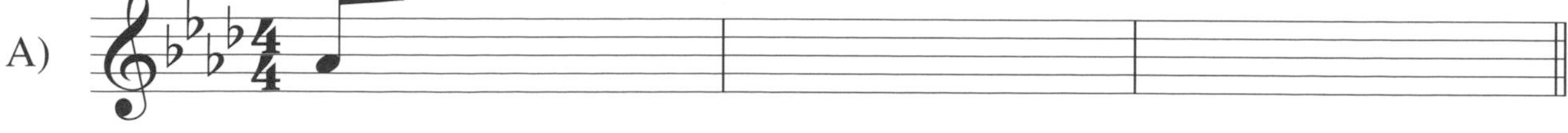

TRACK 327
B)
TRACK 328
C)
TRACK 329
D)
Key of F Minor
TRACK 330
A)
TRACK 331
B)
TRACK 332
C)
TRACK 333
D)
3

ECHO DRILLS

For these drills, listen to the phrase and then echo it back. (**Instructors:** See Appendix for notation of these exercises. Alternatively, these can be found on the accompanying audio.)

Rhythm Echoes

These four exercises feature *two-measure* phrases in 4/4. Clap the rhythms back during the breaks. Listen for the triplets!

TRACK 334

A) 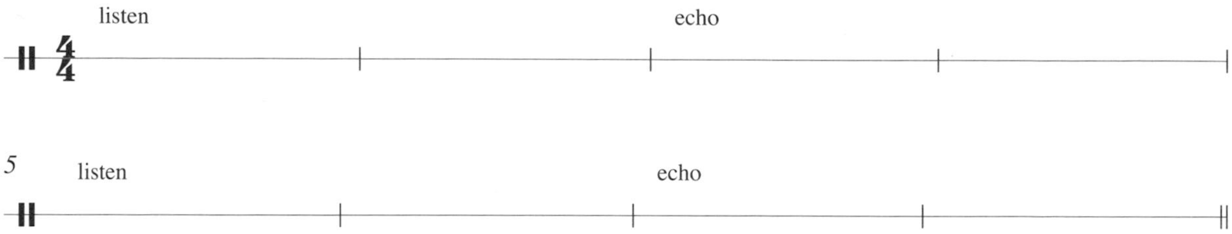 listen echo

5 listen echo

TRACK 335

B) 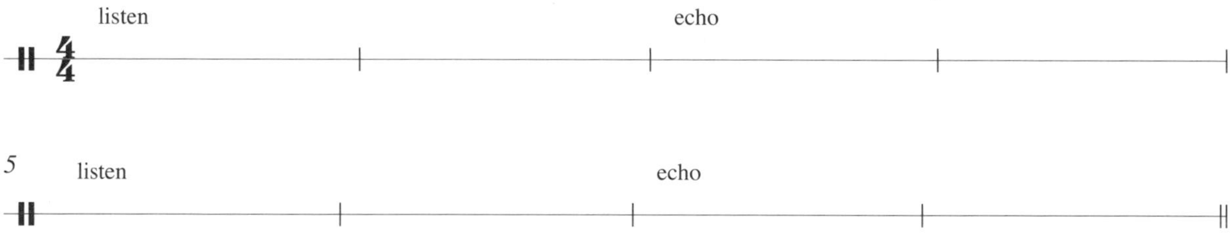 listen echo

5 listen echo

TRACK 336

C) 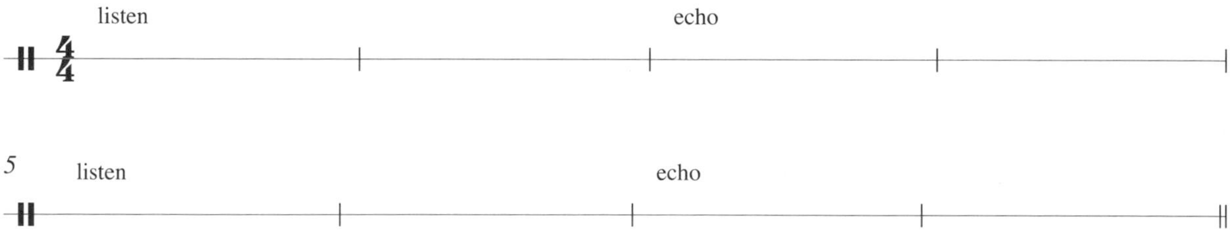 listen echo

5 listen echo

TRACK 337

D)

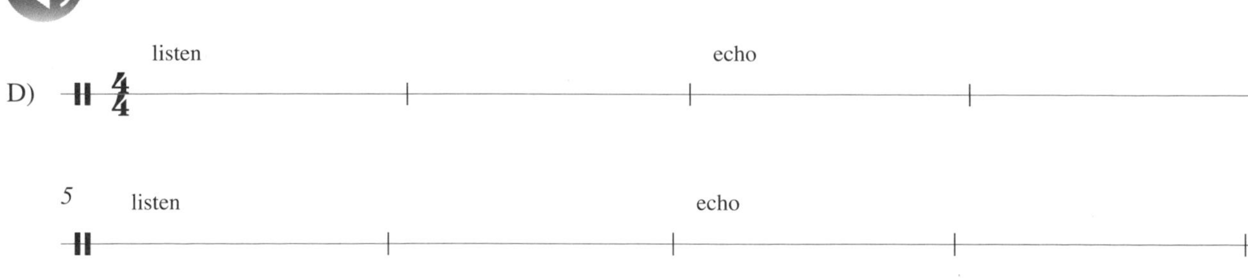

Melodic Echoes

In these four exercises, you'll hear a *two-bar* melody in 4/4 followed by two bars of silence. Sing the melody back during the break.

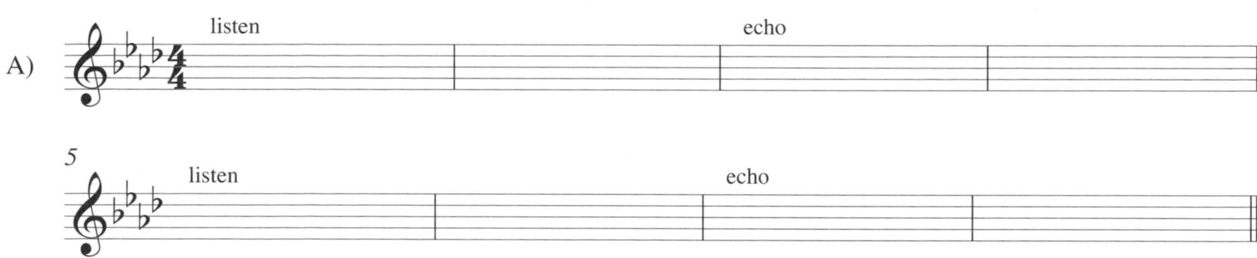

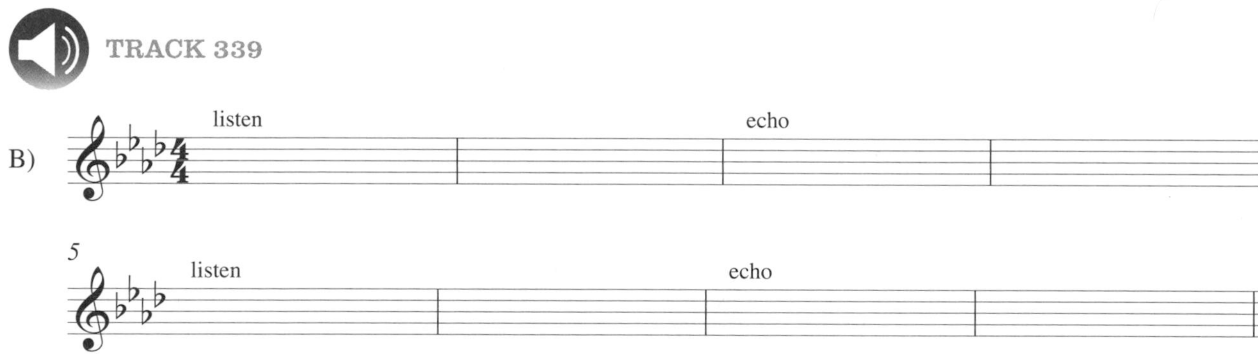

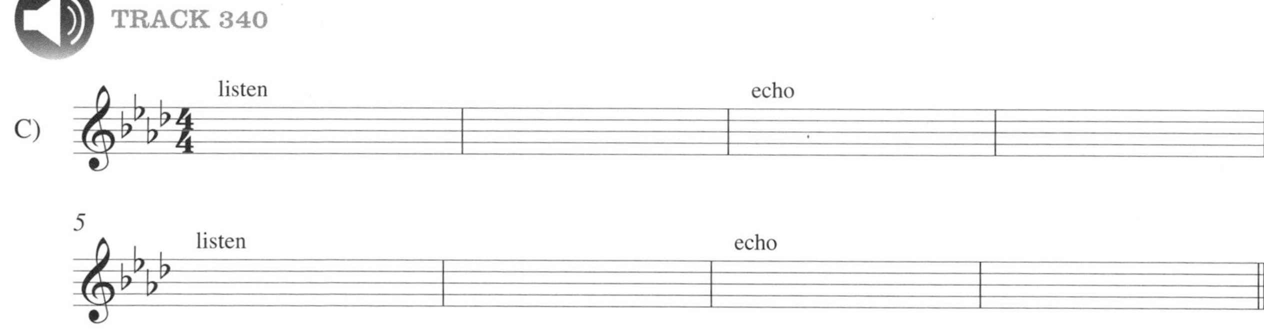

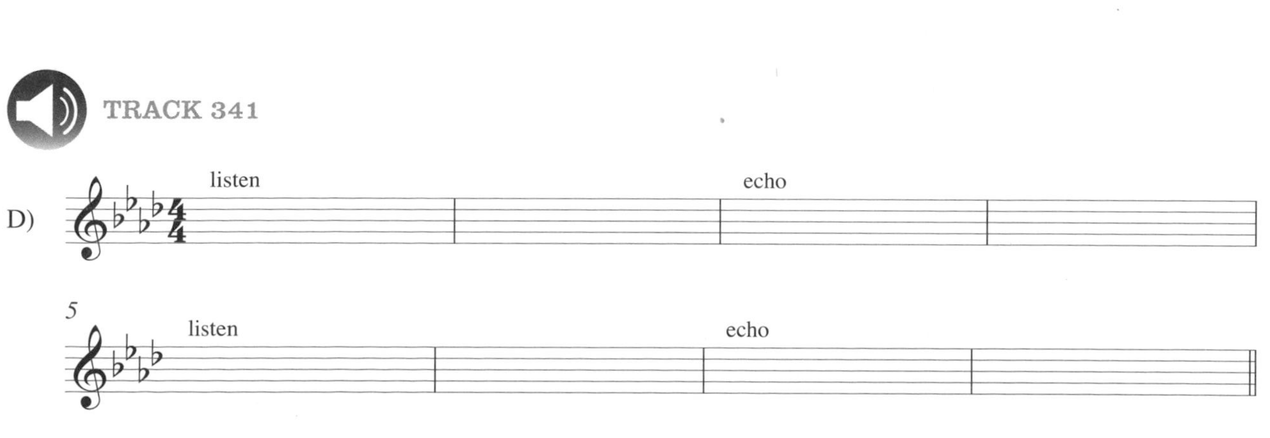

CHAPTER 12

EXERCISES IN B MAJOR AND G♯ MINOR

The last pair of keys we'll look at is B major and its relative minor, G# minor.

THE SCALES

We have a total of five sharps in the keys of B major and G# minor. Let's see how this works.

B Major Scale

First, write out the letter names spanning from tonic to tonic:

B C D E F G A B

After examining these notes on the piano keyboard, we see we need to make alterations to get the intervallic formula. In this case, raise the notes C, D, F, G, and A a half step each.

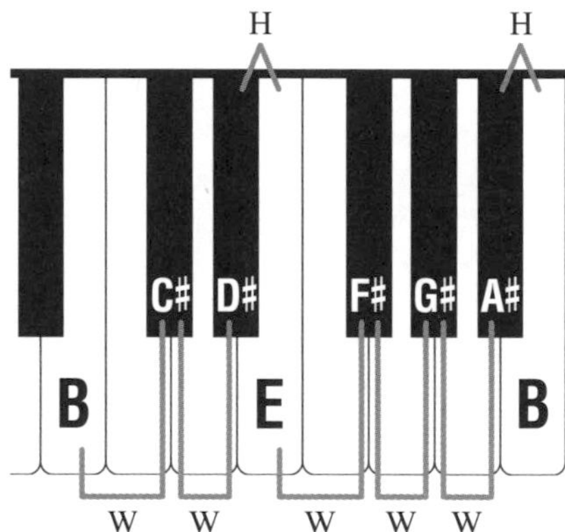

Therefore, we now know that the B major scale is spelled B–C#–D#–E–F#–G#–A#, and the key signature for B major is five sharps: F#, C#, G#, D#, and A#.

G♯ Minor Scale

G# minor is the relative minor of B major, so its key signature also contains five sharps.

The Other Two Keys in the Circle

With this chapter, we will have covered 10 of the 12 possible keys in the Circle of Fifths. The ones we won't cover are the two least common: D♭ major and F♯ (or G♭) major. D♭ major contains five flats: B♭, E♭, A♭, D♭, and G♭. The key at the bottom of the circle (opposite the key of C) can be called F♯ or G♭ major, because either way there are six accidentals. If called F♯ major, it contains six sharps: F♯, C♯, G♯, D♯, A♯, and E♯. (The note E♯ is enharmonically the same as F, but is spelled E♯ in the F♯ major scale because every letter name must be represented.) If called G♭ major, it contains six flats: B♭, E♭, A♭, D♭, G♭, and C♭. (Again, the C♭ would not be named B, because there is already a B♭ in the G♭ major scale.)

We opted to omit these two keys so we can cover a few other concepts in the remaining chapters. By now, you know the routine. You know how to build the scale by adhering to the intervallic formula, and therefore are able to figure out their key signatures (even though we just told you above). In Chapter 17, we'll discuss transposition. You'll learn how any of the exercises in this book can be transposed to one of these keys should you choose to do so.

RHYTHM STUDY

With the addition of 16th notes, we expand our rhythmic palette once more. A 16th note is twice as fast as an eighth note and is so named because there are 16 of them in a measure of 4/4. To count 16th notes, we add "e" and "a" syllables in between the beat number and the "and" when counting eighth notes, so the beats are counted: 1 e + a 2 e + a, etc.

Notice that 16ths are beamed together, similarly to eighth notes. They are generally more common in slower tempos, as the faster the song is, the more challenging it is to perform them. We'll slow the tempo down a bit for the following exercises and look at 16ths only in simple meters for this chapter.

Rhythmic Drills

Clap the following rhythms together as a class or in smaller groups.

Rhythmic Dictation

Listen to the following rhythms and write them down. Each example will be played twice.

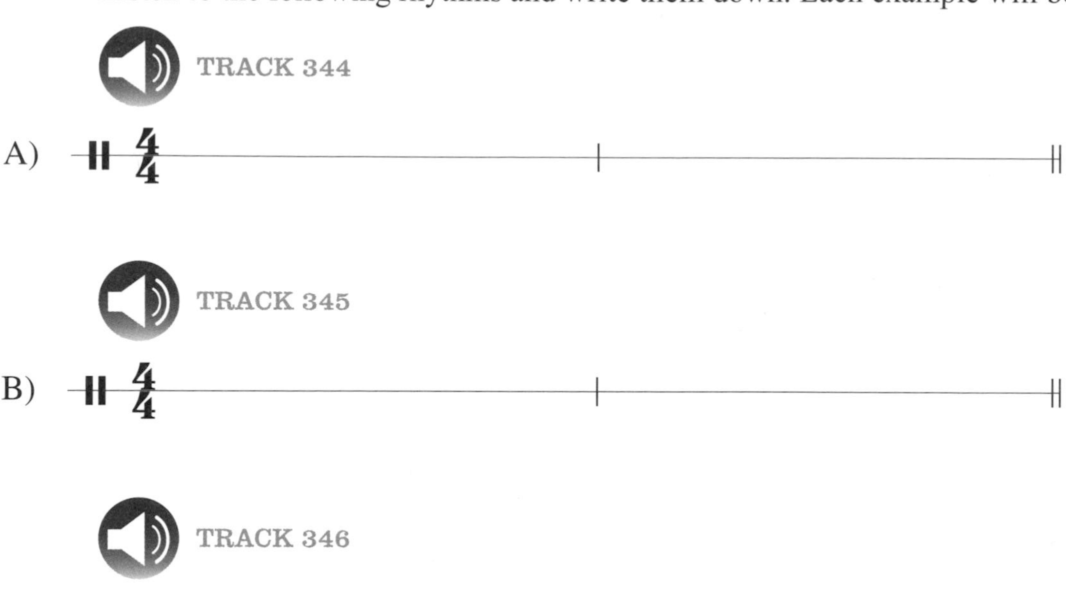

TRIAD STUDY

In this chapter, we're going to work on recognizing all seven triad arpeggios in a major key. We've already looked at the three major triads (I, IV, and V) as well as the three minor triads (ii, iii, and vi). The last triad is diminished, and is built from the 7th degree. In the key of B major, this is A#°.

Regarding the "1-7 line" idea, the vii° chord contains the 7th degree and does not contain the tonic. It sounds somewhat similar to the V chord since it shares two notes, but it shouldn't be difficult to tell them apart, because the diminished 5th interval (present in the vii° chord but not in the V chord) is usually easy to hear.

Taken altogether then, here are all seven diatonic triads in the key of B major.

TRACK 349

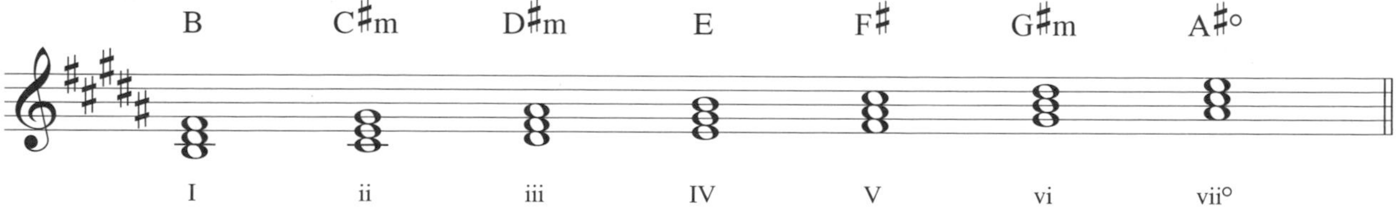

As with intervals, the more you hear these chords in different progressions, the more quickly you'll be able to pick them out with your ears only. It's not uncommon for someone with a well-trained ear, when given the key, to be able to write out a chord chart only by ear upon first hearing the song. Obviously, it's easier to do when there are fewer chords, but you'd be surprised how easy this becomes with a bit of practice.

Triad Dictation

Now let's try picking out these triads by ear. Determine which diatonic arpeggio in the key of B major you're hearing: I (B), ii (C♯m), iii (D♯m), IV (E), V (F♯), vi (G♯m), or vii° (A♯°). The examples will appear in either harmonic (chords) or melodic (arpeggios) fashion. You'll first hear some tonicizing chords.

TRACK 350

A) ___ G) ___

B) ___ H) ___

C) ___ I) ___

D) ___ J) ___

E) ___ K) ___

F) ___ L) ___

SIGHT-SINGING EXERCISES

These examples contain all the intervals, and feature all the triad arpeggios, we've learned.

Key of B Major

TRACK 351

A) 

TRACK 352

B) 

Key of G♯ Minor

The diminished triad in a minor key appears on the 2nd degree. In our case, it's an A♯° in the key of G♯ minor.

Taken altogether then, here are all seven diatonic chords in the key of G♯ minor.

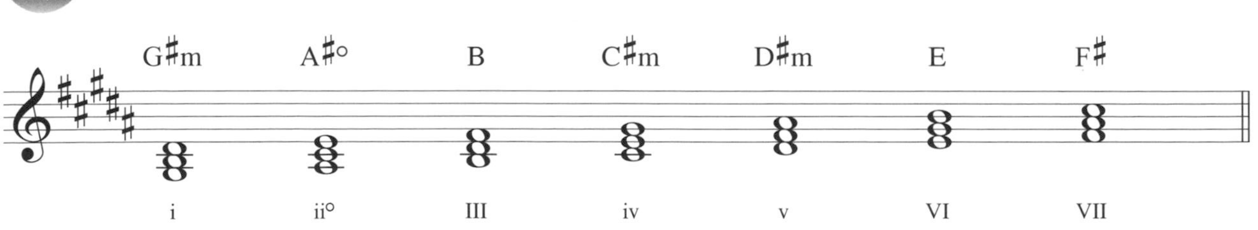

Now let's sing through some exercises in G♯ minor that concentrate on the arpeggios of the key, as well as intervals that span the octave.

TRACK 359

A)

TRACK 360

B)

TRACK 361

C)

TRACK 362

D)

TRACK 363

E)

TRACK 364

F)

MELODIC DICTATION EXERCISES

In these exercises, you'll hear the instructor play a melody twice, and you'll write it down by ear. (**Instructors:** See Appendix for notation of these exercises. Alternatively, these can be found on the accompanying audio.)

Key of B Major

A)

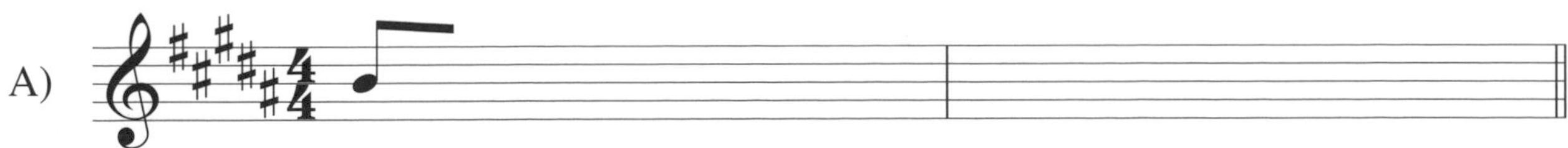

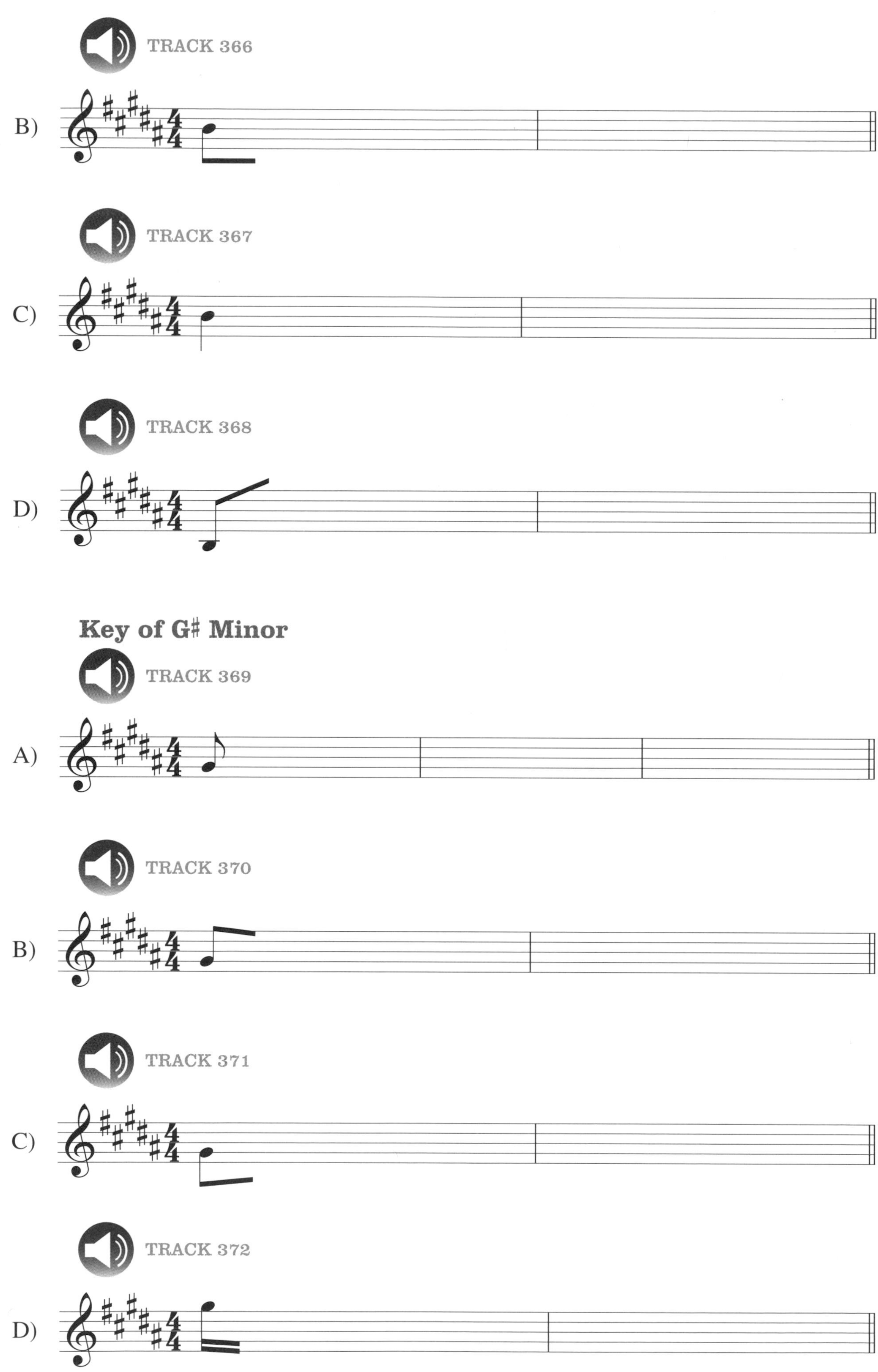
TRACK 366
B)
TRACK 367
C)
TRACK 368
D)
Key of G♯ Minor
TRACK 369
A)
TRACK 370
B)
TRACK 371
C)
TRACK 372
D)

ECHO DRILLS

For these drills, listen to the phrase and then echo it back. (**Instructors:** See Appendix for notation of these exercises. Alternatively, these can be found on the accompanying audio.)

Rhythm Echoes

Since we've added 16th notes, we'll go back to one-bar phrases here.

TRACK 373

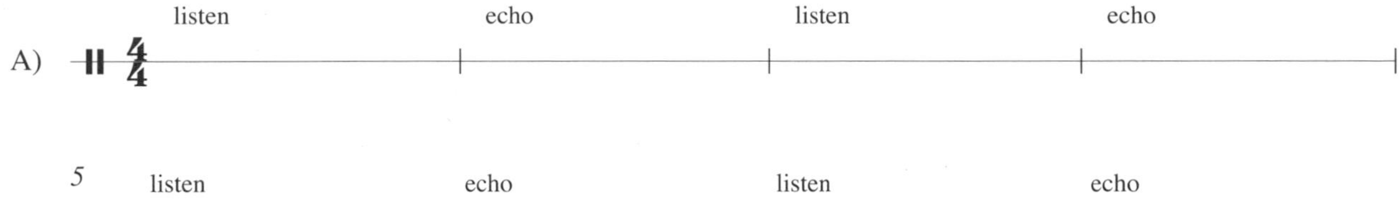

TRACK 374

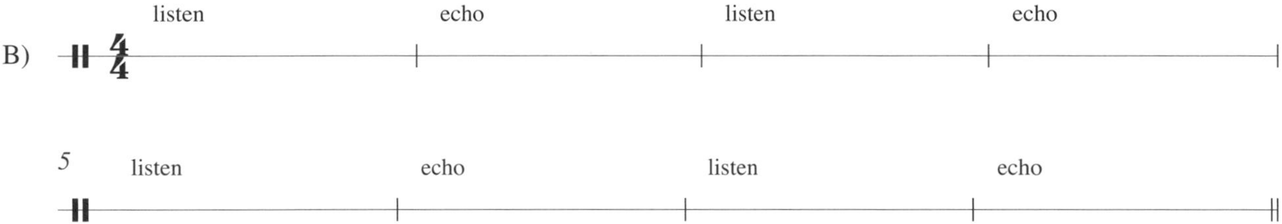

TRACK 375

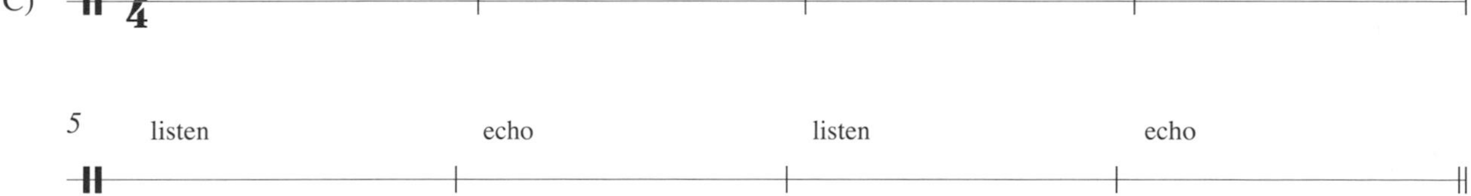

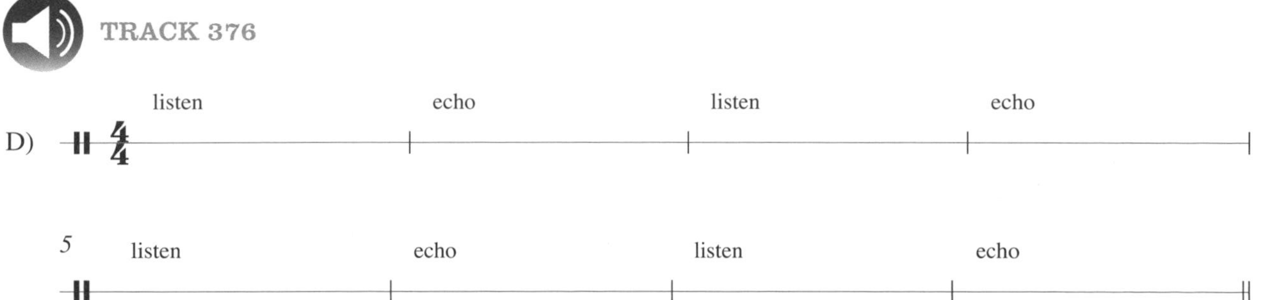

Melodic Echoes

You'll hear a one-bar melody in 4/4 followed by one bar of silence. Sing the melody back during the break.

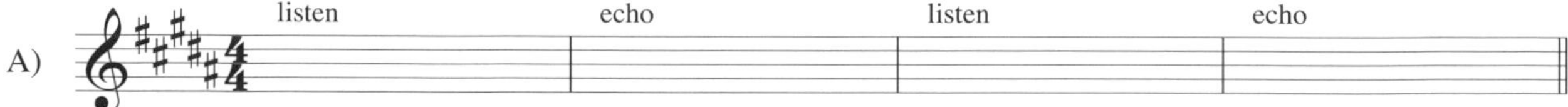

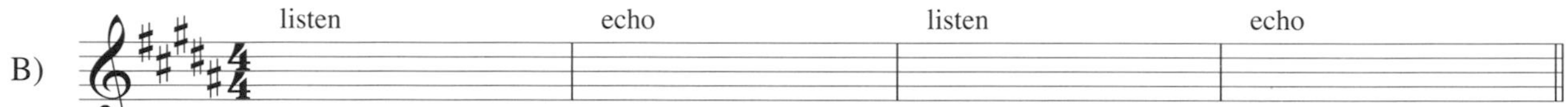

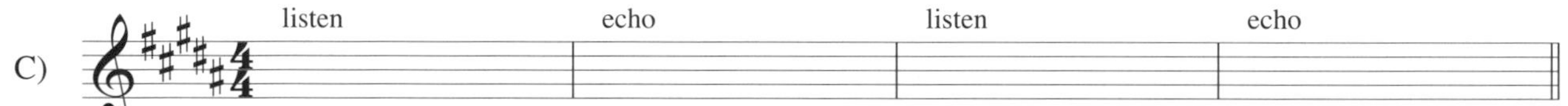

D) listen echo listen echo

CHAPTER 13

PENTATONIC AND BLUES SCALES

In addition to major and minor scales, there are several other scales commonly used in Western music. Some of the most common are pentatonic and blues scales. They're the focus of this chapter.

PENTATONIC SCALES

A pentatonic scale contains five notes instead of the standard seven in a major or minor scale. ("Penta" means five, so it makes sense!) There are two main types of pentatonic scales: the *major pentatonic*, and the *minor pentatonic*.

Major Pentatonic

The major pentatonic scale is a leaner, five-note version of the major scale. This scale is common in pop, rock, country, jazz—pretty much you name it. It omits the 4th and 7th degrees from the major scale, so we're left with 1–2–3–5–6. In the key of C major, this means omitting F and B, leaving C–D–E–G–A.

TRACK 381

Minor Pentatonic

The minor pentatonic scale is a stripped-down version of the minor scale, omitting the 2nd and 6th degrees for a numeric formula of 1–3–4–5–7. In the relative key of A minor, this again means omitting the notes F and B, leaving A–C–D–E–G. Notice the similarity to the C major pentatonic scale; it contains all the same notes. Therefore, pentatonic scales can be relatives, just like major and minor scales.

TRACK 382

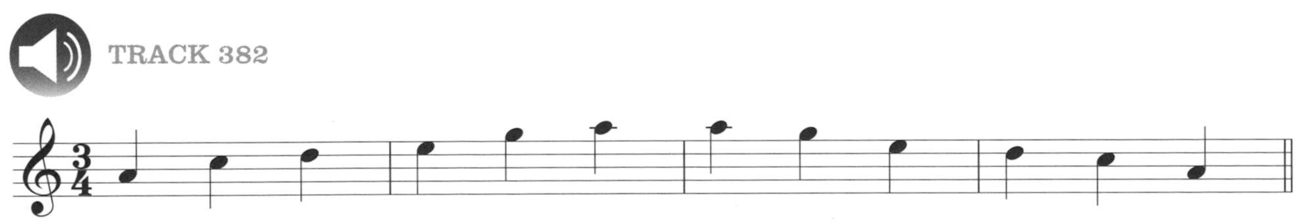

BLUES SCALE

The blues scale is a six-note scale that adds a chromatic passing tone to the minor pentatonic scale. The term *chromatic* (with regards to scales and melodies) refers to notes progressing in consecutive half steps. The added note appears between the 4th and 5th degrees of a minor pentatonic scale, which makes its numeric formula 1–3–4–♯4 (or ♭5)–5–7. In A minor, this is A–C–D–D♯ (or E♭)–E–G.

TRACK 383

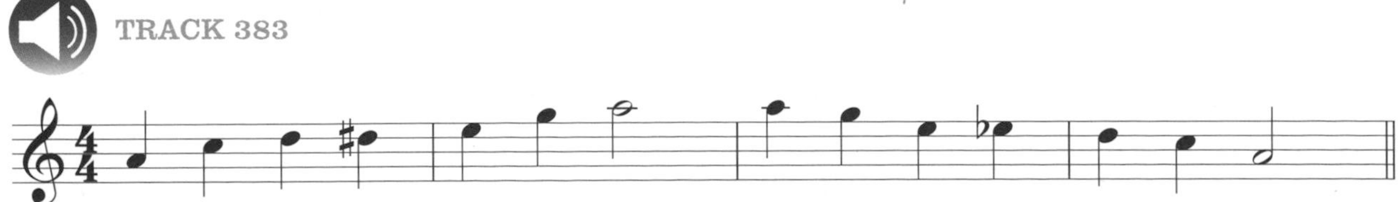

Other Blues Scales

The blues scale need not be identified as a "minor" blues scale. The term blues scale on its own is generally accepted to mean the minor pentatonic with the added ♭5th. There is a sequence of notes sometimes referred to as a major blues scale, but the standardization of such a scale is not established; you'll encounter conflicting examples of which notes are contained in such a scale. For our purposes, we'll stick to the above-mentioned definition of the standard blues scale.

RHYTHM STUDY

Let's include some challenging 16th-note rhythms that feature syncopation by employing, among other things, 16th-note rests (𝄿) and dotted eighth notes (3/4 of a beat). Again, we'll stick with simple meters throughout the chapter.

Rhythmic Drills

Clap the following rhythms together as a class or in smaller groups.

Rhythmic Dictation

Listen to the following rhythms and write them down. Each example will be played twice.

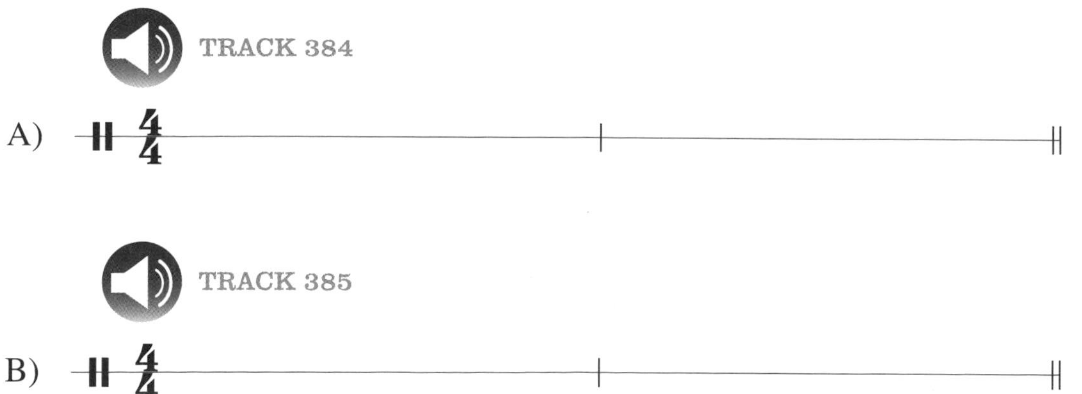

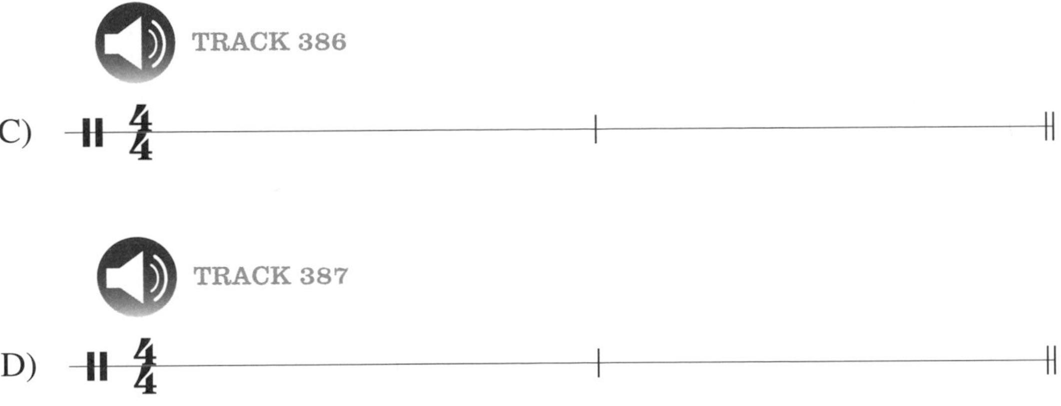

Scale Study

Since we're looking at pentatonic scales, now is a good time to discuss *parallel* key relationships, as opposed to *relative*. Relative major and minor keys share the same key signature (and therefore the same notes), while parallel keys share the same tonic but contain different notes. Whereas the relative minor of C major is A minor, the *parallel* minor of C major is *C minor*.

What does this have to do with pentatonic scales? Well, in bluesy music, in which pentatonic scales are heavily featured, we frequently encounter this type of *modal mixture* or parallel key relationship. In a blues song in the key of C major, for example, you may find that the vocal melody makes use of the C major pentatonic scale, but the guitar solo makes use of the C minor pentatonic scale. Or each one may combine both scales, depending on the phrase.

In these exercises, we're going to work on hearing different intervals as they relate to the parallel keys of C major and C minor. To get an idea of how this sounds, listen to the following example of C major pentatonic followed by C minor pentatonic.

The same can be done with chords. When we mix modes this way, we say that we are "borrowing chords" from the parallel key. For example, listen to the following progression, which is clearly in the key of C major.

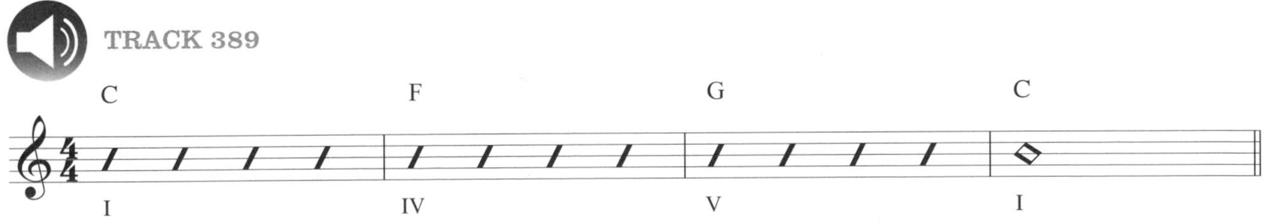

Now listen to this progression, which has two "borrowed chords" from the parallel key of C minor.

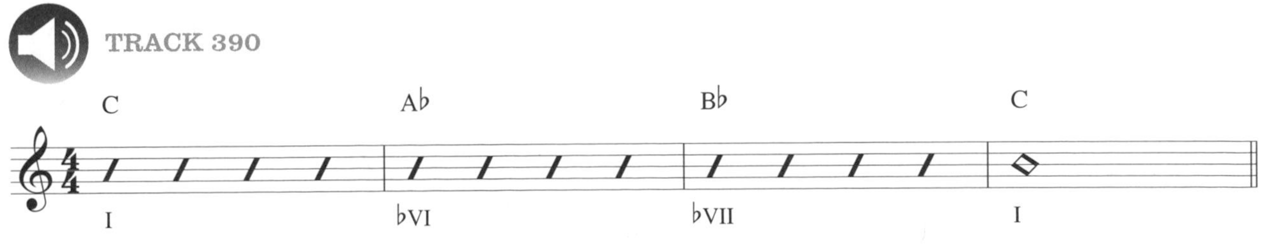

To restate what was said in Chapter 12: As with intervals, the more you hear these chords in different progressions, the more quickly you'll be able to pick them out with your ears only. It's not uncommon for someone with a well-trained ear, when given the key, to be able to write out a chord chart only by ear upon first hearing the song. Obviously, it's easier to do when there are fewer chords, but you'd be surprised how easy this becomes with a bit of practice.

Scale Identification

Now we'll identify these scales by ear. Determine whether you're hearing a major pentatonic, minor pentatonic, or a blues scale. The scales will be played in several different keys.

SIGHT-SINGING EXERCISES

Let's work on singing melodies from the pentatonic and blues scales.

Major Pentatonic

These six exercises utilize six different keys.

TRACK 396

E)

TRACK 397

F)

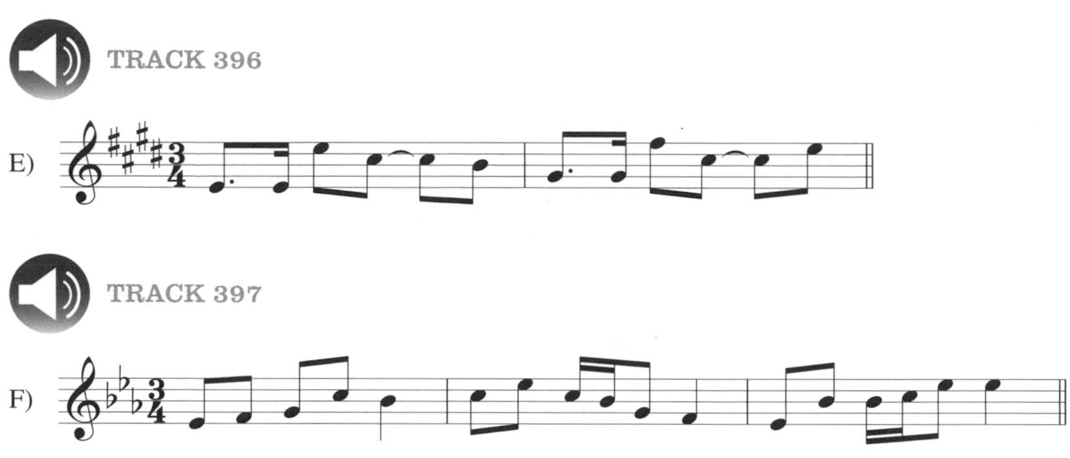

Minor Pentatonic and Blues Scale

These six melodies come from either the minor pentatonic or blues scale, in various keys.

TRACK 398

A) 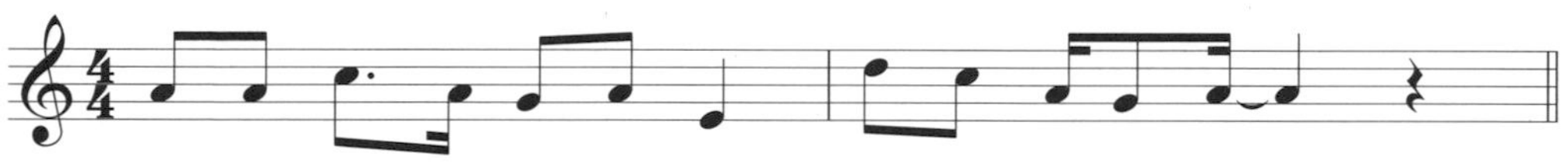

TRACK 399

B) 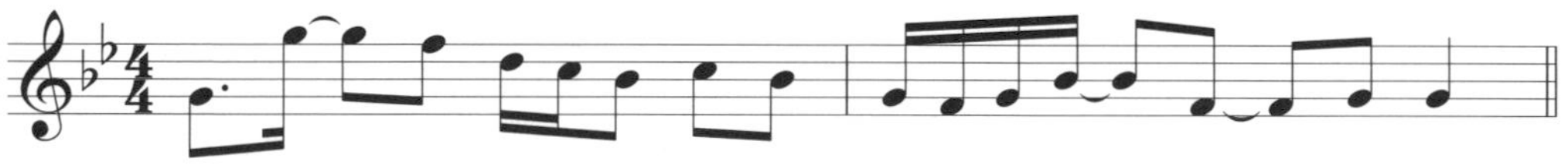

TRACK 400

C) 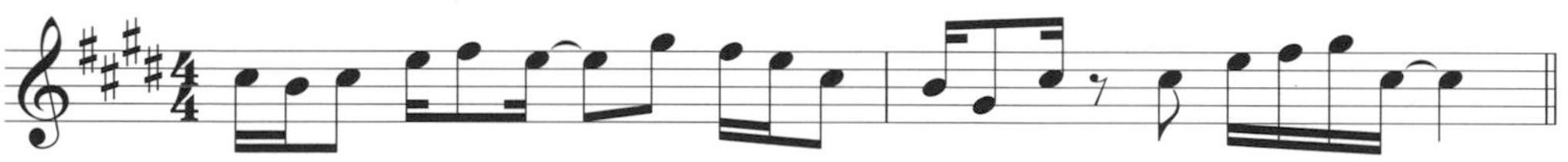

TRACK 401

D) 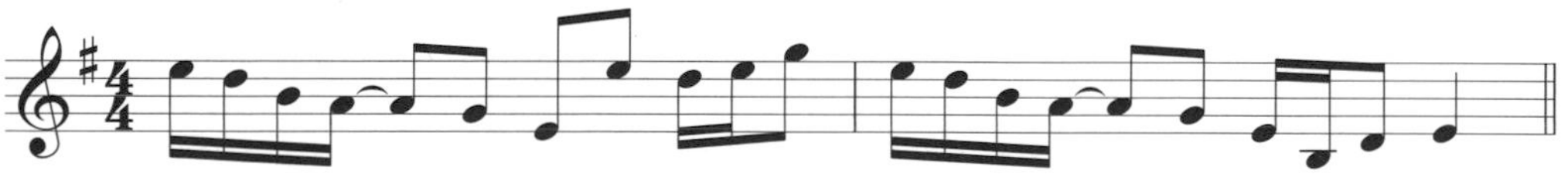

TRACK 402

E) 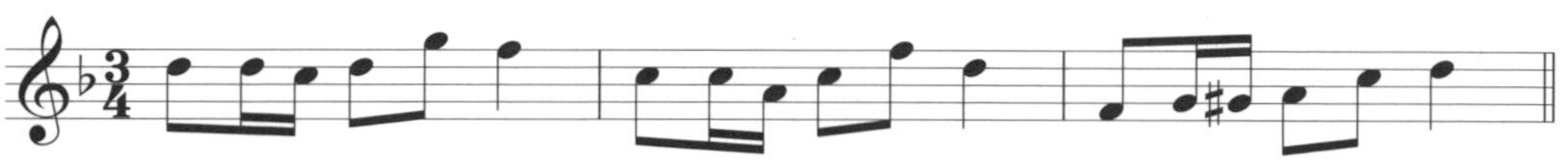

TRACK 403

F) 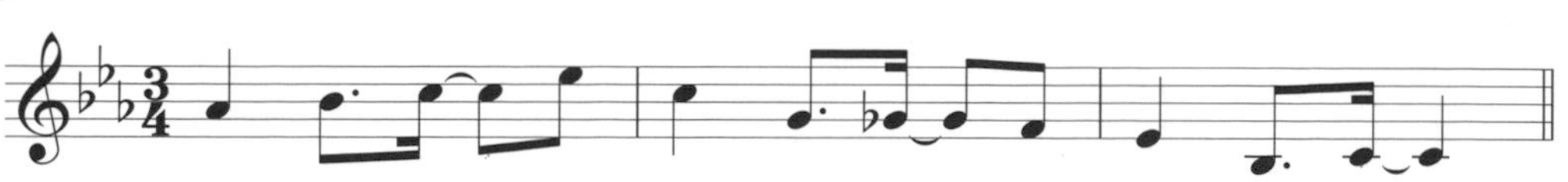

MELODIC DICTATION EXERCISES

In these exercises, listen to the instructor play a melody twice, then write it down by ear. Various keys are covered, so tonicizing chords are played before each example. (**Instructors:** See Appendix for notation of these exercises. Alternatively, these can be found on the accompanying audio.)

Major Pentatonic

TRACK 404

C Major

A) 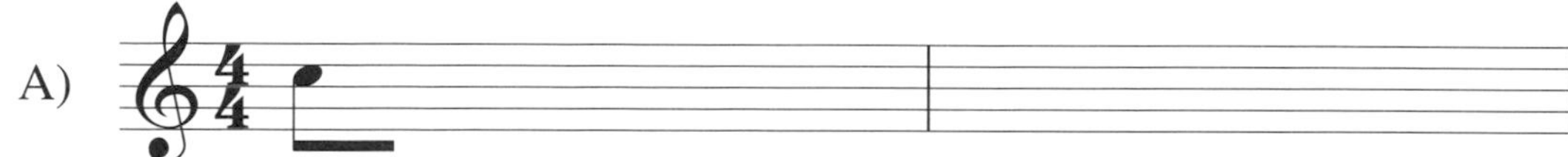

TRACK 405

A Major

B) 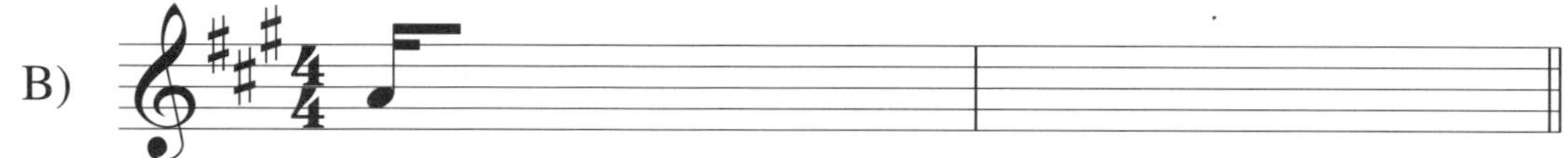

TRACK 406

G Major

C) 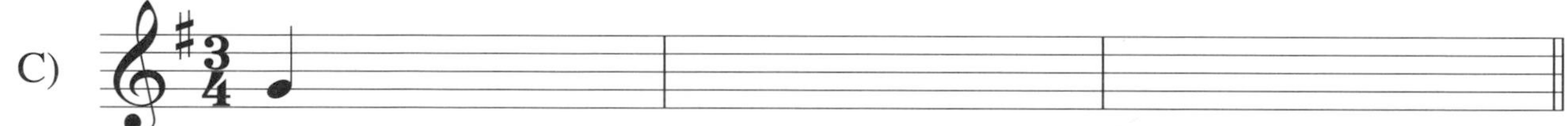

TRACK 407

F Major

D) 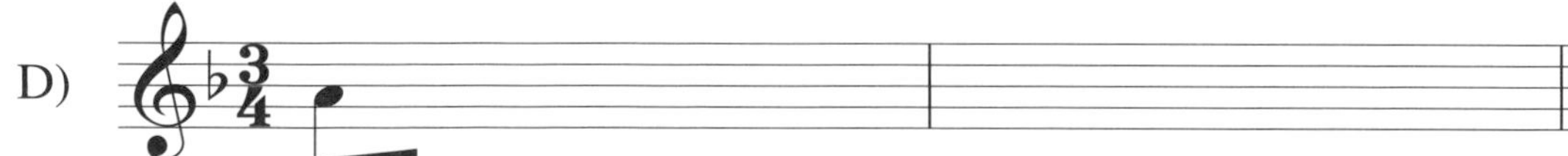

Minor Pentatonic and Blues Scale

TRACK 408

A minor

A) 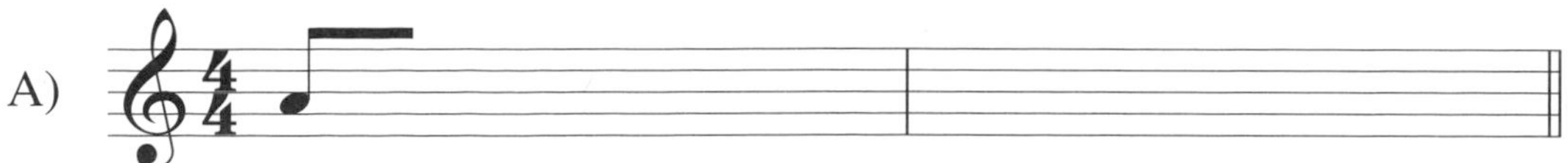

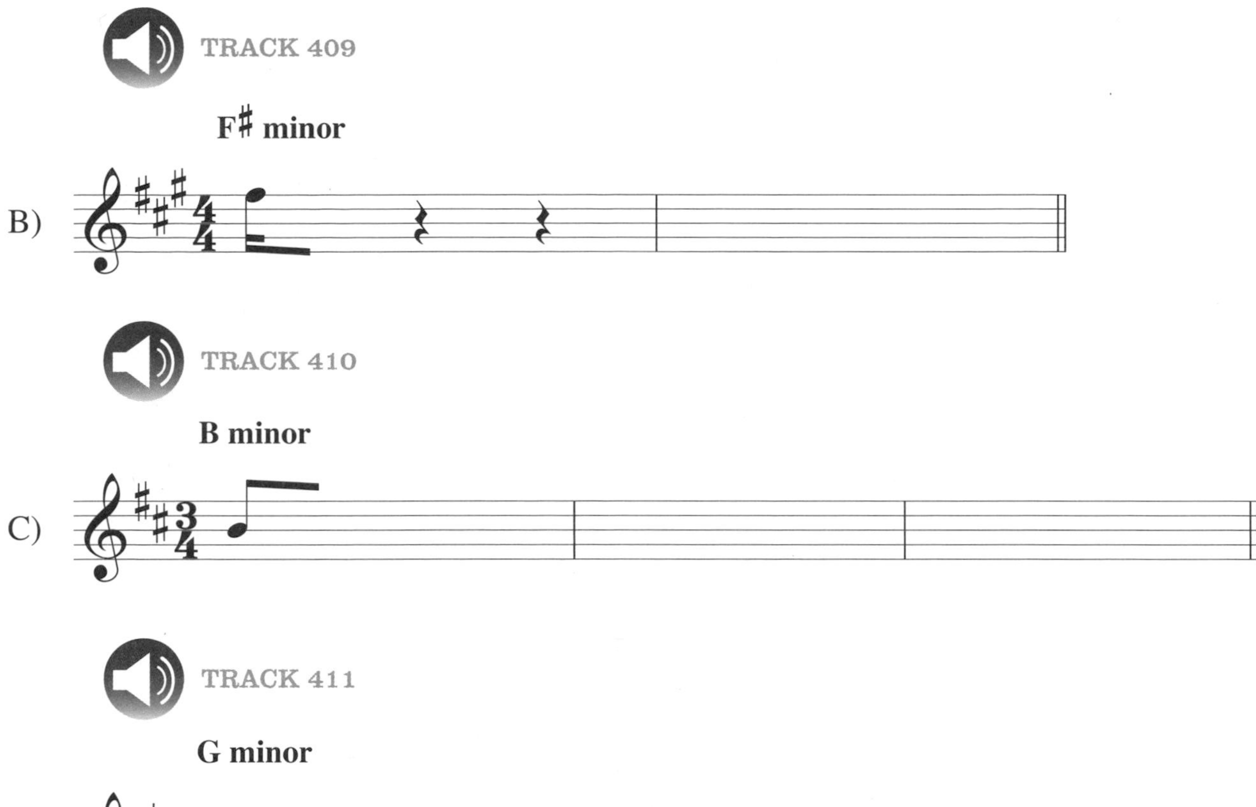

ECHO DRILLS

For these drills, listen to the phrase and then echo it back. (**Instructors:** See Appendix for notation of these exercises. Alternatively, these can be found on the accompanying audio.)

Rhythm Echoes

Listen to each bar of rhythm and echo it back by clapping in the breaks.

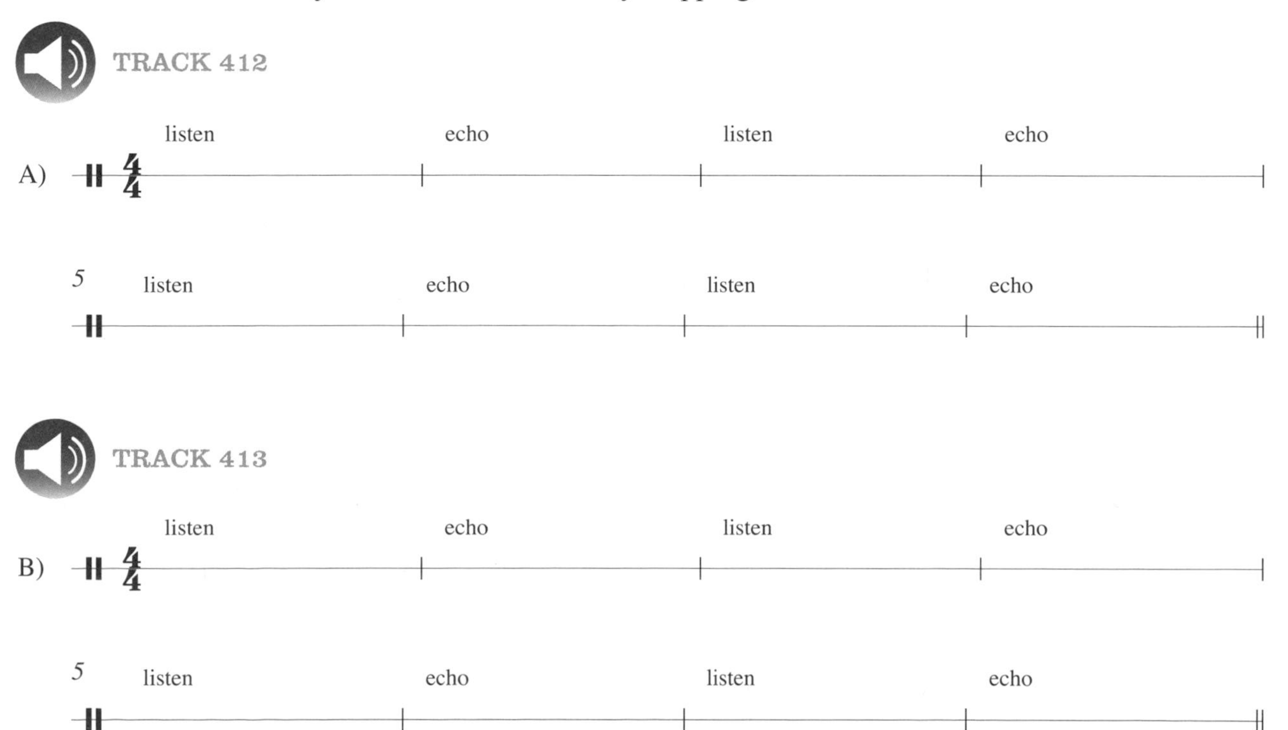

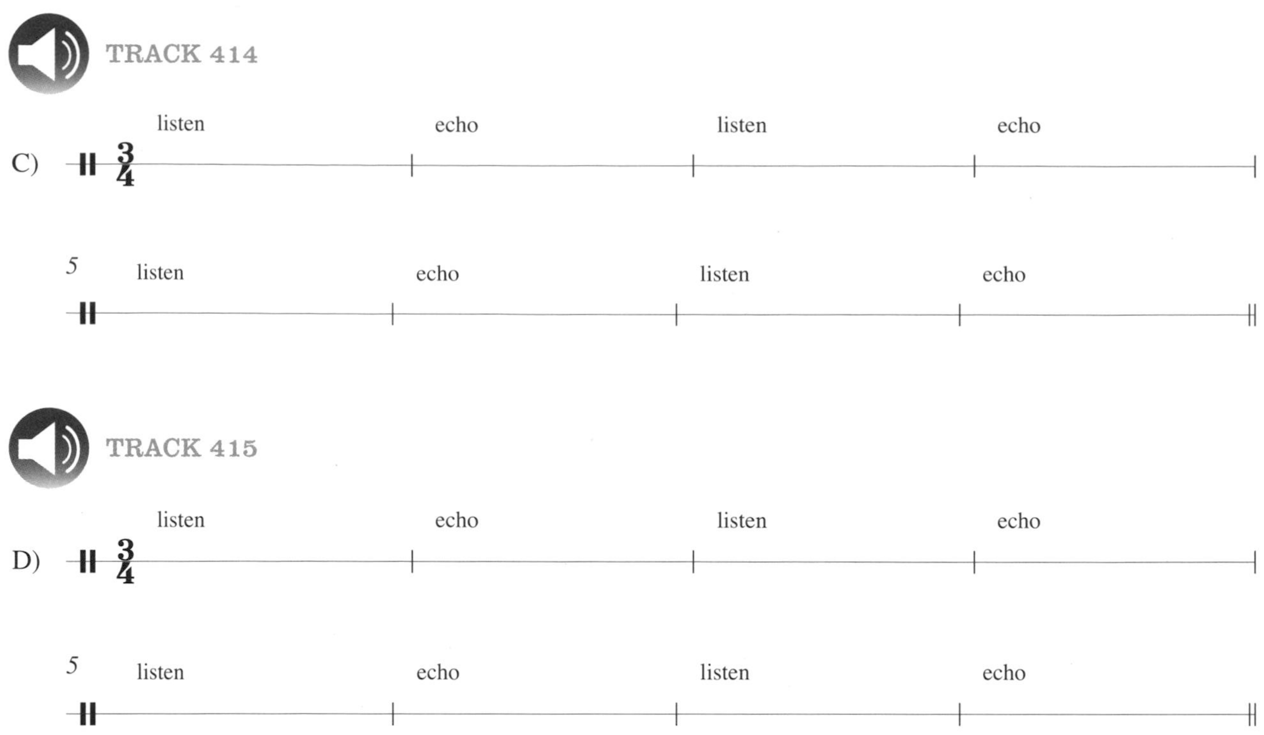

Melodic Echoes

In these four examples, you'll hear a one-bar melody in 4/4 followed by one bar of silence. Sing the melody back during the break. Various keys are covered, so tonicizing chords are played before each example.

TRACK 416

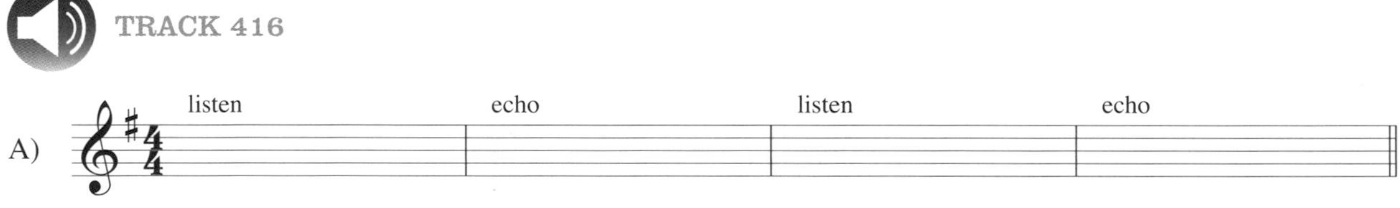

TRACK 417

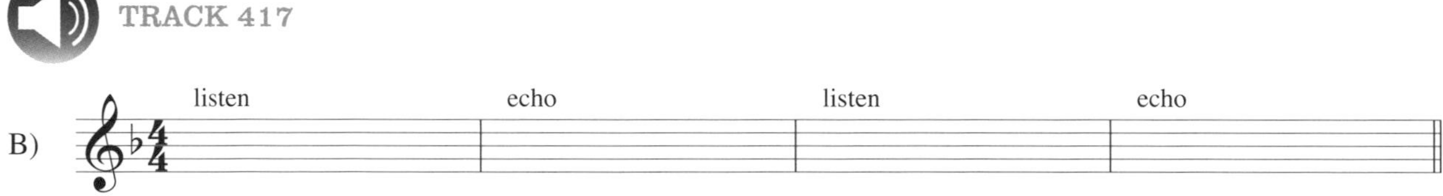

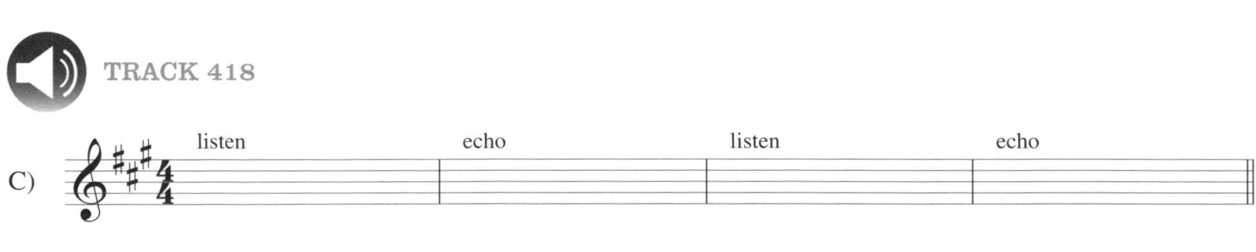

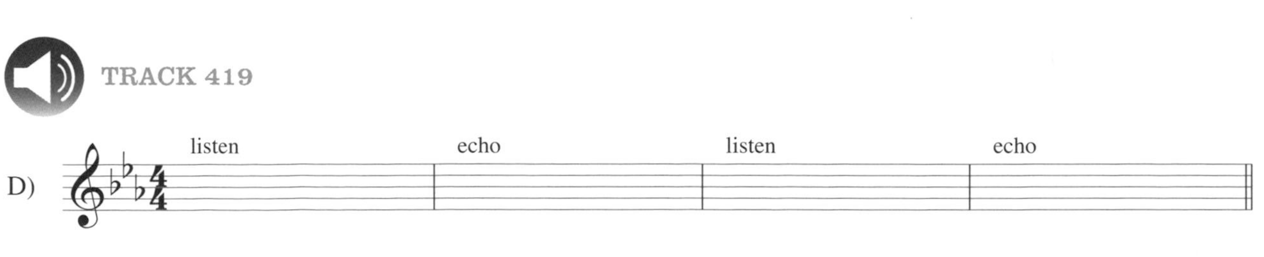

CHAPTER 14

THE MIXOLYDIAN MODE

The modes date back over a millennium. The short story is that different scales are created by treating the seven notes in a major scale as the tonic. For example, in a C major scale (C–D–E–F–G–A–B), C is the tonic by default. But seven *modes* of the C major scale can be created by treating the other notes as the tonic as well.

MODES: THE RELATIVE PICTURE

If we play the notes of the C major scale, but treat the 2nd, D, as the new tonic, the result is D–E–F–G–A–B–C. The intervallic formula (W-H-W, etc.) and/or numeric (1-2-♭3, etc.) formulas created here are different than the major or minor scales we've encountered thus far. Each of these seven modes of the major scale has its own name. Using the C major scale as our base, here are the modes we can generate from it:

Mode #	Mode Name
1	C Ionian: C–D–E–F–G–A–B (the same as the C major scale)
2	D Dorian: D–E–F–G–A–B–C
3	E Phrygian: E–F–G–A–B–C–D
4	F Lydian: F–G–A–B–C–D–E
5	G Mixolydian: G–A–B–C–D–E–F
6	A Aeolian: A–B–C–D–E–F–G (the same as the A minor scale)
7	B Locrian: B–C–D–E–F–G–A

This may seem like a lot to take in, but it's important to realize that it's only an extension of the relative key concept. In fact, A Aeolian is the relative minor of C major. Earlier we said the only difference between a C major scale and an A minor scale is that in the former, we're treating C as the tonic, and in the latter, we're treating A as the tonic. The seven modes of the major scale are derived by continuing the process of treating other notes of the scale as the tonic.

MODES: THE PARALLEL PICTURE

We can also treat the modes as scales on their own, with their own intervallic/numeric formula. To do this, think of the major scale as the standard and treat all others as variations of it. Being the standard, its numeric formula is simply 1–2–3–4–5–6–7. To create any other scale, we raise (sharp) or lower (flat) any of the degrees.

Using the key of C again, the C major scale is 1–2–3–4–5–6–7, which is C–D–E–F–G–A–B. To create a C minor scale (or C Aeolian mode), we lower the 3rd, 6th, and 7th degrees by a half step to get C–D–E♭–F–G–A♭–B♭. The numeric formula for the Aeolian mode (or minor scale), then, is 1–2–♭3–4–5–♭6–♭7. Its intervallic formula is W–H–W–W–H–W–W. Look back to Chapter 2; you'll see that this formula matches the one arrived at for the minor scale. Again, this is not the relative relationship; this is a parallel relationship, so the tonic stays the same (C, in this case), but the notes change.

If we go through all the modes and define their numeric formula, as compared to the major scale, here's the result:

- **Ionian** (major scale)**:** 1–2–3–4–5–6–7
- **Dorian:** 1–2–♭3–4–5–6–♭7
- **Phrygian:** 1–♭2–♭3–4–5–♭6–♭7
- **Lydian:** 1–2–3–♯4–5–6–7
- **Mixolydian:** 1–2–3–4–5–6–♭7
- **Aeolian** (minor scale)**:** 1–2–♭3–4–5–♭6–♭7
- **Locrian:** 1–♭2–♭3–4–♭5–♭6–♭7

THE MIXOLYDIAN FORMULA

Look at the Mixolydian formula given above. The only difference between it and a major scale is the lowered 7th degree. So if C Ionian is spelled C–D–E–F–G–A–B, then C Mixolydian is spelled C–D–E–F–G–A–B♭.

TRACK 420

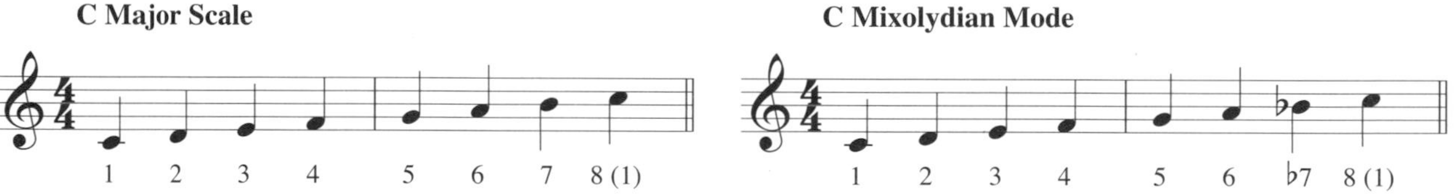

We can do this with any key. Lower the 7th degree of a major scale and its *parallel* Mixolydian mode results. (Again, this is not the same relationship as the relative one outlined above and seen in the relative majors and minors.) Here's the same thing in the key of G.

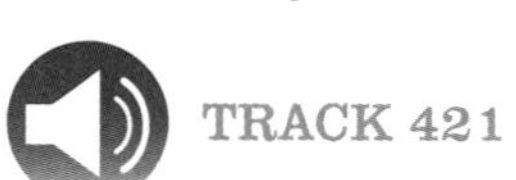
TRACK 421

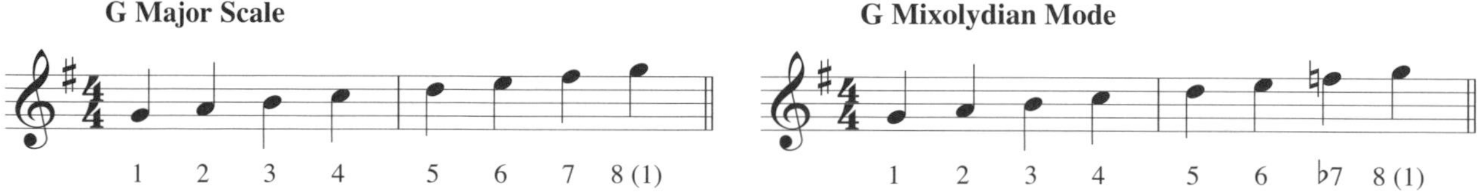

RHYTHM STUDY

Now let's apply 16th notes to compound meters to learn how they sound. There's no standard, agreed-upon way to count 16th notes in compound meter, as there is with 4/4 ("1 e + a"). If the tempo is slow enough, you may be able to count every eighth note by number and include "and" in between, such as this:

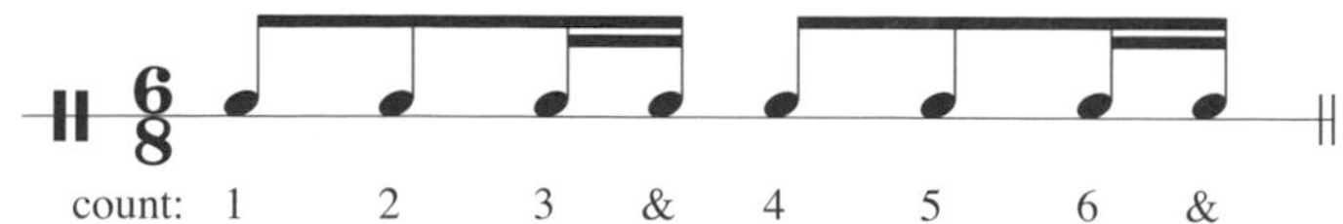

Even at a moderate tempo, that can be quite a mouthful. Often, we end up counting with dotted-eighth-note beats (two in 6/8 and four in 12/8) and make up syllables for the remaining notes—syllables that flow easily off the tongue. Here are two such possibilities:

Rhythmic Drills

Clap the following rhythms together as a class or in smaller groups.

Rhythmic Dictation

Listen to the following rhythms and write them down. Each example will be played twice.

What About Key Signatures?

You may wonder which key signature should be used when dealing with music created from a specific mode. For example, if the piece of music is to be set in C Mixolydian—spelled C–D–E–F–G–A–B♭—should there be no key signature (C major) or one flat (F major)? There's no established consensus on this; you'll see examples of both, depending on where you look.

You might find it easiest to use the key signature for the major scale and then add the accidentals on every 7th tone. The two examples that follow, for instance, use a C major key signature. This allows us to easily recognize the tonic of the song, an important piece of information.

SIGHT-SINGING EXERCISES

Let's work on singing melodies that use the Mixolydian mode. We'll cover several different keys and time signatures.

C Mixolydian (C–D–E–F–G–A–B♭)

TRACK 426

A) 

B) 

F Mixolydian (F–G–A–B♭–C–D–E♭)

TRACK 428

A) 

B) 

MELODIC DICTATION EXERCISES

In these exercises, listen to the instructor play a melody twice, then write it down by ear. Various keys are covered, so tonicizing chords are played before each example. Notice the 9/8 time signature in Examples E and F. This is another compound meter. Whereas 6/8 has two (dotted-eighth) pulses per measure, and 12/8 has four, 9/8 has three pulses per measure. (**Instructors:** See Appendix for notation of these exercises. Alternatively, these can be found on the accompanying audio.)

C Mixolydian

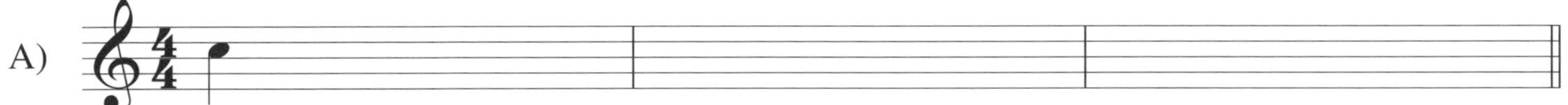

B♭ Mixolydian

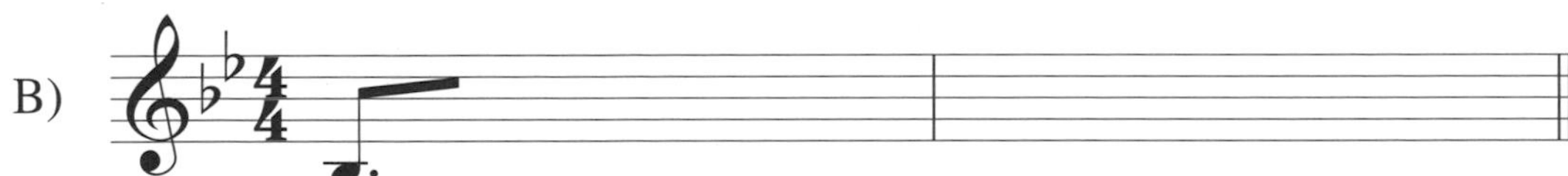

A Mixolydian

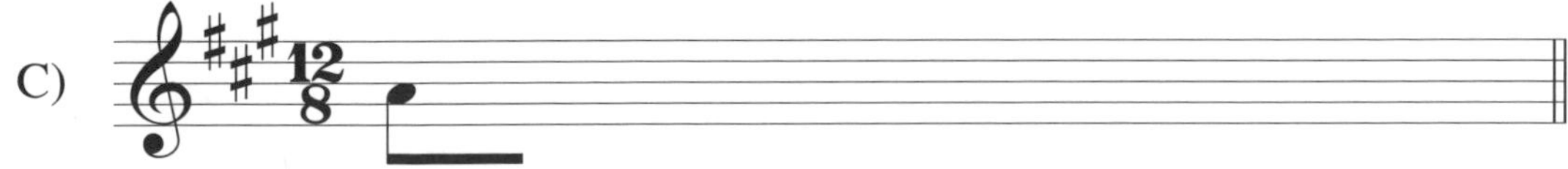

F Mixolydian

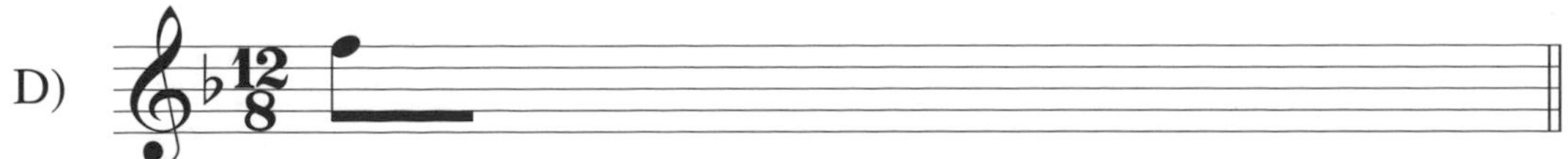

D Mixolydian

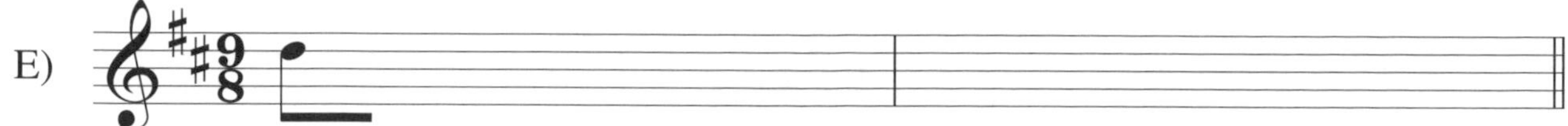

E♭ Mixolydian

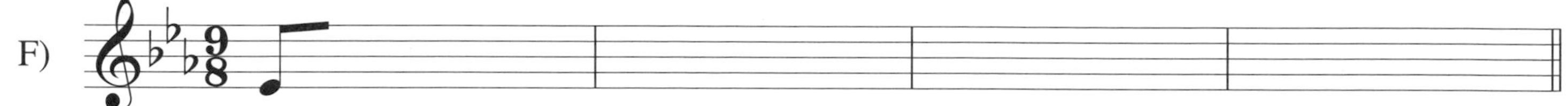

ECHO DRILLS

For these drills, listen to the phrase and then echo it back. (**Instructors:** See Appendix for notation of these exercises. Alternatively, these can be found on the accompanying audio.)

Rhythm Echoes

In these four exercises, listen to each bar of rhythm and echo it back by clapping in the breaks.

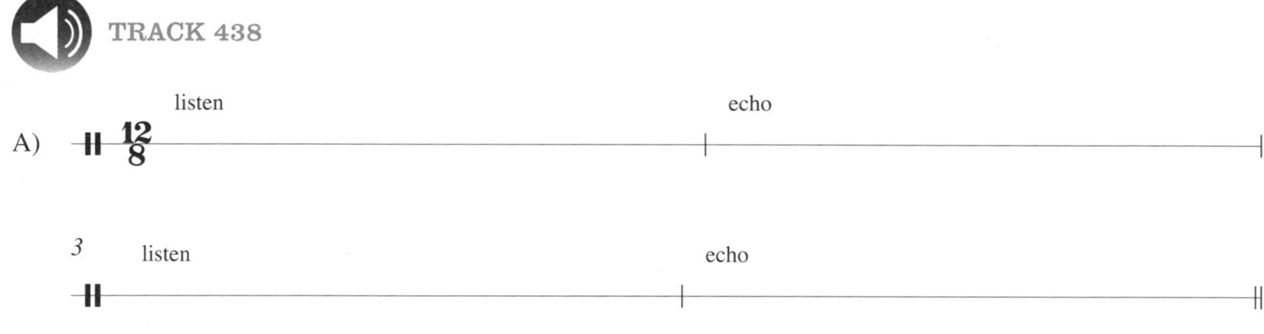

echo

B)

3 listen echo

TRACK 441

D) listen echo

3 listen echo

Melodic Echoes

In these four exercises, you'll hear a one-bar melody in 12/8 followed by one bar of silence. Sing the melody back during the break. Various keys are covered, so tonicizing chords are played before each example.

TRACK 442

A)

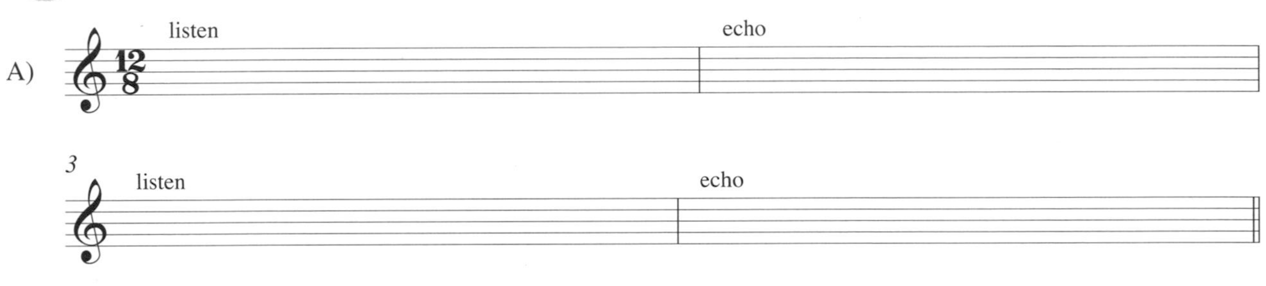

TRACK 443

B)

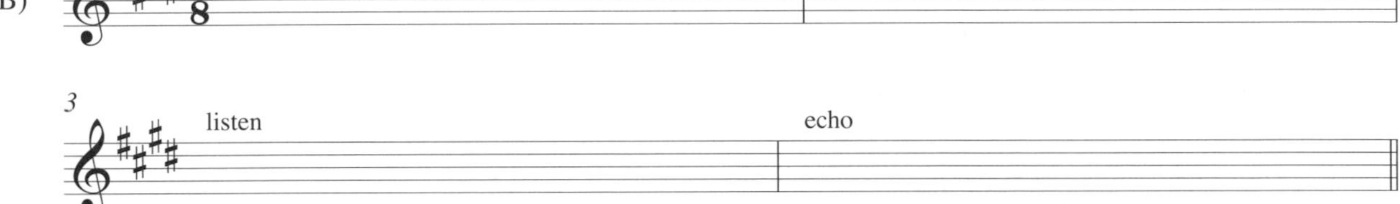

TRACK 444

C)

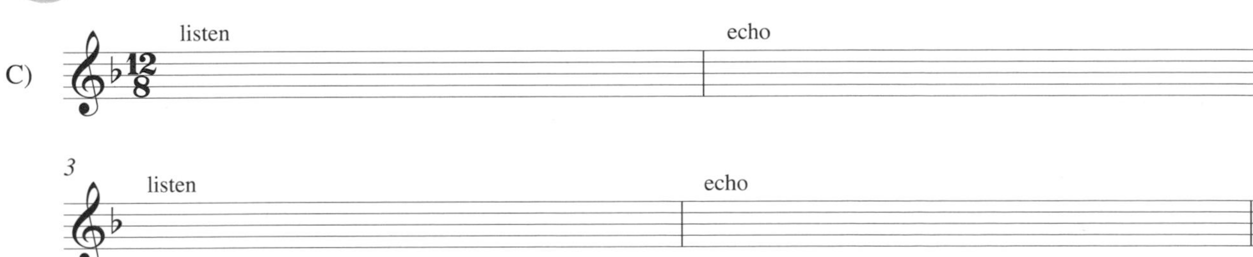

TRACK 445

D)

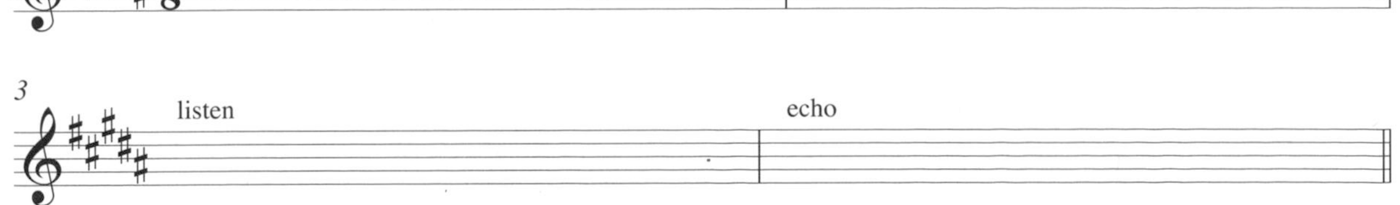

CHAPTER 15
THE DORIAN MODE

In Chapter 14, we learned about the modes and how each can be considered a scale on its own, with a unique intervallic/numeric formula. In this chapter, we focus on the Dorian mode.

THE DORIAN FORMULA

As we saw earlier, the numeric formula for the Dorian mode is 1–2–♭3–4–5–6–♭7. Since it has a minor 3rd degree (as opposed to Ionian or Mixolydian, for example, which have a major 3rd), we call this a minor mode. Comparing C Dorian to a C minor scale (C Aeolian), we note that the only difference is a raised 6th degree in the Dorian scale.

Again, we can easily transpose this idea to another key. Let's take the key of F♯ minor, which has a key signature of three sharps. The F♯ minor scale is spelled F♯–G♯–A–B–C♯–D–E. To make this an F♯ Dorian mode, we need only raise the 6th degree a half step to get F♯ Dorian: F♯–G♯–A–B–C♯–D♯–E.

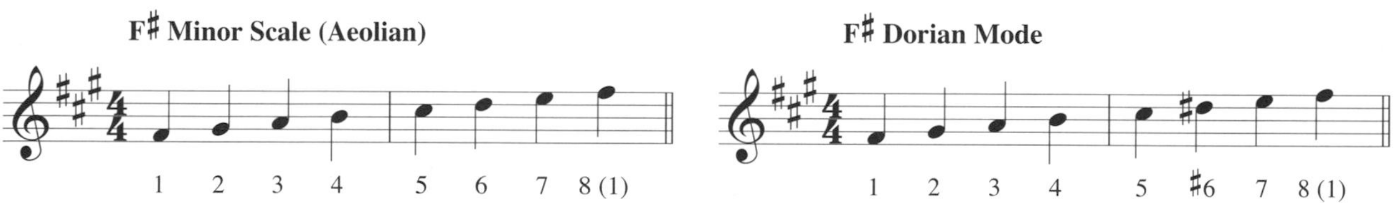

MODAL CHORD PROGRESSIONS

A modal chord progression is one in which the chords are derived from a mode rather than the standard major or minor scale. For example, a telltale sign that a song contains a Dorian mode progression is a minor i chord with a major IV chord. As you know, the chord built from the 4th degree of a minor scale is normally minor, but in the Dorian mode, the 6th scale degree is raised a half step. This 6th scale degree is the 3rd of the chord built from the 4th degree. In A minor, for example, the iv chord is normally Dm. But when you raise the 6th degree of the scale, F, to F♯, you're raising the Dm chord's minor 3rd (F) to a major 3rd (F♯).

Compare the sound of these two progressions. First, here's a standard A minor chord progression: i–iv, or Am–Dm.

TRACK 448

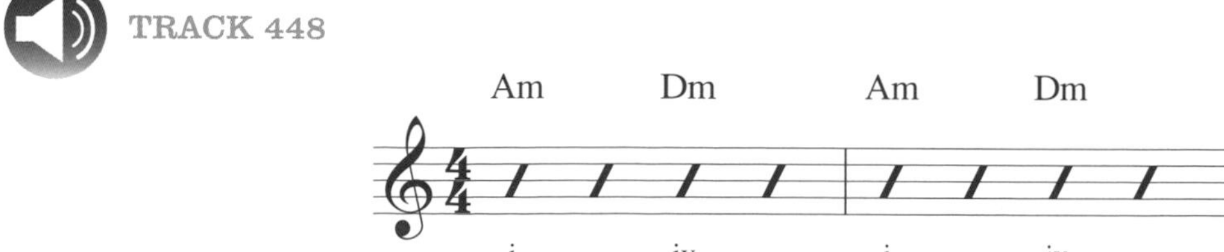

Now, here is a modal progression in A Dorian: i–IV, or Am D.

We looked at the Mixolydian mode in the previous chapter. A distinguishing feature of a Mixolydian progression is a ♭VII chord. Instead of the diminished chord built from the 7th degree in a major scale, when the 7th degree in a Mixolydian mode is lowered, a major triad built from the ♭7th degree results. In the key of C major, this is a B♭ chord.

Listen to this typical C major progression using a V chord (G), which contains the natural 7th degree (B) as its major 3rd.

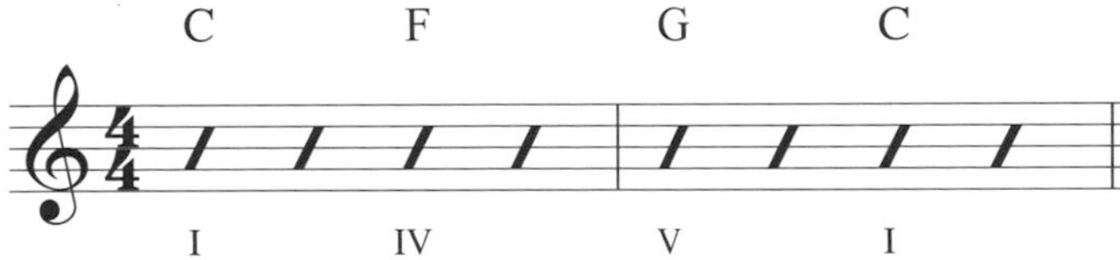

The following C Mixolydian progression substitutes a ♭VII chord (B♭) for the V chord. Compare it with the sound of Track 450.

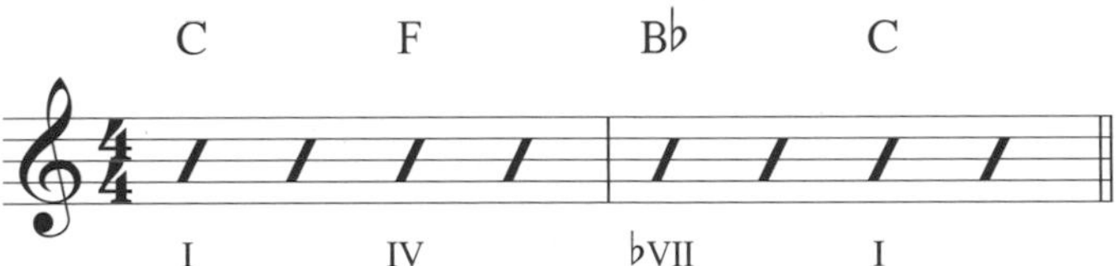

Lowering the 7th by half step is essentially lowering the major 3rd of the V chord to a minor 3rd. Consequently, another strong indicator of a Mixolydian progression is a major I chord with a minor v chord. In the key of C major, this is a Gm chord. We discussed the ♭VII chord because it's more popular than the minor v chord, although it is used as well.

What does all this mean? It's a useful red flag when you're sight-reading a melody. If you see one of these chords—a major IV chord in a minor key, or a ♭VII (or minor v) chord in a major key—it's a safe bet that the melody over those chords is derived from the Dorian or Mixolydian mode, respectively.

RHYTHM STUDY

Let's get a little more sophisticated with our 16th notes in compound meters. While these rhythms will be the most difficult to read thus far, many songs feature rhythms like these all over the place.

Rhythmic Drills

Clap the following rhythms together as a class or in smaller groups.

A) 

B)

C)

D)

Rhythmic Dictation

Listen to the following rhythms and write them down. Each example will be played twice.

TRACK 452

A)

TRACK 453

B)

TRACK 454

C)

TRACK 455

D)

SIGHT-SINGING EXERCISES

And now let's sing some melodies using the Dorian mode. We'll cover several different keys and time signatures.

A Dorian (A–B–C–D–E–F♯–G)

G Dorian (G–A–B♭–C–D–E–F)

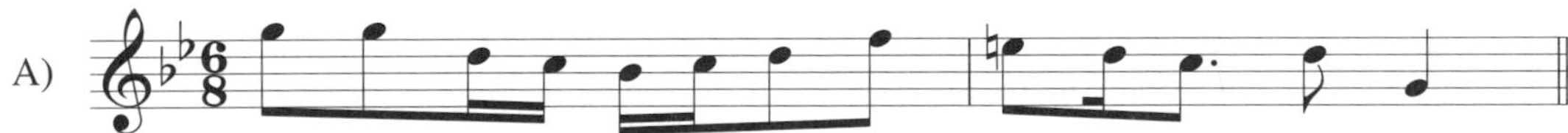

E Dorian (E–F♯–G–A–B–C♯–D)

MELODIC DICTATION EXERCISES

In these exercises, listen to the instructor play a melody twice, then write it down by ear. Various keys are covered, so tonicizing chords are played before each example. (**Instructors:** See Appendix for notation of these exercises. Alternatively, these can be found on the accompanying audio.)

A Dorian

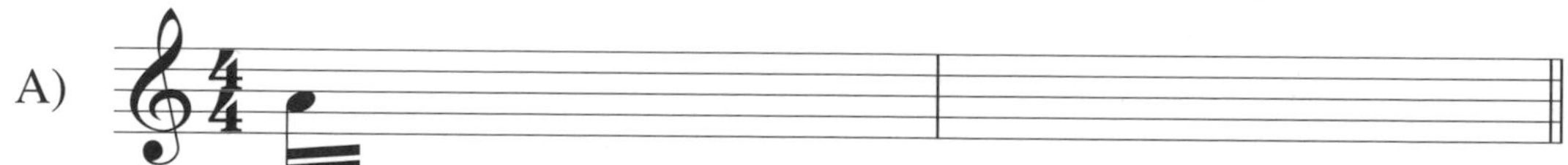

F Dorian

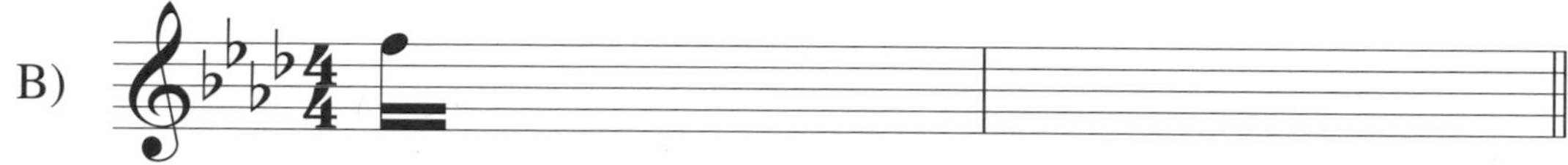

C Dorian

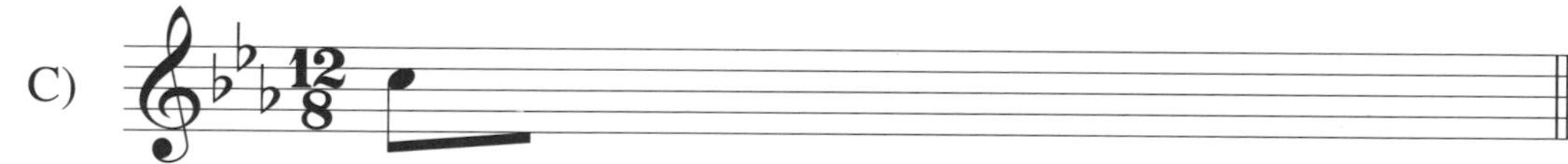

E Dorian

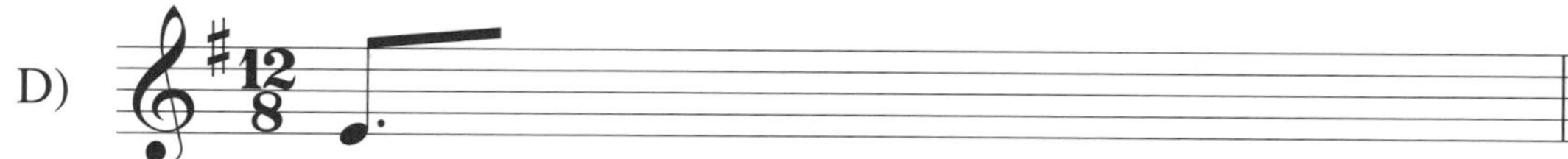

G Dorian

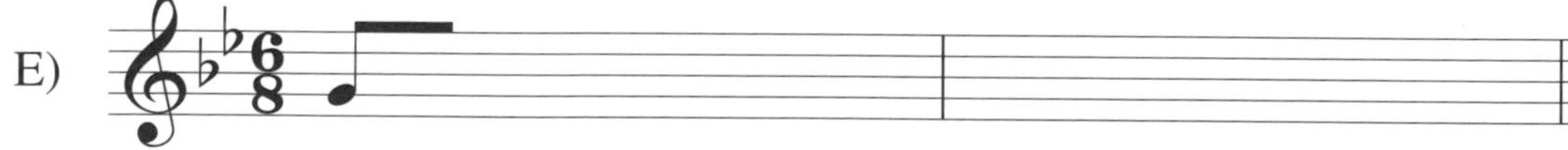

B Dorian

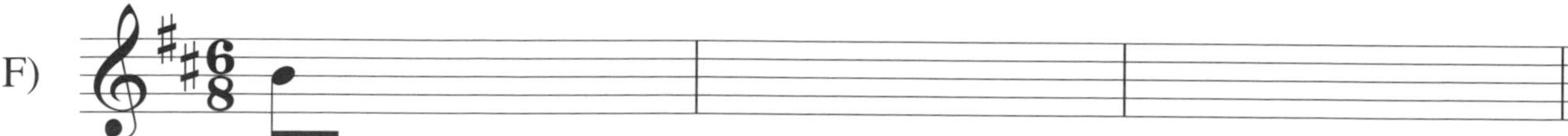

ECHO DRILLS

For these drills, listen to the phrase and then echo it back. (**Instructors:** See Appendix for notation of these exercises. Alternatively, these can be found on the accompanying audio.)

Rhythm Echoes

In these four exercises, listen to each bar of rhythm and echo it back by clapping in the breaks.

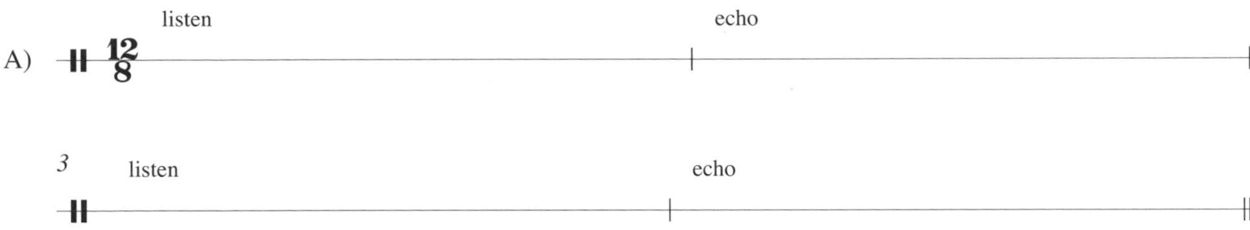

TRACK 469

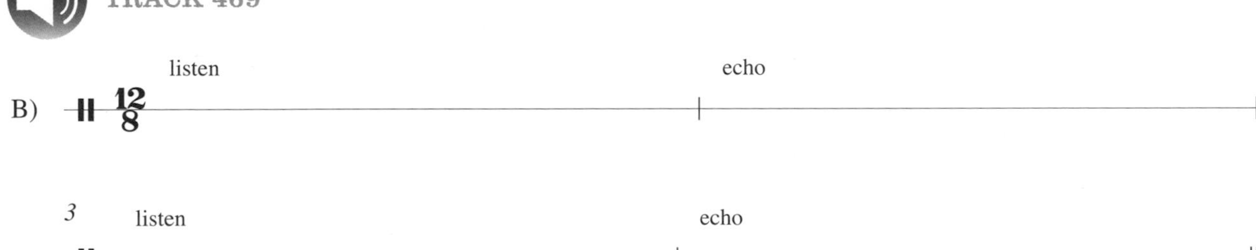

TRACK 470

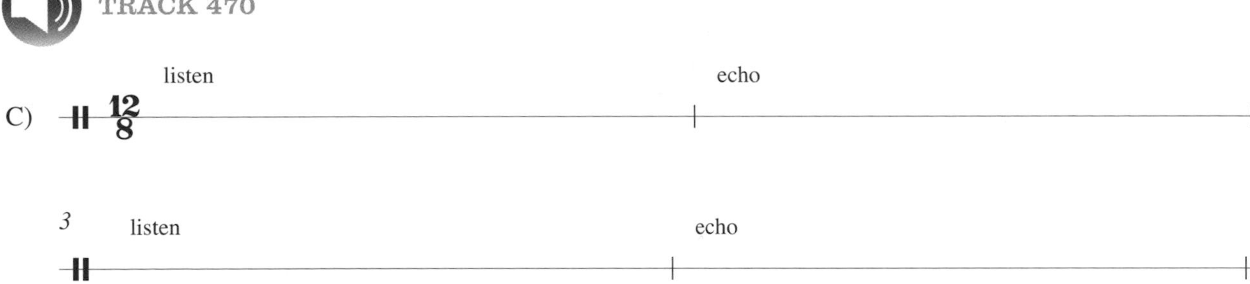

TRACK 471

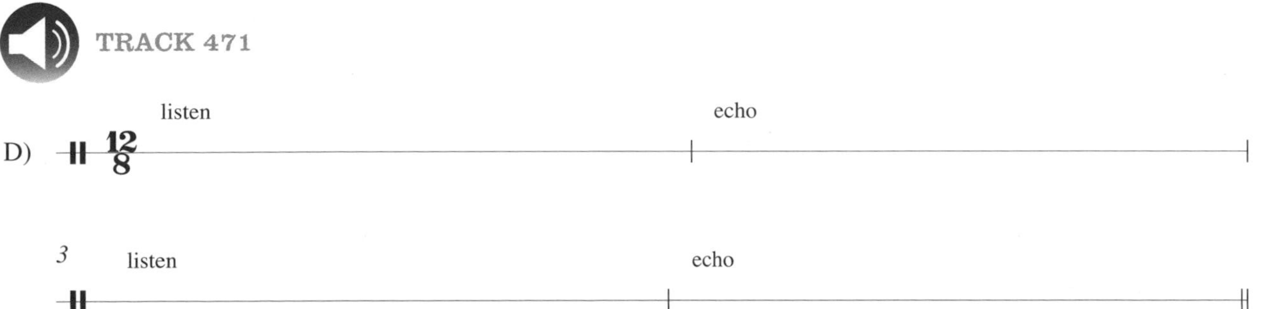

Melodic Echoes

In these four exercises, you'll hear a one-bar melody in 12/8 followed by one bar of silence. Sing the melody back during the break. Various keys are covered, so tonicizing chords are played before each example.

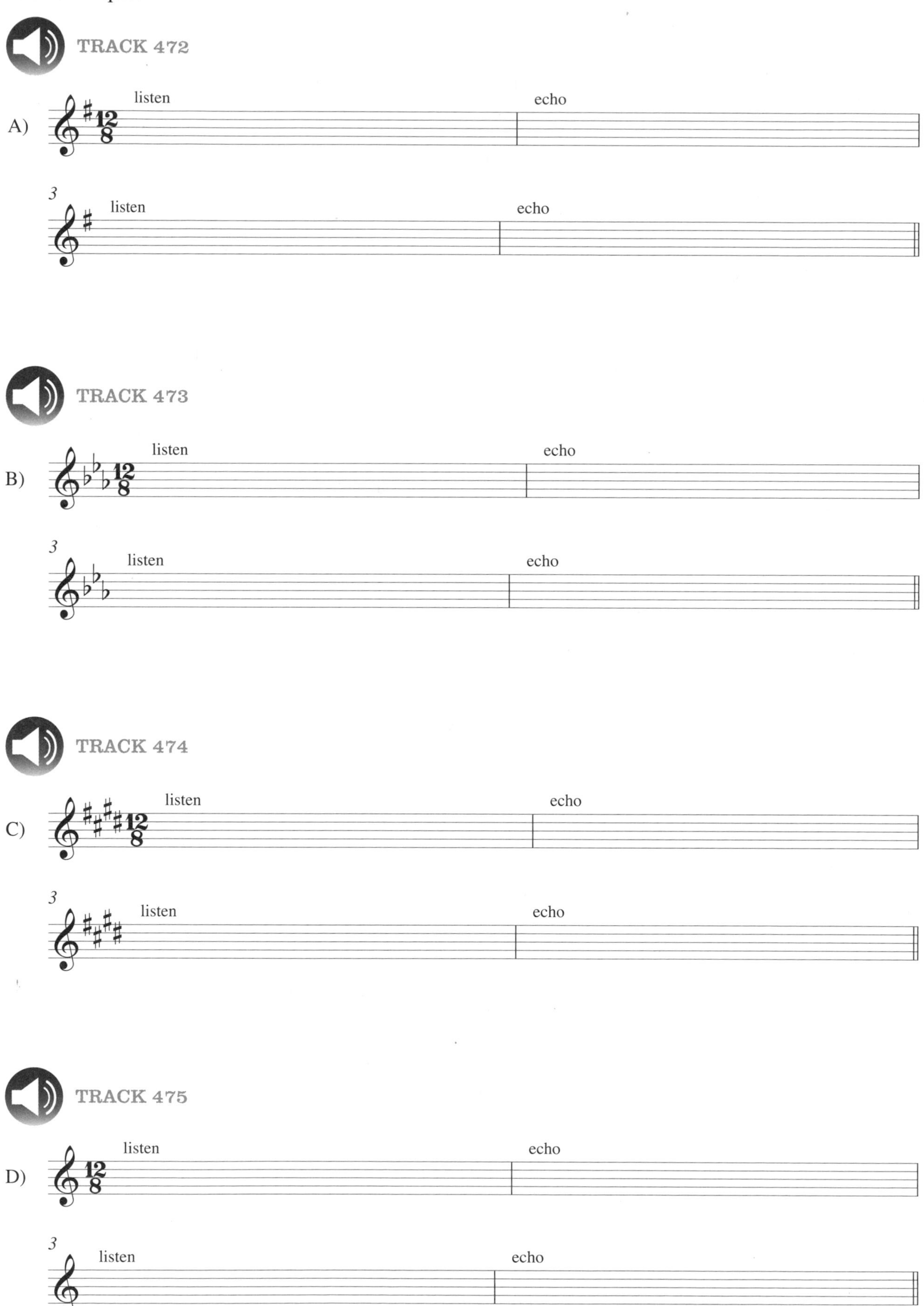

CHAPTER 16
HARMONIC AND MELODIC MINOR SCALES

In addition to the standard minor scale (also called the "natural minor" scale) we learned early on, or even the Dorian mode, there are other minor scales in use. The two we'll look at here are the *harmonic minor* and the *melodic minor*.

THE HARMONIC MINOR SCALE

The harmonic minor scale is similar to the minor scale, but has a raised (or major) 7th degree. (See Chapter 2 for a refresher on the minor scale.) In the key of A minor, then, it is spelled A–B–C–D–E–F–G♯. Listen to the difference between the A natural minor scale and the A harmonic minor scale.

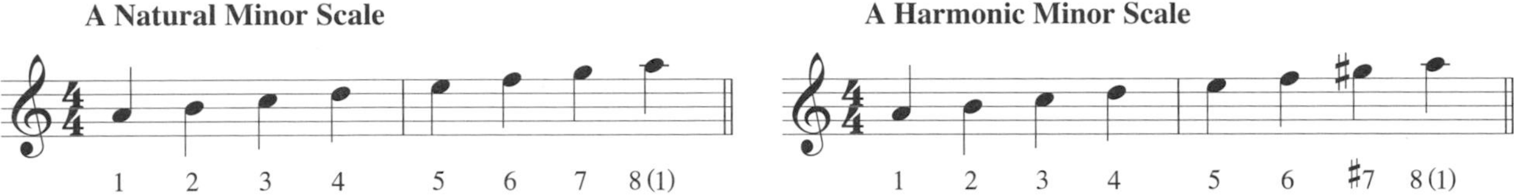

It's a striking sound you've heard before many times. Although it is sometimes heard in pop music, it's not terribly common.

A Closer Look

Why does this scale exist? In Chapter 10 (page 82), we learned that the 7th degree in a major scale is called the leading tone. This is because, being a half step away from the tonic, it *leads* the ear there. If we play the notes of a C major scale from C up to B and stop there, it sounds unresolved. This is one reason the V chord leads so perfectly to the I chord: it contains that leading tone as its major 3rd. In the key of C, this is a G chord, spelled G–**B**–D.

In minor keys, however, there is no leading tone relationship by default. A minor scale has a ♭7th degree in it, so there's a whole step between the ♭7th and tonic. This makes a big difference in terms of harmonic pull. In a minor key, the v chord is normally a minor chord because of this; the ♭7th degree of the scale is the minor 3rd of the v chord. In the key of A minor, for example, the v chord is Em, spelled E–**G**–B. This G note is the ♭7th scale degree (A–B–C–D–E–F–**G**). The result: a I–V–I chord progression sounds powerful in a major key, while a i–v–i progression in a minor key sounds comparatively weak.

The solution? Make the v chord in a minor key a major V chord! This practice began centuries ago and is still used in many styles of music today. To make the Em chord (the v chord in A minor) into an E major chord, we raise G to G♯. And if we change the G note in an A minor scale to G♯, we have—you guessed it—the A harmonic minor scale.

Listen to the difference between a i–v–i (Am–Em–Am) progression and a i–V–i (Am–E–Am) progression in the key of A minor.

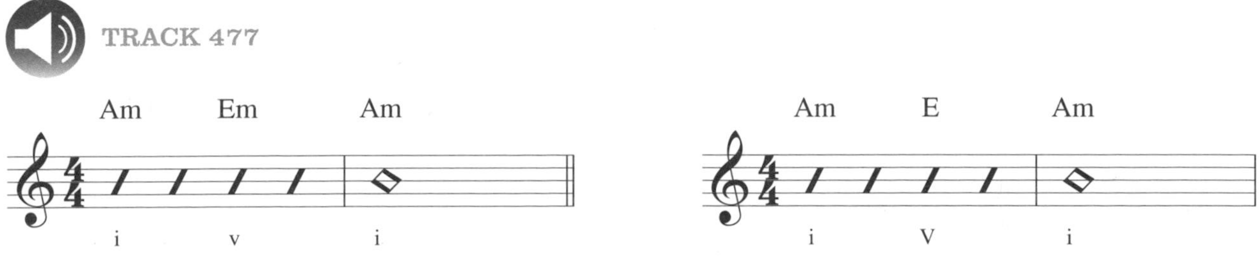

The difference is night and day. And that's where the harmonic minor scale comes from.

THE MELODIC MINOR SCALE

The harmonic minor scale was created, and life seemed good. At last, there was the strong V–i cadence that had been so lacking in minor-key compositions. However, when people tried to sing this new harmonic minor scale, it was a bit awkward, due to the augmented 2nd interval between the ♭6th and 7th scale degrees. In Chapter 9, we briefly discussed augmented 2nds and mentioned that they do occasionally pop up. This is a perfect example.

In the A harmonic minor scale, from F (♭6th) to G♯ (7th) is the distance of three half steps, a minor 3rd. But in this case, it can't be called a minor 3rd. Why not? All together now: "Because only two letter names are involved, F and G."

So, after composers had heard enough complaining from singers, they decided to do something about it. "What if we also raise the 6th degree by a half step?" This became the melodic minor scale. In the key of A minor, this is A–B–C–D–E–F♯–G♯. Let's compare the sound of the A natural minor, harmonic minor, and melodic minor scales to hear the difference.

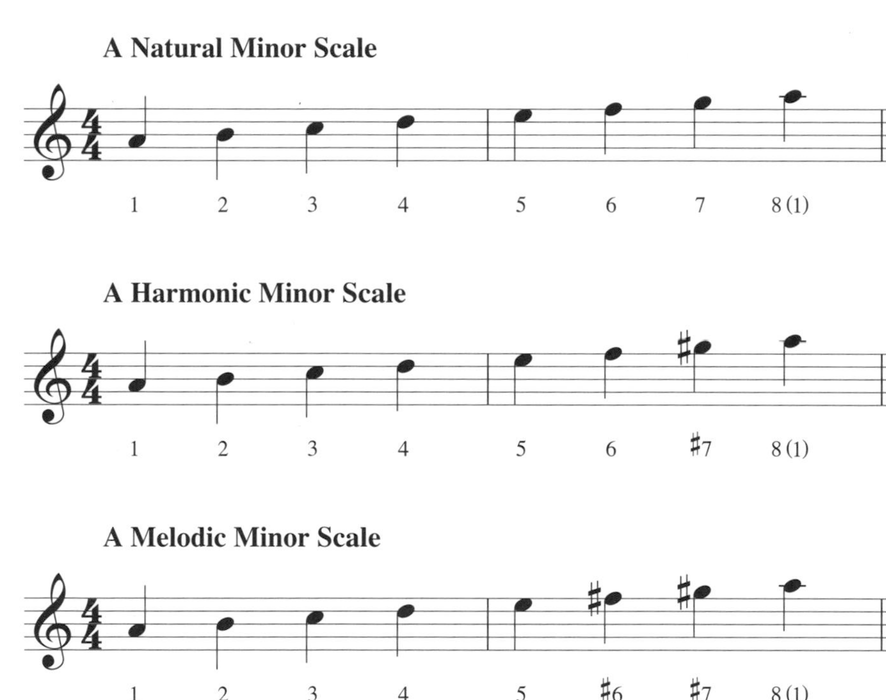

These scales, especially the melodic minor, were altered in this way only during ascending phrases. When descending, they almost always reverted back to the natural minor scale.

Certain jazz music ignores this rule, using the ascending melodic minor form continually, regardless of melodic direction. This is sometimes called the *jazz melodic minor scale*.

A Closer Look

When we raise the 6th degree of a minor scale, we affect the harmony created in the chords of that scale. The most obvious—and most prominently exploited—result is that the minor iv chord becomes a major IV chord. So, rather than this somewhat awkward-to-sing phrase that would be derived from the A harmonic minor scale (notice the augmented 2nd interval)…

… the minor iv chord could be made a major IV chord by raising the F to F♯, thus replacing the awkward augmented 2nd with a major 2nd.

As with the modal progressions of last chapter, these chords are an indication that the melody probably will be derived from these scales. This is not to say that a minor iv chord never occurs in a minor key; there are plenty of them. Often, it depends on the direction of the melodic line. Although the melodic minor scale is more popular in classical music and jazz, we need look no further than one of the best-known songs of all time to hear it used in a pop idiom. In the Beatles' classic "Yesterday," the line "I'm not half the man I used to be" runs straight up the D melodic minor scale from A all the way to F.

RHYTHM STUDY

Our final rhythm study for the book is the most difficult of all, incorporating several different meters and many mixed rhythms.

Rhythmic Drills

Clap the following rhythms together as a class or in smaller groups.

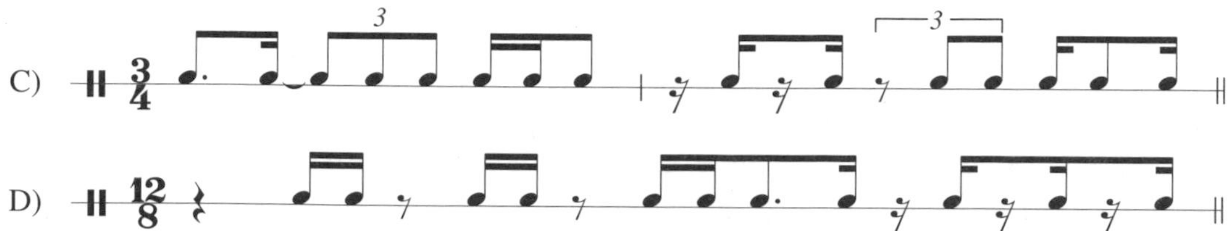

Rhythmic Dictation

Listen to the following rhythms and write them down. Each example will be played twice.

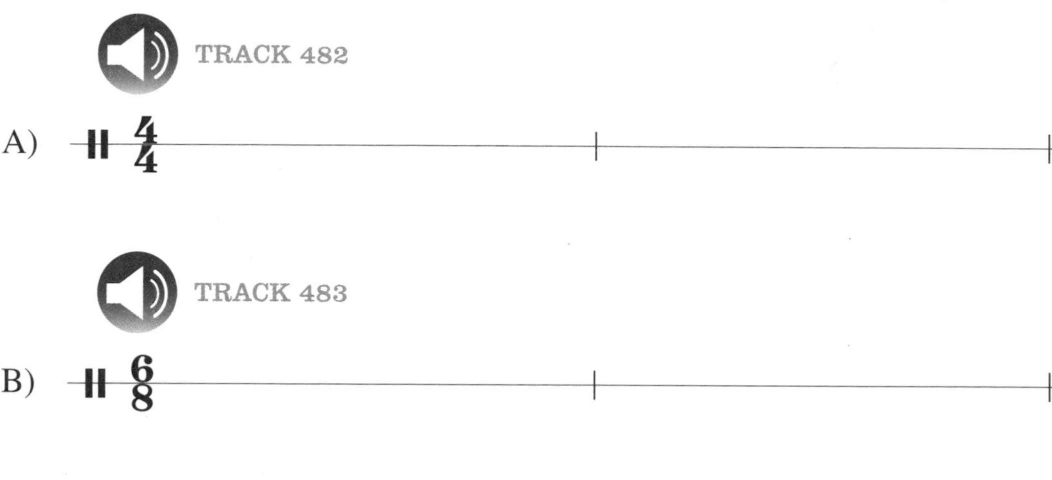

TRACK 484

SIGHT-SINGING EXERCISES

Let's sing some melodies from the harmonic and melodic minor scales. We'll cover several different keys and time signatures. Keep an eye on the accidentals, as the descending phrases often revert back to natural minor.

A Harmonic Minor (A–B–C–D–E–F–G♯)

D Harmonic Minor (D–E–F–G–A–B♭–C♯)
TRACK 488
A)
TRACK 489
B)
B Harmonic Minor (B–C♯–D–E–F♯–G–A♯)
TRACK 490
A)
TRACK 491
B)
A Melodic Minor (A–B–C–D–E–F♯–G♯)
TRACK 492
A)
TRACK 493
B)
C Melodic Minor (C–D–E♭–F–G–A–B)
TRACK 494
A)
TRACK 495
B)

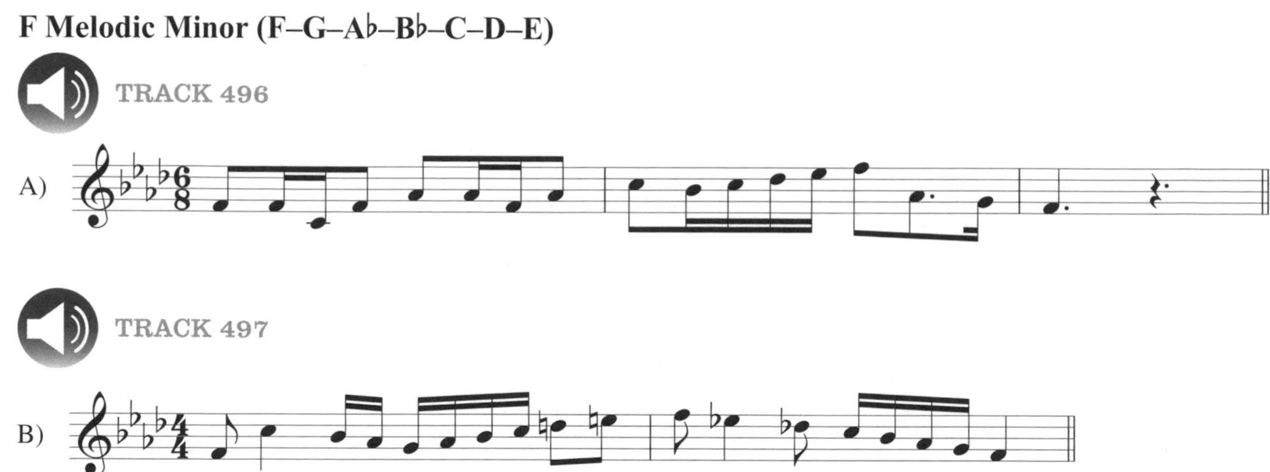

MELODIC DICTATION EXERCISES

In these exercises, listen to the instructor play a melody twice, then write it down by ear. Various keys are covered, so tonicizing chords are played before each example. Remember to use courtesy accidentals. (**Instructors:** See Appendix for notation of these exercises. Alternatively, these can be found on the accompanying audio.)

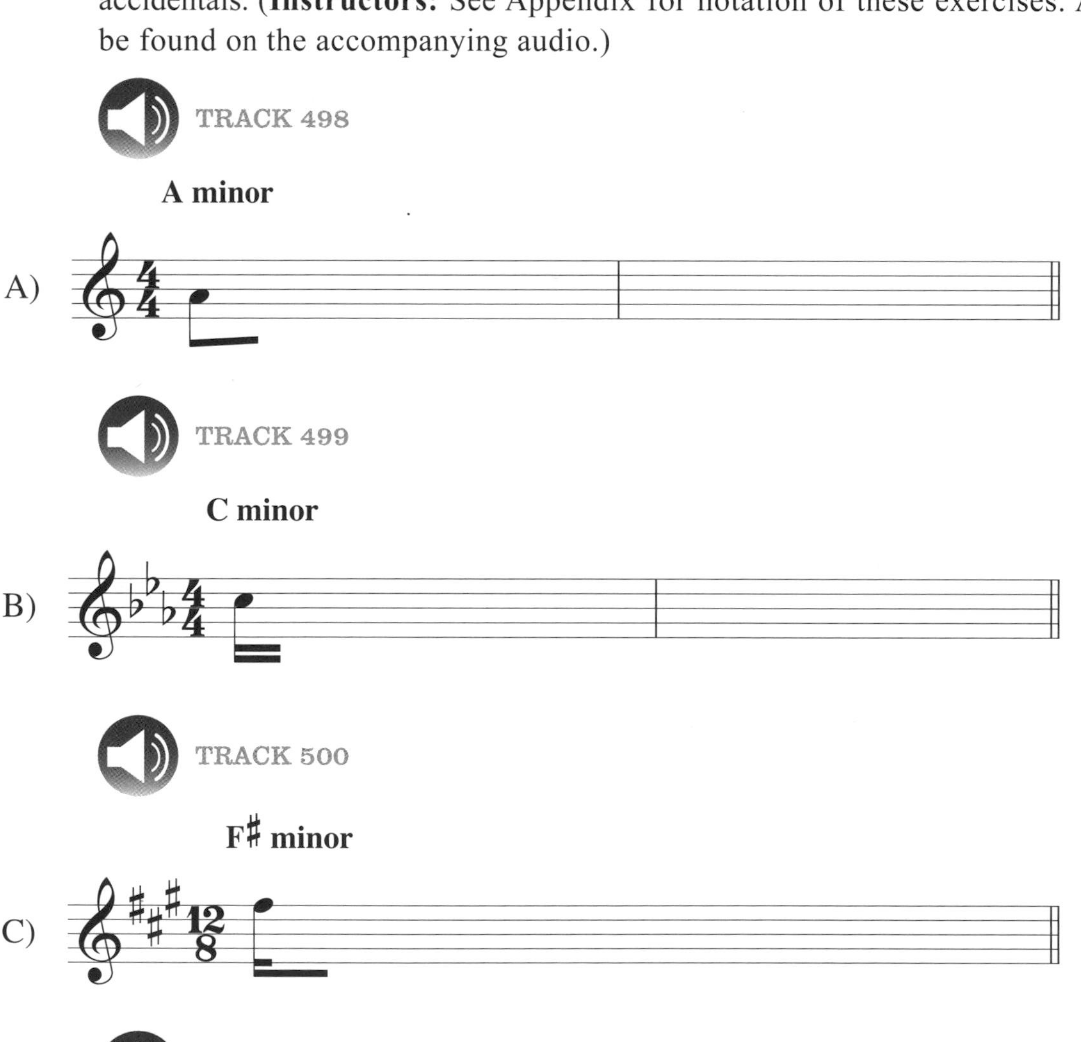

TRACK 501

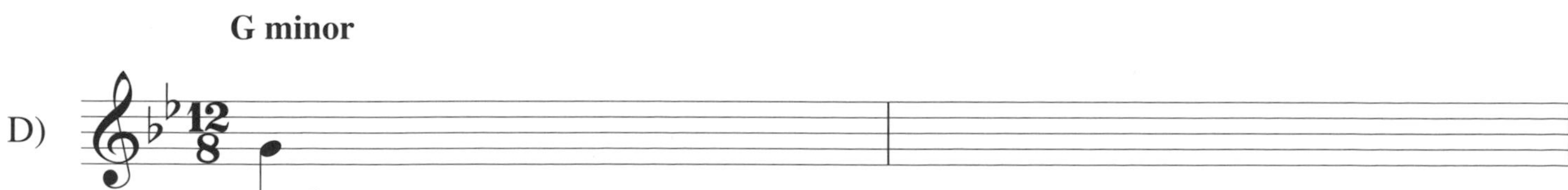

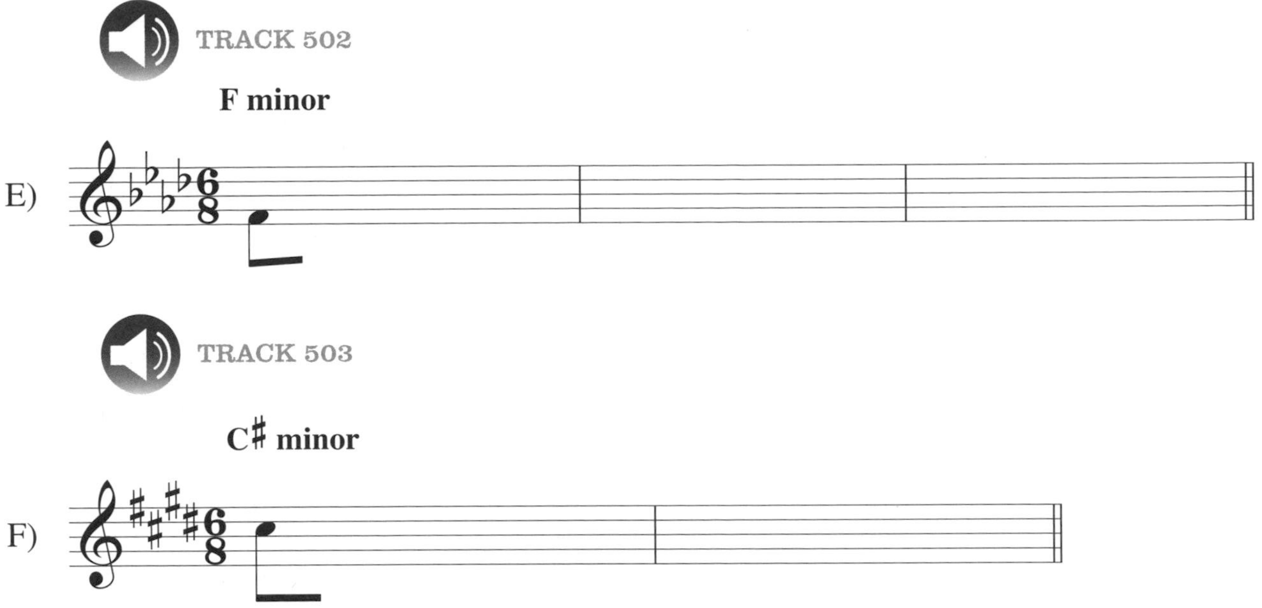

ECHO DRILLS

For these drills, listen to the phrase and then echo it back. (**Instructors:** See Appendix for notation of these exercises. Alternatively, these can be found on the accompanying audio.)

Rhythm Echoes

In these four exercise, listen to each bar of rhythm and echo it back by clapping in the breaks.

TRACK 507

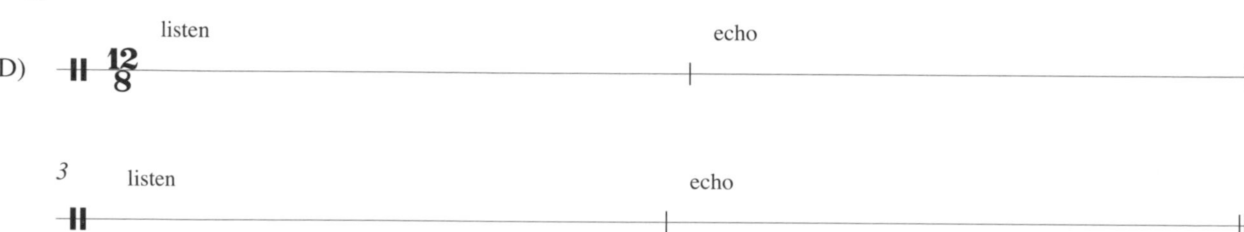

Melodic Echoes

In these four exercises, you'll hear a one-bar melody followed by one bar of silence. Sing the melody back during the break. Various keys are covered, so tonicizing chords are played before each example.

TRACK 508

A) listen echo listen

4 echo listen echo

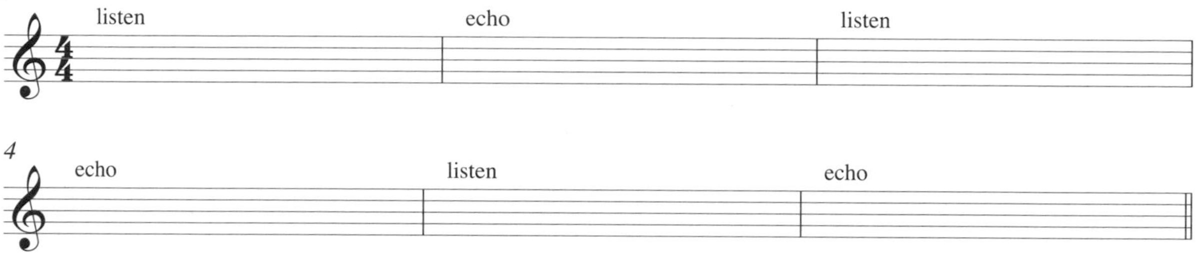

TRACK 509

B) listen echo listen

4 echo listen echo

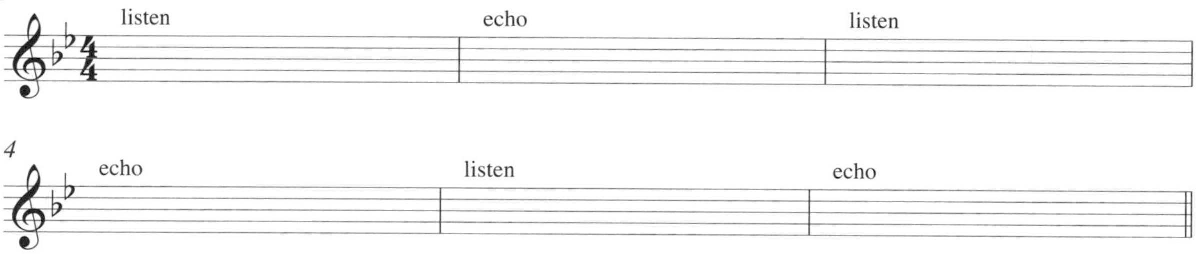

TRACK 510

C) listen echo

3 listen echo

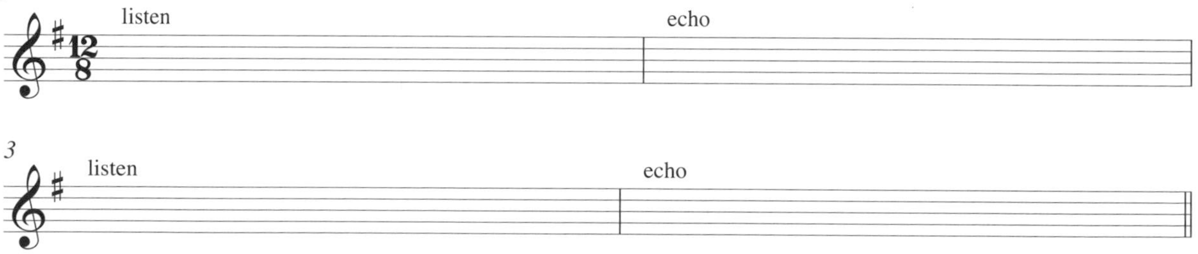

TRACK 511

D) listen echo

3 listen echo

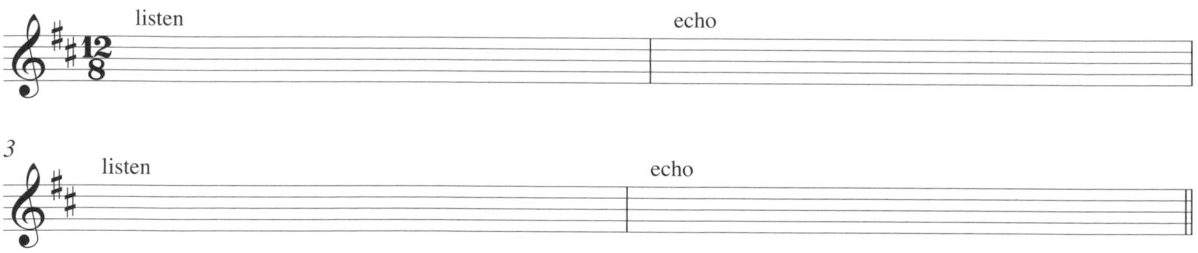

CHAPTER 17
READING A CHART AND TRANSPOSING

If you plan to work as a musician in any professional capacity—especially one that involves performing popular music often—the skills of chart-reading and transposition are essential. In this chapter, we'll look at each in detail.

READING A CHART

There are several different types of musical charts (or "scores"). Some are highly detailed transcriptions of a performance, others are complete orchestral scores for dozens of instruments, and some are nothing more than chord symbols and bar lines. However, there are elements common to each type; understanding them is crucial if you want to be able to keep your place.

Style and/or Tempo Marking

The *tempo head* is often the first bit of information in a piece of music. Its purpose is to give a rough (or more specific) idea of how the piece should sound. The stylistic marking could say something like "Slowly, with feeling"—or it could be general, like "Moderately." It might be specific regarding musical genre, as in "Moderate Jazz Swing." In classical music, Italian terms are often used. Here are the most common:

- **Adagio:** Slowly
- **Andante:** Walking pace
- **Moderato:** Moderately
- **Allegretto:** Moderately fast
- **Allegro:** Fast and bright
- **Presto:** Very fast

Often, there's a descriptor paired with a BPM (beats per minute) marking, like this:

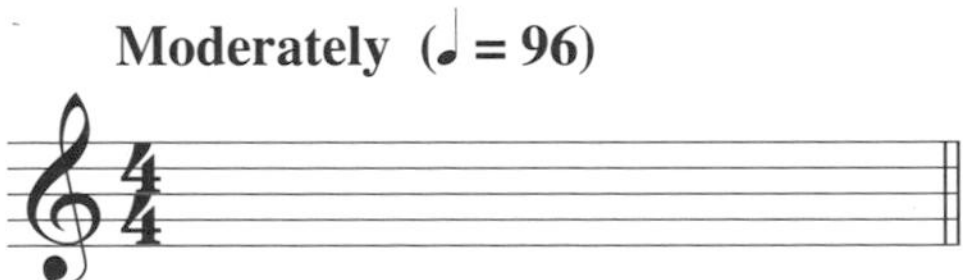

The BPM is a specific marking that can be matched with a metronome. While many older-styled metronomes allow you to move the BPM by pre-assigned increments, modern digital metronomes enable you to set the BPM to any number you like.

Key Signature and Meter

By now, you are familiar with key signature and meter. However, don't just glance at the beginning and assume that's that. Scan through the chart to see if the key or meter changes at a certain point; this can be jarring if you're not prepared for it.

When a key signature changes, there is usually a double thin bar line preceding it; the new key signature is written immediately after the double bar line.

If the key is changing to C major (A minor), natural signs cancel the previous key signature.

If either (key signature or meter) changes at the end of a system, that information should appear at the end of that system to give ample warning.

Repeats and Bracketed Endings

A *repeat sign* instructs you to go back to a certain measure and play/sing the same music again, the second time continuing through the repeat sign. Usually, there are two repeat signs at work: a left and a right. If there is no left sign (which normally comes first), go back to the beginning of the piece and repeat from there. Study the following examples.

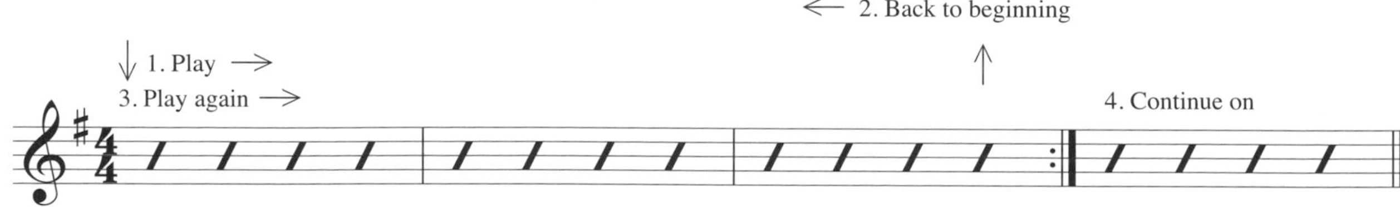

Normally, though, we pass through the left sign first and then come to the right. At that point, go back and repeat from the left sign, continuing on through the right sign.

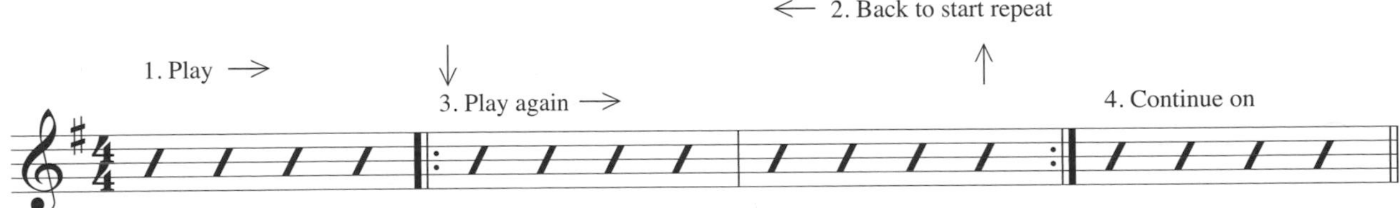

Sometimes, a passage is to be repeated several times. A simple direction, such as "Play 4 times," indicates that the material between the repeat signs is played four times before continuing on.

Composers and engravers often use *bracketed* (or *numbered*) *endings*, in which only the end is changed during a repeat. Play from the left repeat sign to the right, which is enclosed by a bracket with "1" in it. Then go back and start from the left repeat sign as normal. This time, though, skip over the "1" bracket and go straight to the "2" bracket, continuing on from there.

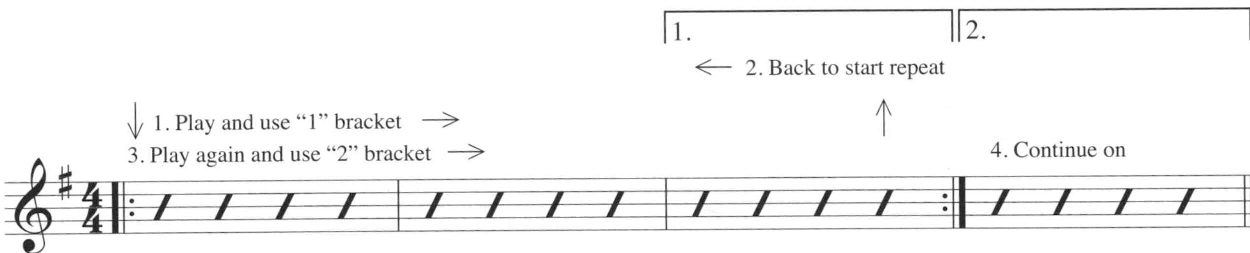

These bracketed endings can include not only second endings, but also third, fourth, etc. In this case, there is a right repeat sign at the end of the second ending, indicating a return to the left repeat sign, after which the first and second endings are skipped, leaping directly to the third, and so on.

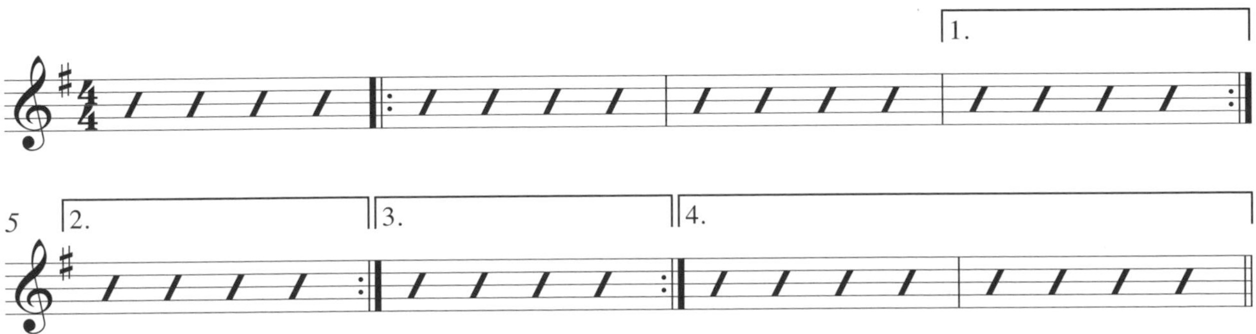

Routing Directions and Shortcuts

A routing direction is another common paper/ink saver. Again, these are all Italian terms.

D.S. al Fine (Dal Segno al Fine)

D.S. means "to the sign." The "sign" is the symbol that looks like a titled "S" with a line through it and a dot on each side. Return to this spot when you reach D.S. The "al Fine" bit basically means "to the end." If you reach a double-thin bar line and see this direction, return to the sign ("segno") and play again to "Fine." (Always ignore the "Fine" direction until directed to it.)

In the following example, you would:

- Play to "D.S. al Fine"
- Go back to measure 3 (where the sign is)
- Play to the end of measure 8 (where "Fine" is)

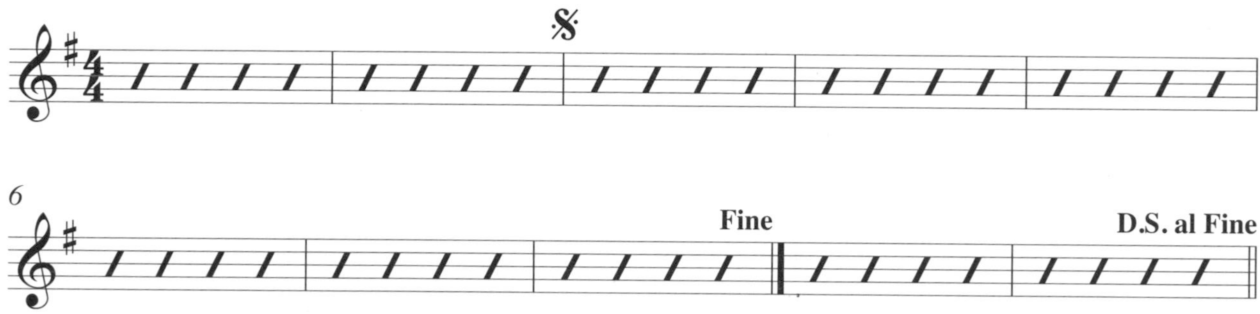

D.S. al Coda (Dal Segno al Coda)

Coda is the Italian word for "tail." It's a section tacked onto the end of a piece. When you see this direction, go back to the sign and play until the "To Coda" direction. (Again, ignore "To Coda" until directed to it.) At that point, skip to the Coda section, which is marked with the crosshair-looking symbol.

In the following example, you would:

- Play to "D.S. al Coda"
- Go back to measure 3 (where the sign is)
- Play to the end of measure 7 (where "To Coda" is)
- Skip to the Coda and play to the end

D.C. al Fine (Da Capo al Fine)

D.C. means "to the beginning" (literally, "to the head"). This is a variation on D.S. al Fine in which, instead of going back to the sign, we go back to the beginning and play until "Fine."

In the following example, you would:

- Play to "D.C. al Fine"
- Go back to measure 1 and start over
- Play to the end of measure 8 (where "Fine" is)

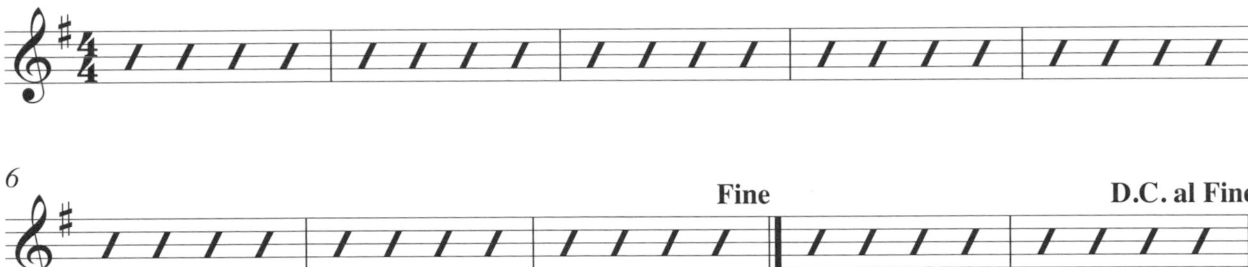

D.C. al Coda (Da Capo al Coda)

This is a variation of the previous "D.S. al Coda." Instead of going back and playing from the sign, we play from the beginning to the "To Coda" direction, at which point we jump to the Coda.

In the following example, you would:

- Play to "D.C. al Coda"
- Go back to measure 1
- Play to the end of measure 6 (where "To Coda" is)
- Skip to the Coda and play to the end

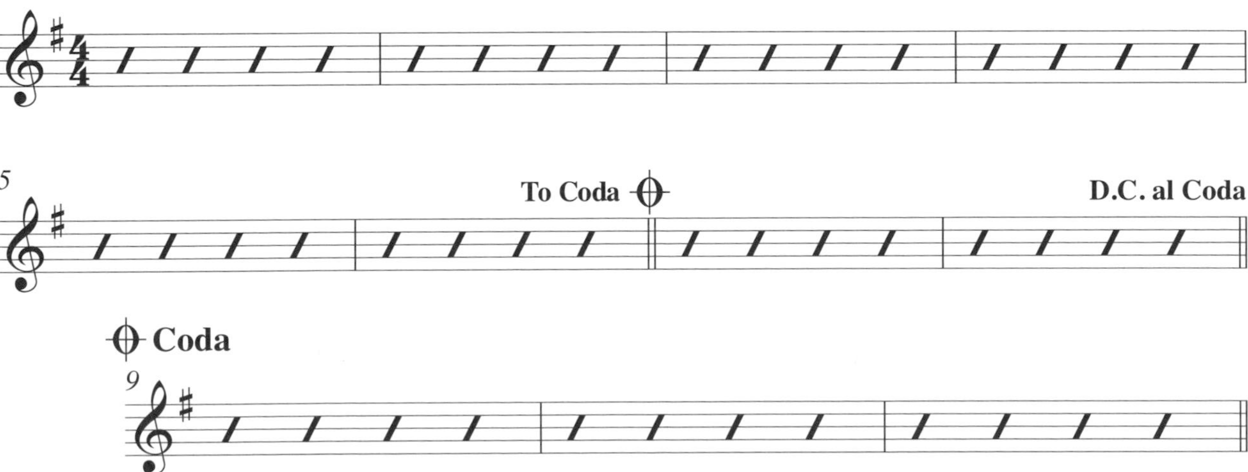

If there are repeats within the range of these directions, they will usually tell you specifically what to do.

In the following example, you would:

- Play to "D.S. al Fine (no repeat)"
- Go back to measure 3 (where the sign is)
- Ignore the repeat signs and play to the end of measure 6 (where "Fine" is)

In the following example, you would:

- Play to "D.S. al Fine (take 2nd ending)"
- Go back to measure 3 (where the sign is)
- Skip over the 1st ending to the 2nd ending and play to the end of measure 7 (where "Fine" is)

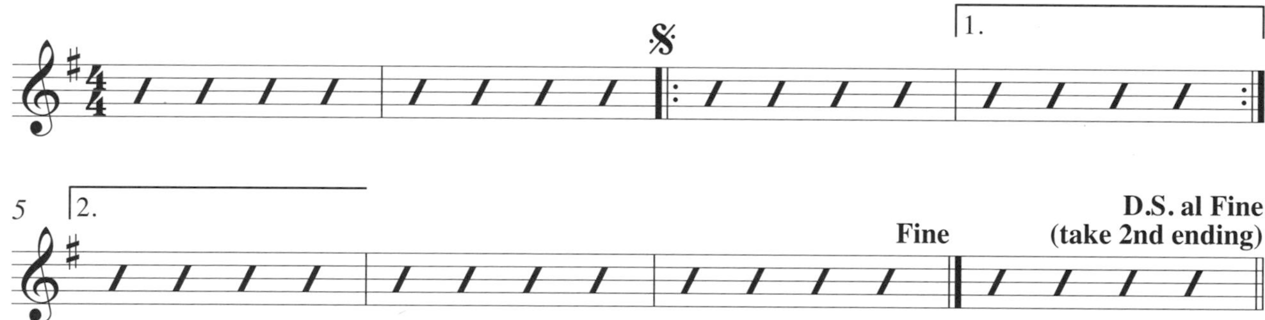

TRANSPOSING

To *transpose* a piece of music means to play it or sing it in a different key. For example, a C major song with the notes C–D–E–F–G (which runs straight up the C major scale) transposed to D major, would be D–E–F♯–G–A. Singers often transpose songs, because we all have different vocal ranges. If a song sits well for a high tenor voice, for example, it might need to be transposed down a few steps for a baritone voice.

The Beauty of Numbers

Numeric formulas and analysis come in handy when transposing. Since the numbers have no note names attached to them, they can be applied to any key. Let's take a look at how this works.

Remember that the numeric formula for the major scale is the standard: 1–2–3–4–5–6–7. Now assign each of those numbers to a specific note of the major scale. In G major, G is 1, A is 2, B is 3, and so on. (Remember that the key signature for G major is one sharp, so 7 would be F♯.) In B♭ major, 1 = B♭, 2 = C, 3 = D, 4 = E♭, and so on. As long as you know key signatures, it's like painting by numbers.

Look at the following phrase in C major:

First, write out the scale under the numeric formula:

1	2	3	4	5	6	7
C	D	E	F	G	A	B

That's the road map. Now write the matching number below each note in the musical phrase.

Now we're ready for the transposition. Let's transpose it to A major. First, write out the numbers with the new scale beneath them.

1	2	3	4	5	6	7
A	B	C#	D	E	F#	G#

Now transfer the numbers written below the musical phrase to a new staff and add the matching notes from the new key. That's all there is to it!

Chords are just as easy, thanks to the Roman numeral method. Look at this chord progression in C major.

To transpose the progression to a new key, write out the Roman numeral chord formula, then add the note names with the proper chord suffix beneath them. (See page 47 in Chapter 6.) In C major, the Roman numerals look like this:

I	ii	iii	IV	V	vi	vii°
C	Dm	Em	F	G	Am	B°

Next, write the matching Roman numeral below each chord in the progression.

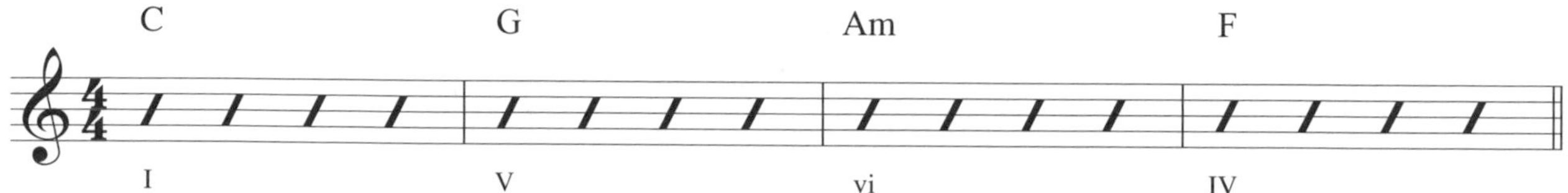

To transpose, first write out the set of Roman numerals and matching chords in the new key. Let's transpose to F major.

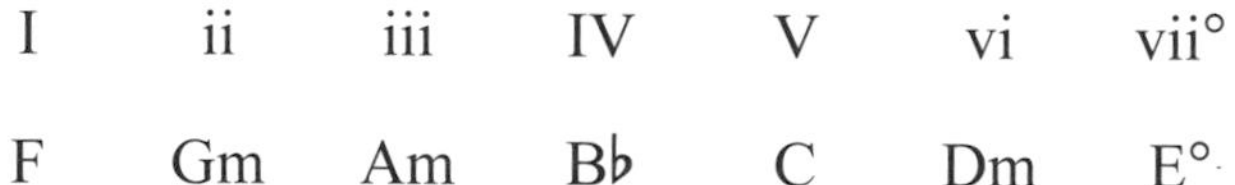

Finally, transfer the Roman numerals from the chord progression to a new staff and add the matching chords from the new key.

With a little practice, you'll be able to do this without even thinking about it. As you become more comfortable with the different key signatures, you'll become ever more facile with it.

Let's put this into practice by transposing a well-known piece of music: Beethoven's "Ode to Joy." Here is the melody in the key of D major:

Now transpose it to the key of B♭ major. (Answer found in the Appendix.)

Ode to Joy

APPENDIX

In this section, you'll find useful bits of information not thoroughly covered previously. Also contained here are the answers for the Dictation quizzes and the notation of the Echo Drills for the instructor's reference.

Vocal Ranges

Everyone has a preset vocal range, though it can be extended a bit with proper training and practice. These fall within four main categories: soprano, alto, tenor, and bass.

Soprano

The highest female voice, usually of the range C4 to C6, is the *soprano*. (The term is also used for a boy's unchanged voice, sometimes referred to as a "treble.") In choirs, sopranos are normally grouped in two sections—soprano I and II—based on which end of this spectrum best fits their voice.

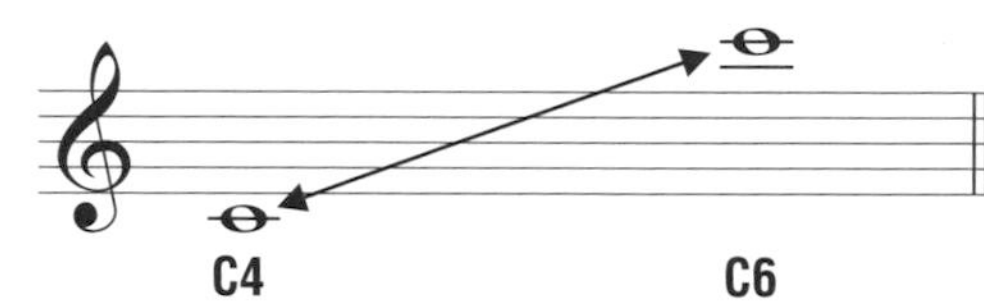

Alto

A lower-pitched female singer is called an *alto*. There are many men in the pop music world who can hit common alto notes, but it's usually done for effect and is not their standard range. The general range for altos is from around F3 (the F below middle C) to F5. As with sopranos, altos are divided into alto I and alto II sections.

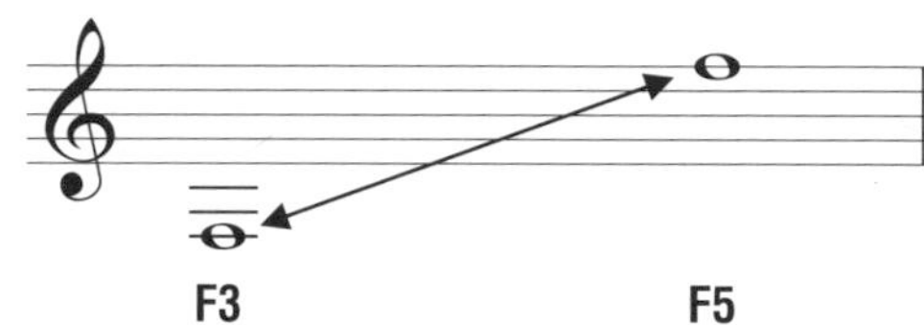

Tenor

The *tenor* range is designated for a high-pitched male voice. A good percentage of pop and rock male singers are/were tenors, including Michael Jackson, Freddie Mercury, Justin Timberlake, and Sting, among others. Note that tenors read treble clef, but they sing an octave lower than they read. The usual written range for a tenor is from about C4 (middle C) to C6. Again, though, due to the transposition, this range actually sounds about an octave lower than the soprano range. Tenors are also divided into tenor I and tenor II sections.

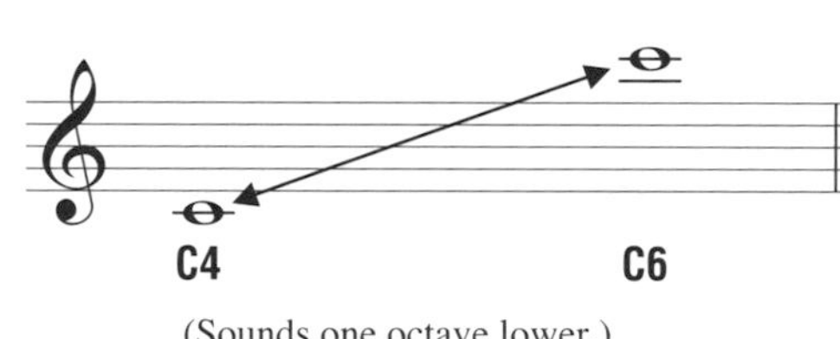

(Sounds one octave lower.)

Bass

At the bottom of the spectrum lie the *basses*. In the pop world, you don't hear too many basses, although they are more prevalent in country music. Basses read bass clef and sing at written pitch. Their range generally extends from around E2 to F4. Basses are divided in two sections as well, but the higher-voiced basses are referred to as *baritones*, while the lower-pitched are simply called basses.

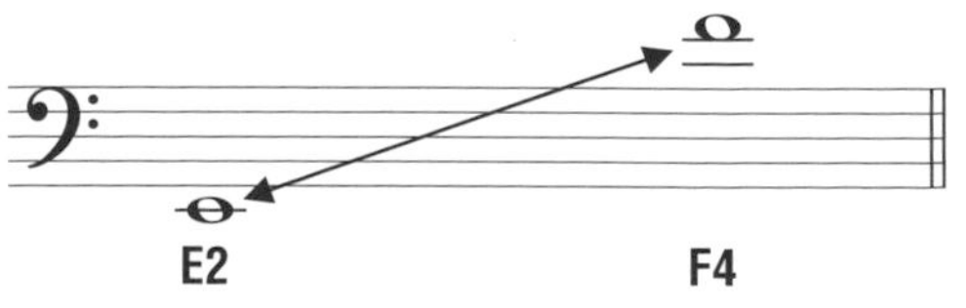

THE CIRCLE OF FIFTHS

The Circle of Fifths is a useful graphic model for memorizing key signatures. It's arranged like a clock, with 12 different major keys (the relative minors are often included as well) spaced evenly around the circle. C major is at the top (12:00) with no sharps or flats. Progressing clockwise around the circle, each key is one 5th higher: C, G, D, A, etc. The keys on the right side of the circle are the sharp keys; the ones on the left are the flat keys.

At the bottom (6:00) is the enharmonic key of F♯ or G♭. This key contains six accidentals: F♯'s key signature is six sharps, and G♭'s key signature is six flats. Progressing counter-clockwise around the circle, we move up by 4ths: C, F, B♭, E♭, etc. This makes sense, because—as we know from Chapter 8—a 5th interval inverted is a 4th, and vice versa. In other words, if we move from C up to G, we move up a 5th. But if we move from C down to G, we move down a 4th.

The Circle clearly shows the cumulative progression of sharps and flats in each key as you move around each side. It's an excellent aid in memorizing the key signatures for all 12 keys.

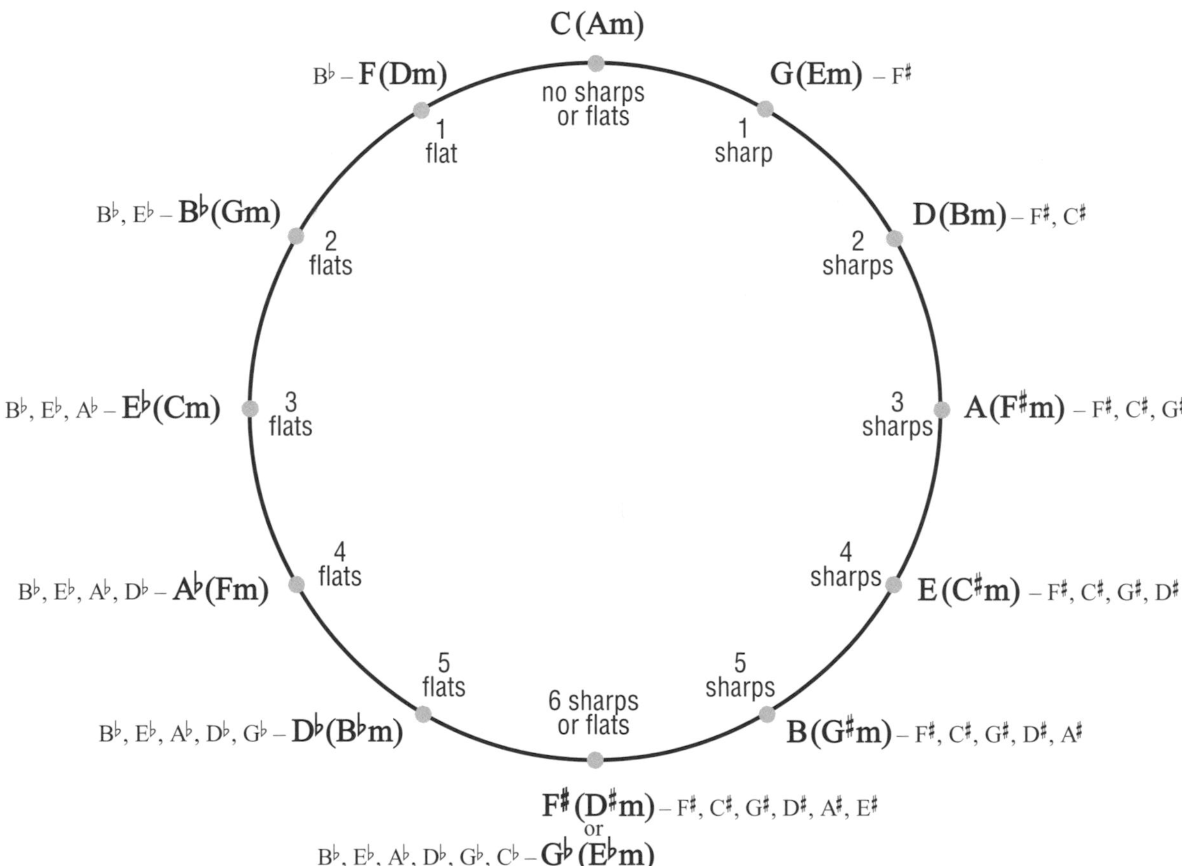

SOLFÈGE SYLLABLES

The solfège syllable system is an alternative to the numeric system for identifying pitches within a key. If you're familiar with the song "Do-Re-Mi" from *The Sound of Music*, you already know most of it. The system assigns a different syllable to each pitch, which is then easily applicable to any key.

Here are the diatonic pitches and their numeric equivalents:

Solfège syllable	Pronunciation	Scale degree
do	doe	1 (tonic)
re	ray	2
mi	mee	3
fa	fah	4
sol	sew	5
la	lah	6
ti	tea	7

Here's an example of how a phrase in G major is sung using solfège syllables:

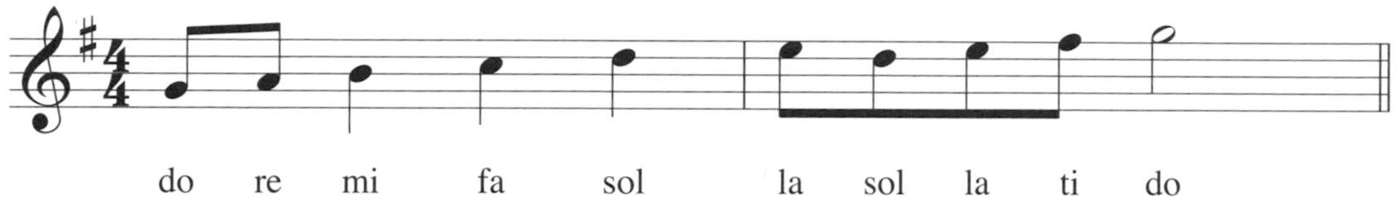

Non-Diatonic Pitches

There are syllables for the five non-diatonic pitches (those outside the major scale) as well, but they change depending on the direction of the melody. Here's how these syllables are named in an ascending chromatic scale (all 12 notes) in the key of C.

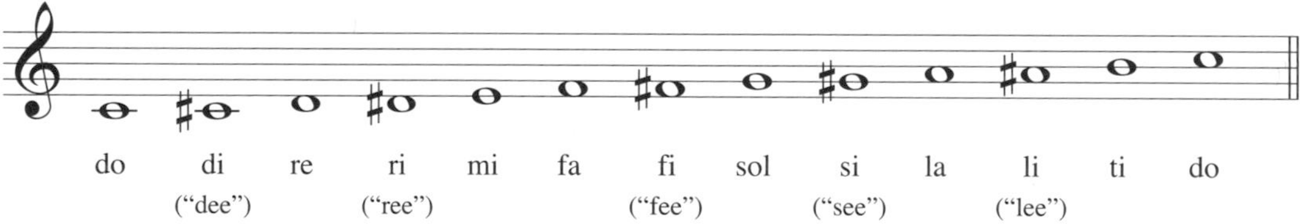

And here's how they look in a descending chromatic scale in C.

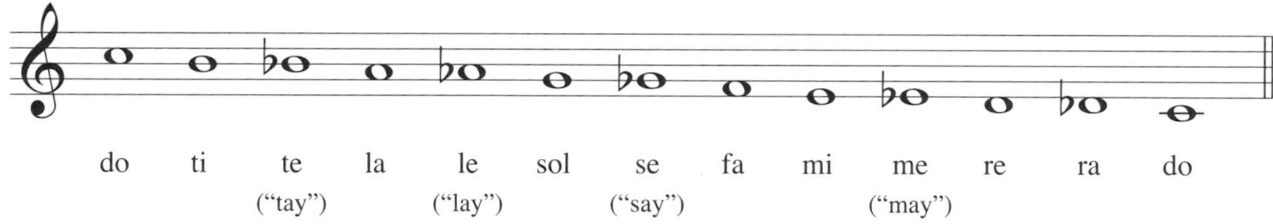

Moveable Do vs. Fixed Do

The solfège system described above is known as the *moveable do* system. This means that "do" is always the tonic, regardless of the key. Another system of solfège, known as "fixed do," also exists, in which "do" is always the note C. In this system, the chromatic syllables above are used just like the names of notes on a piano. It doesn't matter if you're in the key of C or A♭: the note A♭ is always the "le" syllable. In other words, the *moveable do* system is relative, while the *fixed do* system is absolute.

In the opinion of many musicians and teachers, the *fixed do* system is unnecessary, because an absolute system already exists: note names. In other words, why do we need another name for the note C? One possible reason is that it creates one-syllable versions of all the note names; that's easier to sing than "C-sharp," for example. However, the beauty of the *moveable do* system is that melodies are easily transposed to another key. (This was done in Chapter 17 with the number system.) The *fixed do* system does not permit this.

ANSWER KEY

Here you'll find the answers to all the dictation quizzes throughout the book, including Rhythmic Dictation, Interval (or Triad) Dictation, Melodic Dictation, and any other incidental quizzes, as well as the notation for the Echo Drills.

CHAPTER 3

Rhythmic Dictation

Interval Dictation

B) M2; C) m2; D) m2; E) M2; F) m2; G) M2; H) M2

Melodic Dictation

Echo Drills – Rhythm

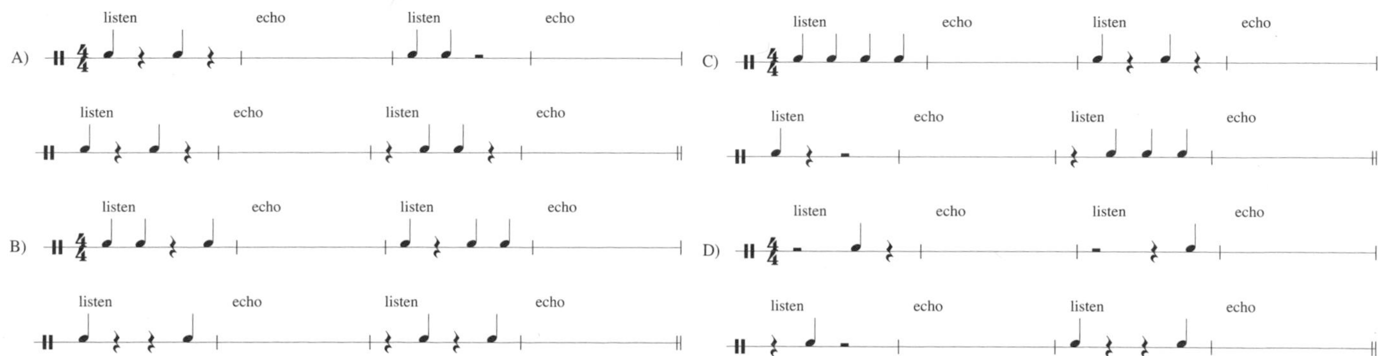

Echo Drills – Melodic

CHAPTER 4

Rhythmic Dictation

Interval Dictation

A) M3; B) m3; C) M3; D) m3; E) M3; F) M3; G) M3; H) m3

Melodic Dictation

Echo Drills – Rhythm

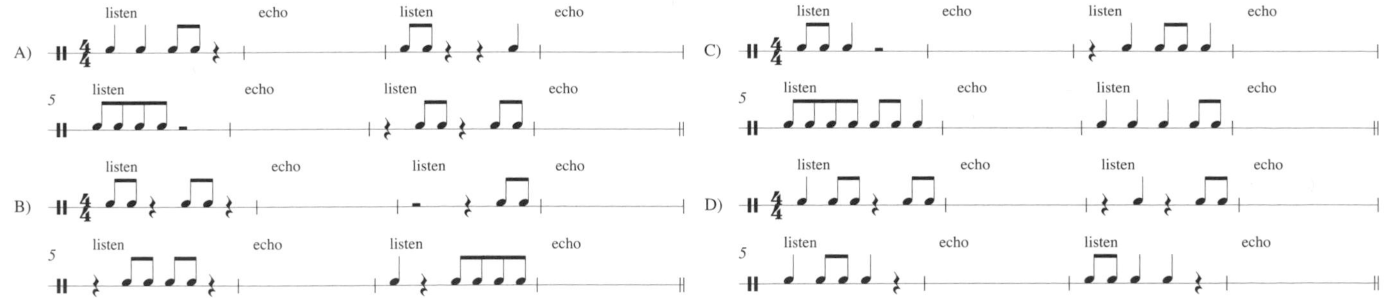

Echo Drills – Melodic

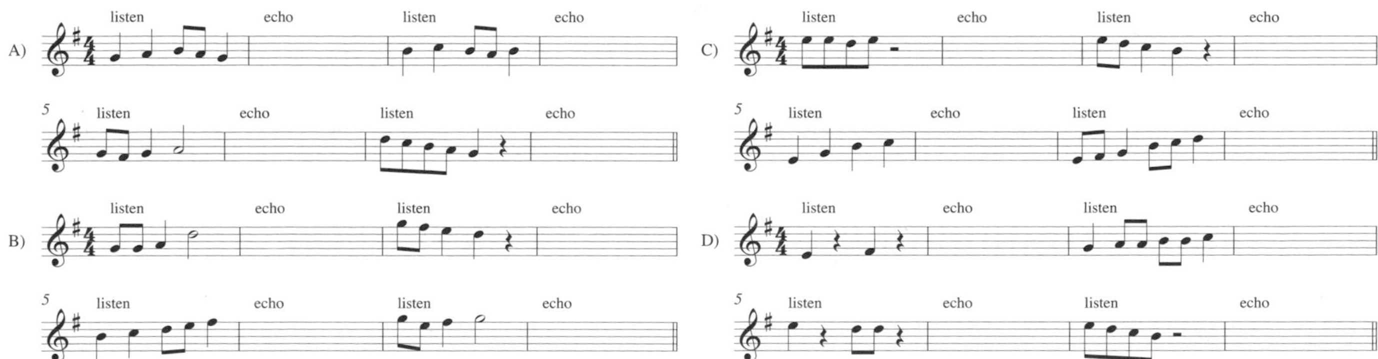

CHAPTER 5

Rhythmic Dictation

Interval Dictation

A) P4; B) P4; C) P5; D) P4; E) P5; F) P5; G) P5; H) P4

Melodic Dictation

Echo Drills – Rhythm

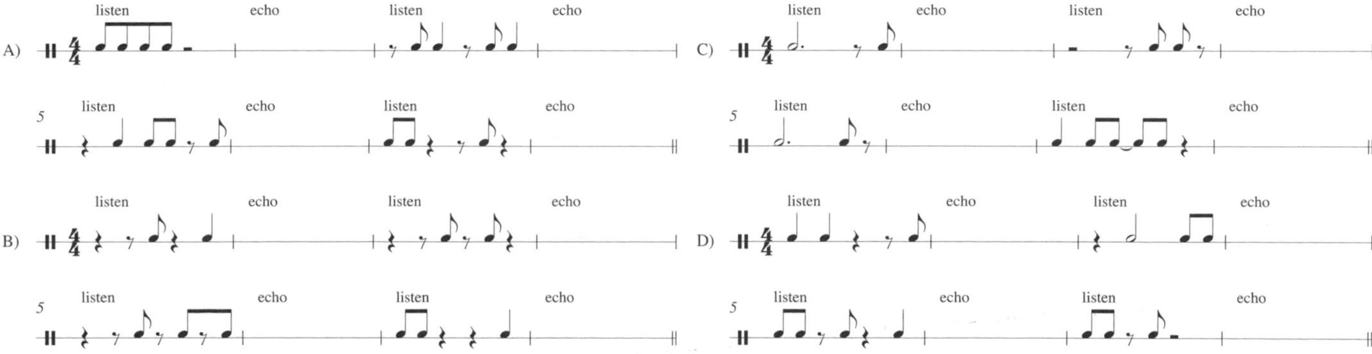

Echo Drills – Melodic

CHAPTER 6

Rhythmic Dictation

Triad Dictation

A) Dm; B) D; C) D+; D) Dm; E) D°; F) D+; G) D; H) D°

Melodic Dictation

Echo Drills – Rhythm

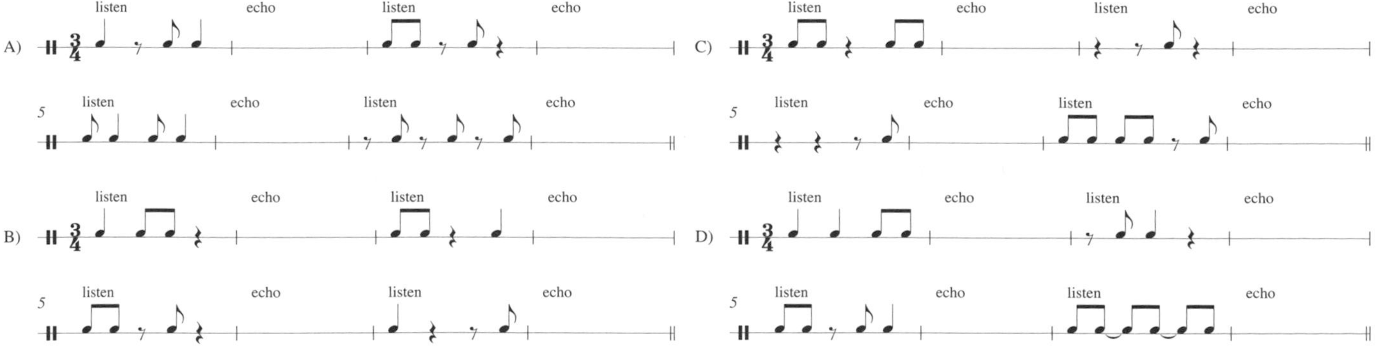

Echo Drills – Melodic

CHAPTER 7

Rhythmic Dictation

Interval Dictation

A) TT; B) A5; C) A5; D) TT; E); TT; F) A5; G) TT; H) A5

Melodic Dictation

Echo Drills – Rhythm

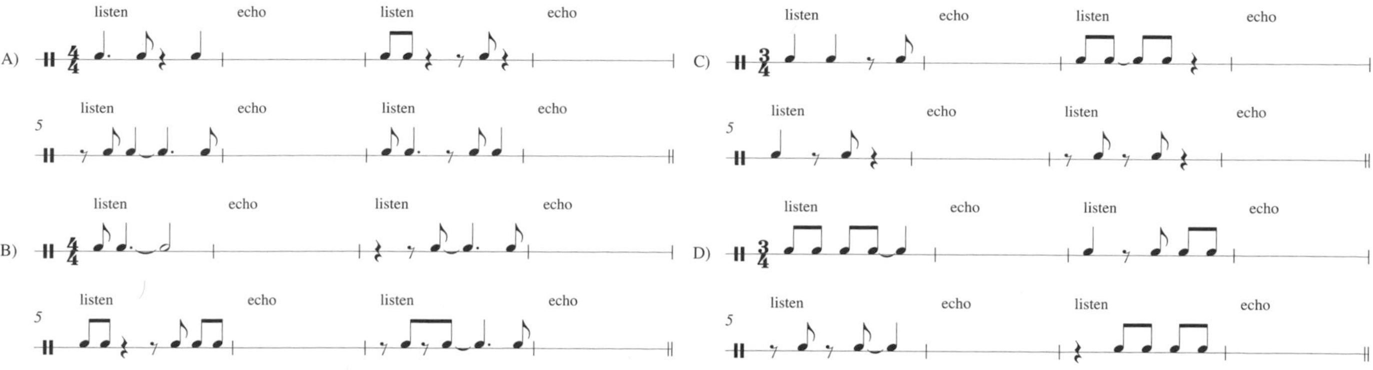

Echo Drills – Melodic

CHAPTER 8

Rhythmic Dictation

Interval Dictation

A) M6; B) M6; C) m6; D) M6; E) m6; F) m6; G) m6; H) M6

Melodic Dictation

Echo Drills – Rhythm

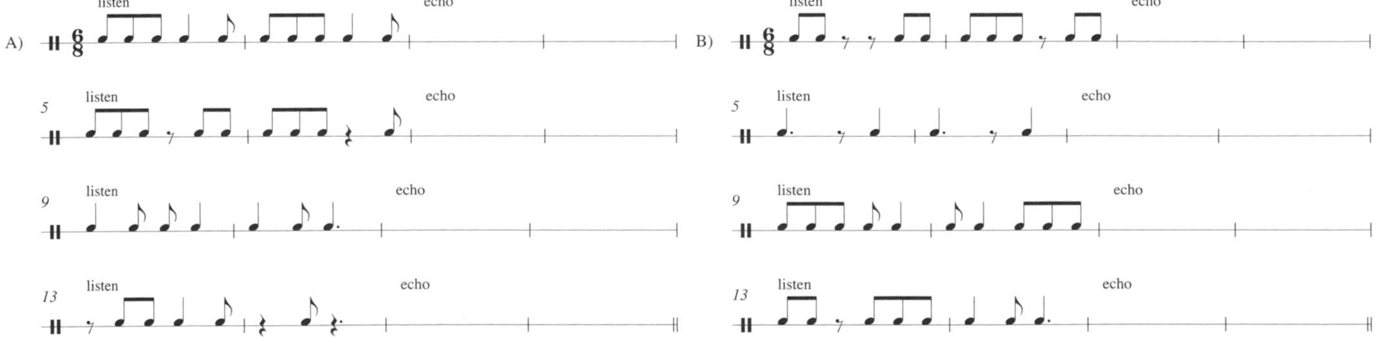

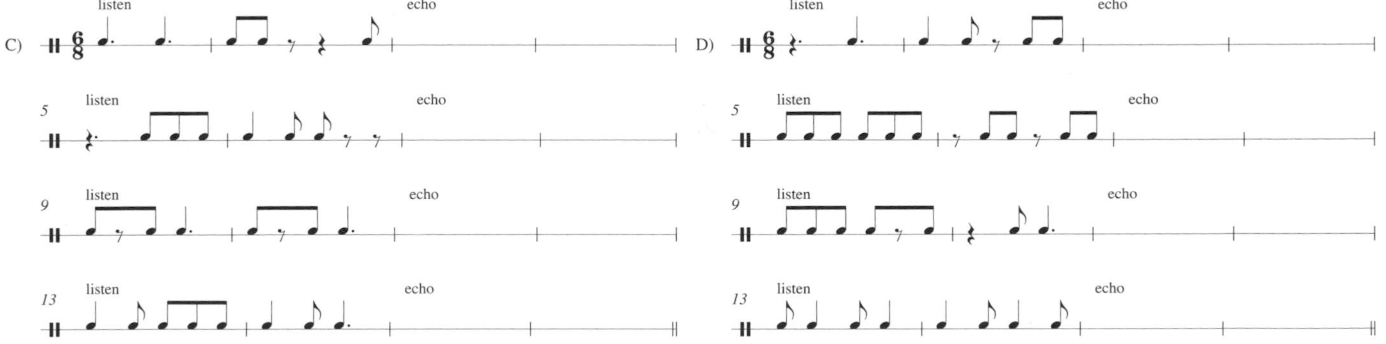

Echo Drills – Melodic

CHAPTER 9

Rhythmic Dictation

A)

B)

C)

D)

Interval Dictation

A) M7; B) m7; C) m7; D) M7; E) m7; F) m7; G) M7; H) M7

Melodic Dictation

Echo Drills – Rhythm

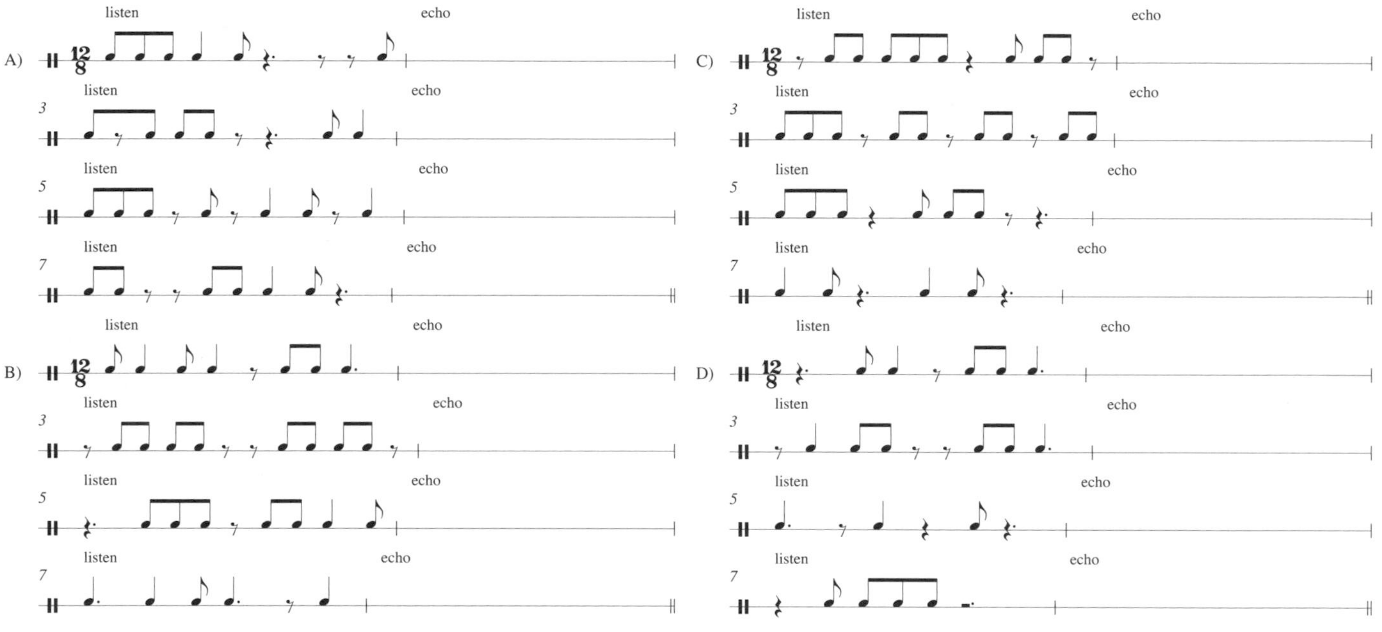

Echo Drills – Melodic

CHAPTER 10

Rhythmic Dictation

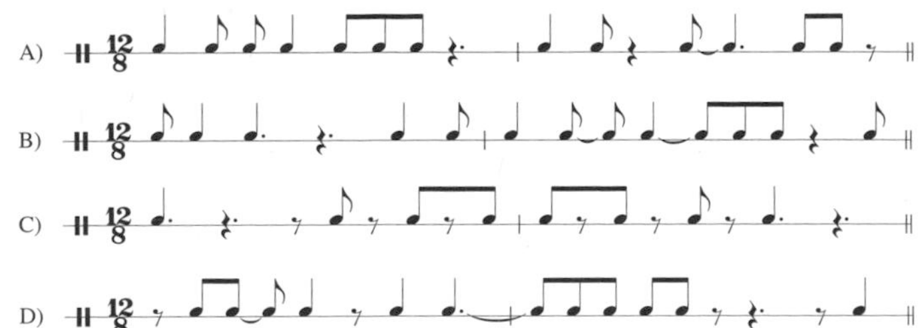

Triad Dictation

A) I; B) IV; C) I; D) V; E) IV; F) V; G) I; H) IV

Melodic Dictation

Echo Drills – Rhythm

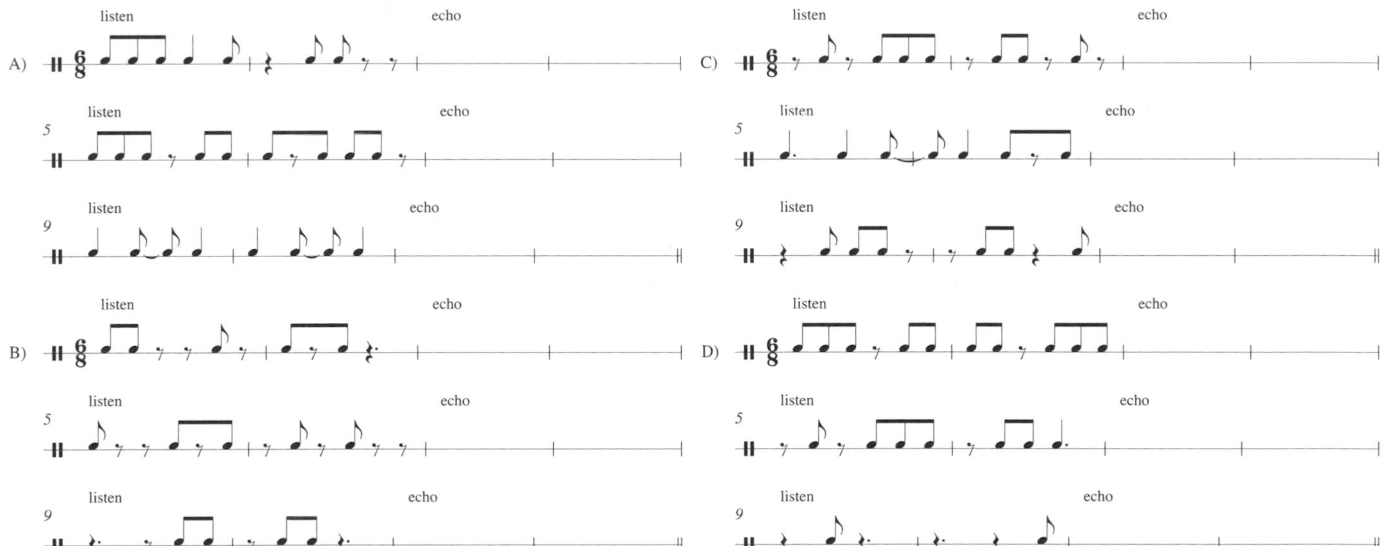

Echo Drills – Melodic

CHAPTER 11

Rhythmic Dictation

Triad Dictation

A) iii; B) vi; C) iii; D) ii; E) vi; F) ii; G) iii; H) vi

Melodic Dictation

Echo Drills – Rhythm

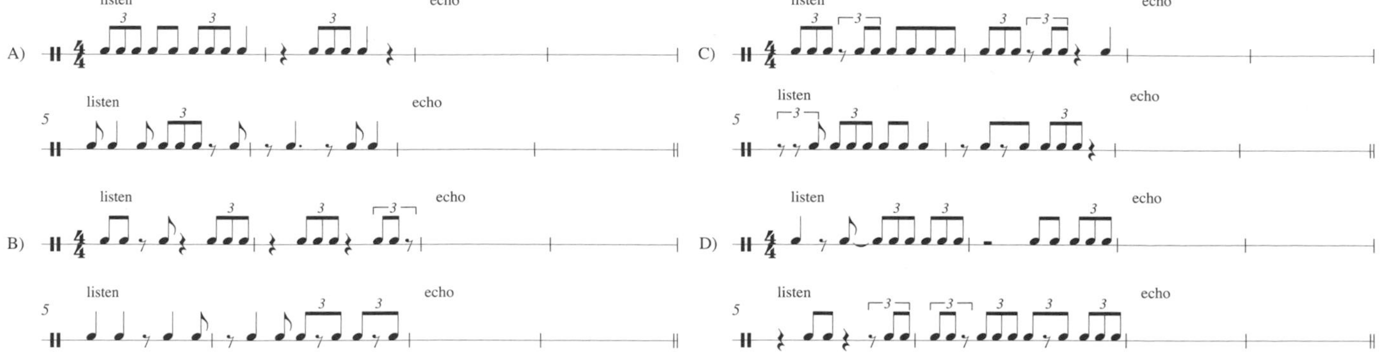

Echo Drills – Melodic

CHAPTER 12

Rhythmic Dictation

Triad Dictation

A) V; B) iii; C) IV; D) I; E) vii°; F) ii; G) vi; H) IV; I) I;

J) V; K) iii; L) vi

Melodic Dictation

Echo Drills – Rhythm

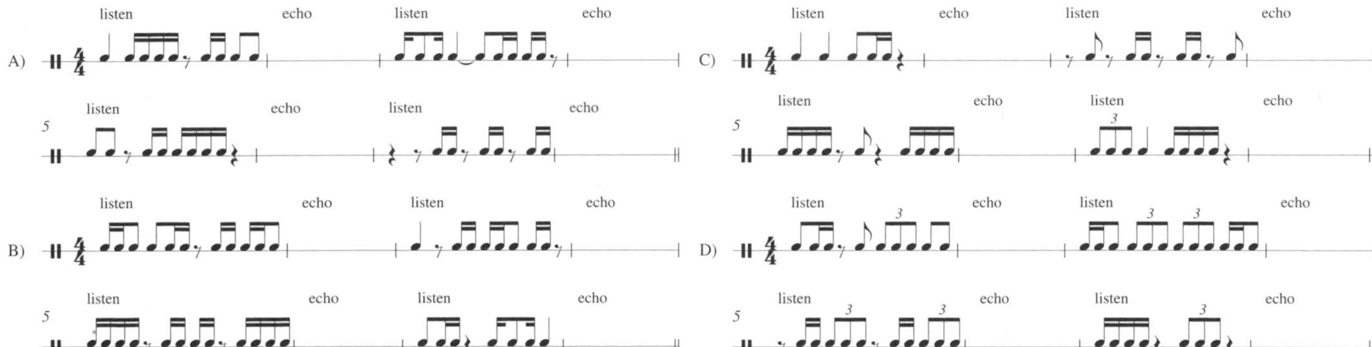

Echo Drills – Melodic

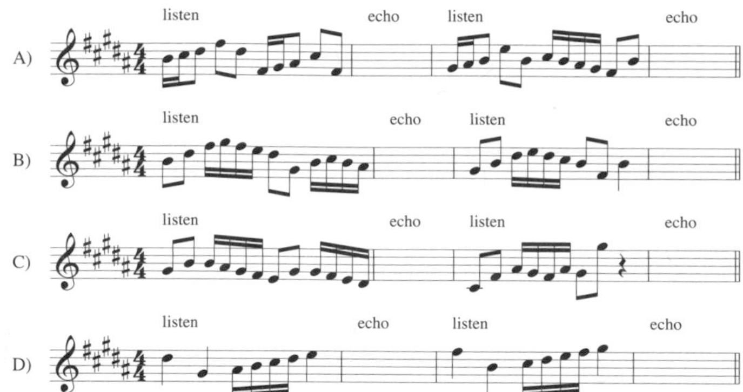

CHAPTER 13

Rhythmic Dictation

Scale Identification

A) major pentatonic; B) blues scale; C) major pentatonic; D) minor pentatonic; E) minor pentatonic; F) blues scale; G) major pentatonic; H) minor pentatonic

Melodic Dictation

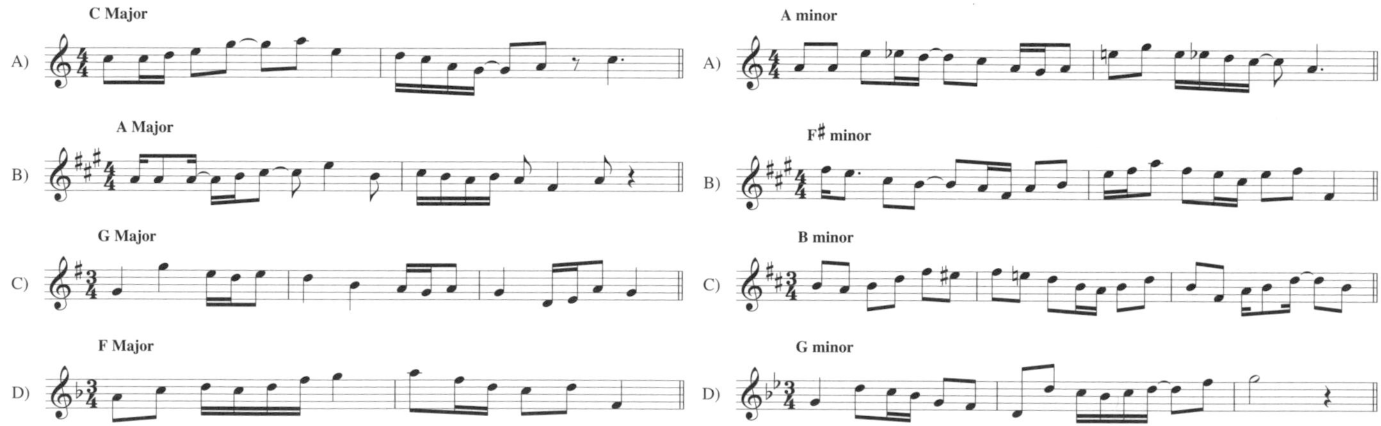

Echo Drills – Rhythm

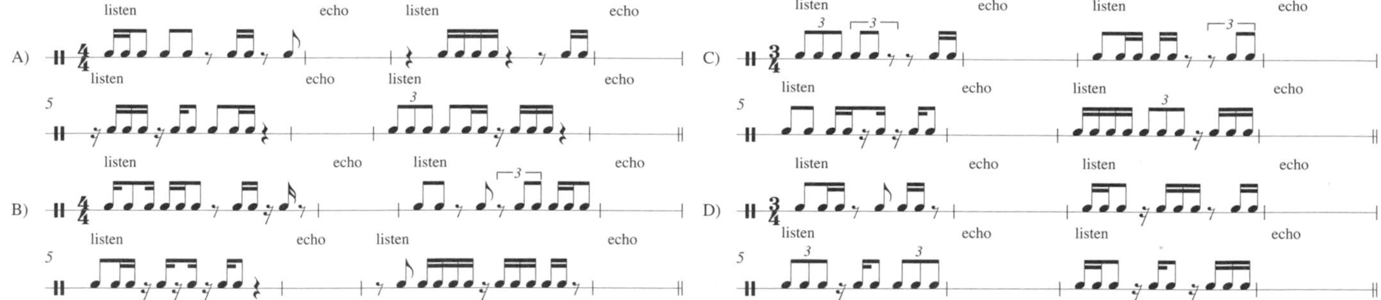

Echo Drills – Melodic

CHAPTER 14

Rhythmic Dictation

Melodic Dictation

Echo Drills – Rhythm

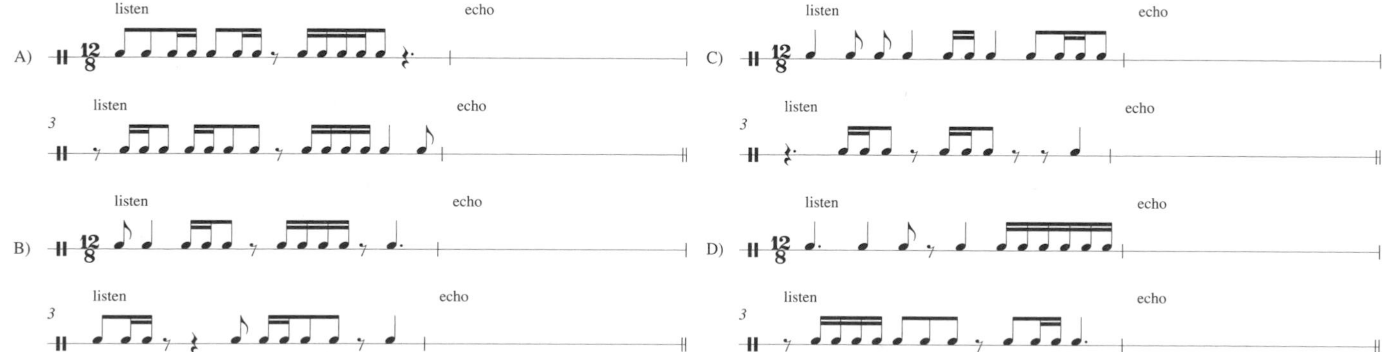

Echo Drills – Melodic

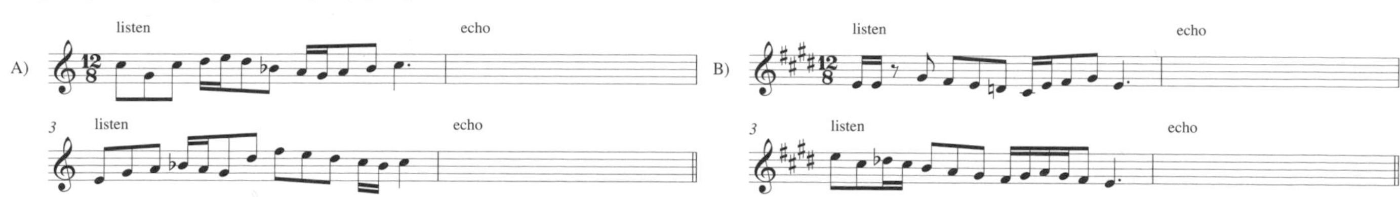

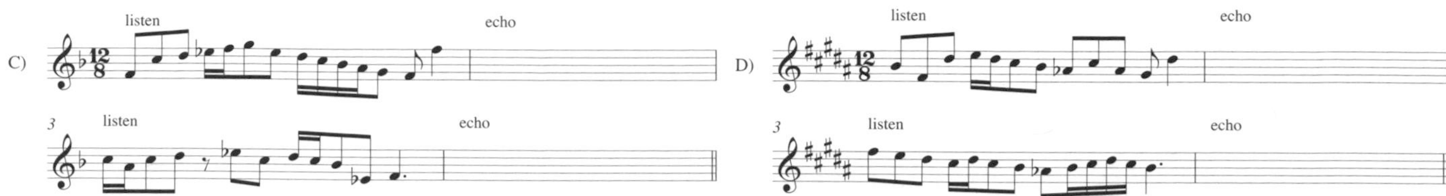

CHAPTER 15

Rhythmic Dictation

Melodic Dictation

Echo Drills – Rhythm

Echo Drills – Melodic

CHAPTER 16

Rhythmic Dictation

Melodic Dictation

Echo Drills – Rhythm

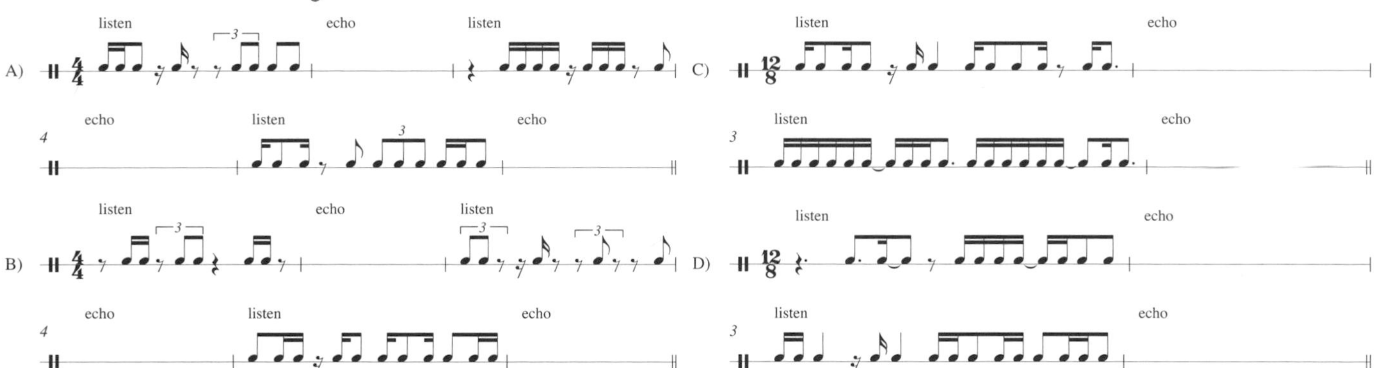

Echo Drills – Melodic

CHAPTER 17

Ode to Joy Transposition Quiz

Ode to Joy

B♭ Major

5

9

13

ABOUT THE AUTHOR

Chad Johnson is a freelance author, editor, and musician. For Hal Leonard LLC, he has authored over 70 instructional books covering a variety of instruments and topics, including *Guitarist's Guide to Scales Over Chords*, *The Hal Leonard Fingerstyle Guitar Method*, *How to Record at Home on a Budget*, *Teach Yourself to Play Bass Guitar*, *Ukulele Aerobics*, *Pentatonic Scales for Guitar: The Essential Guide*, *Pink Floyd Signature Licks*, and *Play Like Robben Ford*, to name but a few. He is a featured instructor on the DVD *200 Country Guitar Licks* (also published by Hal Leonard) and has toured and performed throughout the East Coast in various bands, sharing the stage with members of Lynyrd Skynyrd, the Allman Brothers Band, Jamey Johnson, and others.

When not authoring or editing, he works as a session instrumentalist, composer/songwriter, and recording engineer. His latest band, Sun City, recently released their self-titled debut album, which can be purchased at *www.suncitymusic.bandcamp.com*. Chad currently resides in Dallas with his wife and two children, where he keeps busy with an active freelance career. Feel free to contact him at *chadjohnsonguitar@gmail.com* with any questions or concerns. To keep up to date with Chad's new books and other musical activities, visit him at *www.facebook.com/chadjohnsonguitar*.

Great Harmony & Theory Helpers

HAL LEONARD HARMONY & THEORY – PART 1: DIATONIC

by George Heussenstamm

This book is designed for anyone wishing to expand their knowledge of music theory, whether beginner or more advanced. The first two chapters deal with music fundamentals, and may be skipped by those with music reading experience. Topics include: basic music-reading instruction; triads in root position; triads in inversion; cadences; non-harmonic tones; the dominant seventh chord; other seventh chords; and more.

00312062 .... $27.50

HAL LEONARD HARMONY & THEORY – PART 2: CHROMATIC

by George Heussenstamm

Part 2 – Chromatic introduces readers to modulation and more advanced harmonies, covering: secondary dominants; borrowed chords; the Neapolitan 6th chord; augmented 6th chords; 9th, 11th, and 13th chords; and more. In addition to text, the book features many musical examples that illustrate the concepts, and exercises that allow readers to test and apply their knowledge.

00312064 .... $27.50

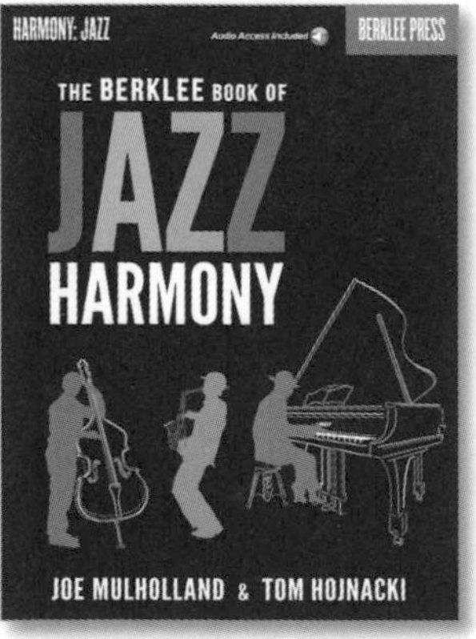

THE BERKLEE BOOK OF JAZZ HARMONY

by Joe Mulholland & Tom Hojnacki

Berklee Press

Learn jazz harmony, as taught at Berklee College of Music. This text provides a strong foundation in harmonic principles, supporting further study in jazz composition, arranging, and improvisation. It covers basic chord types and their tensions, with practical demonstrations of how they are used in characteristic jazz contexts; an accompanying recording lets you hear how they can be applied.

00113755 Book/Online Audio $27.50

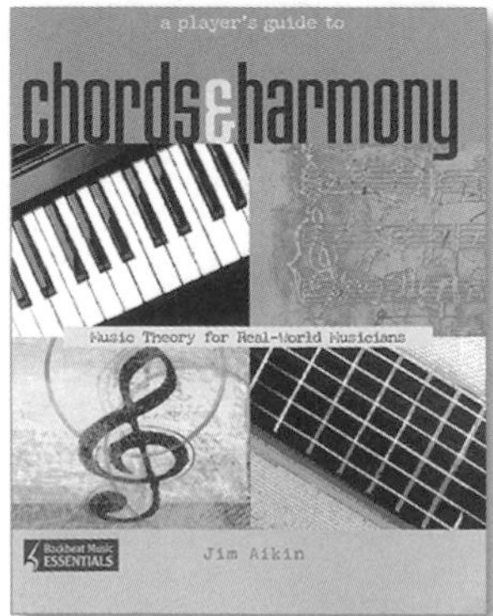

A PLAYER'S GUIDE TO CHORDS AND HARMONY

Music Theory for Real-World Musicians

by Jim Aikin

Backbeat Books

If you'd like to know about music theory but don't want to get bogged down in a stuffy college-level textbook, this guide was written just for you! Covers: intervals, scales, modes, triads and advanced voicings; interpreting chord symbols and reading sheet music; voice leading, chord progressions, and basic song forms; classical, jazz & pop; and more, with helpful quizzes and answers.

00331173 .... $19.95

ENCYCLOPEDIA OF READING RHYTHMS

Text and Workbook for All Instruments

by Gary Hess

Musicians Institute Press

A comprehensive guide to notes, rests, counting, subdividing, time signatures, triplets, ties, dotted notes and rests, cut time, compound time, swing, shuffle, rhythm studies, counting systems, road maps and more!

00695145 .... $19.95

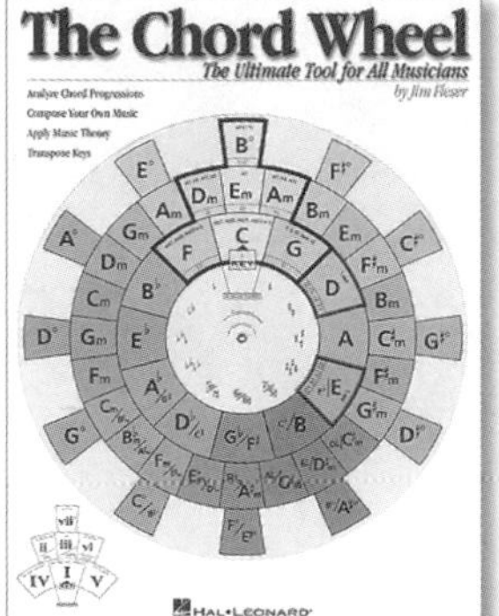

THE CHORD WHEEL

The Ultimate Tool for All Musicians

by Jim Fleser

Master chord theory ... in minutes! *The Chord Wheel* is a revolutionary device that puts the most essential and practical applications of chord theory into your hands. This tool will help you: Improvise and Solo – Talk about chops! Comprehend key structure like never before; Transpose Keys – Instantly transpose any progression into each and every key; Compose Your Own Music – Watch your songwriting blossom! No music reading is necessary.

00695579 .... $14.99

MUSIC THEORY WORKBOOK

For All Musicians

by Chris Bowman

A self-study course with illustrations and examples for you to write and check your answers. Topics include: major and minor scales; modes and other scales; harmony; intervals; chord structure; chord progressions and substitutions; and more.

00101379 .... $12.99

THE ULTIMATE KEYBOARD CHORD CHART

This convenient reference features 120 of the most commonly used chords, easy diagrams, and information on chord theory.

00220016 .... $3.50